Changing the Game
My Journey Through Life and Sports

George A. Selleck, Ph.D.
with Wendy Fayles

How a short, Jewish kid from Compton became an All-American point guard, went head-to-head with Bill Russell, became friends with John Wooden, worked for Ty Cobb, taught Kobe Bryant, turned down the NBA draft to become a Presbyterian minister and psychotherapist, and dedicated his life to helping kids everywhere rediscover the magic of sports and movement

ISBN: 978-1-60679-311-4
Library of Congress Control Number: 2014943674
Book layout: Cheery Sugabo
Cover design: Cheery Sugabo

Coaches Choice
P.O. Box 1828
Monterey, CA 93942
www.coacheschoice.com

Dedication

To my family, who are my support and strength:

>John, Alexis, and Jessica

>Alison, Keith, and Spencer

>Peter, Jenny, Kennedy, and Kia

>Kathleen and Matt

>Dominic and Amanda

>Christian, Cayleb, and Cara

And, finally, to my first wife, Beth, and my final wife, Barbara—lucky is the man who has had one wonderful woman in his life; blessed is the man who has had two.

Acknowledgments

A program like Leading2Play is not a one-person job by any means. It requires a team of individuals who all have unique contributions to make. I am fortunate to have a fantastic team, many of whom I would like to acknowledge. If I forget to mention someone, please keep in mind that I'm almost 80. These things happen.

My heartfelt thanks to:

- Alan Gregerman, highly respected author, business consultant, and teacher, who has been all these and more, over the past several years, as I've sought to bring Leading2Play to life
- Harold "Hap" Wagner, former Stanford teammate and Fortune 500 CEO, who was the first to say, "That's a really good idea!" (in reference to Leading2Play), and who has graciously provided direction and advice through more caffeinated breakfasts than I can remember
- Charles "Jiggs" Davis, not just a classmate but the consummate entrepreneur, whose steady and firm counsel has enabled me to be a much better player than I am, and whose time and support has helped Leading2Play become a real organization, making a real impact
- Jeffrey Davis—photojournalist, filmmaker, and producer—whose experience as a non-profit executive has provided much-needed wisdom and direction to our organizational growth
- Gary Riekes, a friend who lives his passion, respects the dignity, worth, and uniqueness of each individual, and gives his all to each of us
- Paul Jansen, Chris Pulley, and Jocelyn Logan-Friend—not enough can be said about their efforts to introduce and develop Leading2Play in the Fairfax County Public School District. They have been the real pioneers!
- Sam Carver, who chose to use his "gap year" before college by bringing his insight, understanding, and practical knowledge of what kids need as he worked side-by-side with me and the student leadership team of two middle schools in East Palo Alto
- Robert B. Leet, retired banking executive, business consultant, and friend, whose steady hand and thoughtful suggestions have been an integral part of the Leading2Play development and success to date
- Linda Best, former longtime member of the Contra Costa Council, who has brought her acumen and perceptivity to our continuing desire to serve the needs of the underserved West Contra Costa community
- Alex Gomez, board member of the West Contra Costa Business Development Center, who has played a significant leadership role in our efforts in the West Contra Costa area

- Dr. Michael Gibbs, who has encouraged and supported me much as he has the hundreds of youth who attend his well-regarded Camp Bizsmart program to get personal experience working with company founders and CEOs
- David Carver, co-founder of Search Fund Partners, who not only raised a wonderful son, but also brings his own warmth and discernment to our growth, development, and strategic decision-making
- Dr. Fred Neidermeyer, an old friend and colleague, whose expertise in educational program development has served me well through various endeavors, including the Leading2Play curriculum
- Duncan Beardsley, a member of the board at Philanthropic Ventures Foundation, who never fails to impress me with his on-point insights, comments, and suggestions
- Alan McMillen, a friend from our early days at the Long Beach YMCA, whose unfailing good humor has helped keep me going as I deal with the demanding challenges of turning Leading2Play into a viable program
- Gary Petersmeyer, chairman of the board for the Positive Coaching Alliance, former Stanford point guard, and a member of the "gang of three" (along with Alan McMillen and Dave Barram), who has generously offered his support, coaching, and mentoring along this journey of mine
- David Barram, businessman and team player extraordinaire, whose wisdom and experience I am always eager to take advantage of
- Aaron L Miller, who sees the world of youth sports the same way I do, and whose wonderful spirit never fails to serve as a pick-me-up from the inevitable discouragements of this effort
- Matthew Collins, who had the good sense to marry my wife's daughter, and who from day one has volunteered his support of Leading2Play, including actively participating in our very first project in Richmond, CA
- Keith Jones, my son-in-law, who has been with me through so much, and who remains my ongoing link to my daughter, Alison, and grandson, Spencer. Words cannot express how important his advice, patience, and clarity of thought have been.
- Saumil Majmudar, my SportzVillage compatriot, who is working hard to bring the Leading2Play values to the children of India
- And last, but certainly not least, Dr. James Peterson, founder of Coaches Choice, author, and/or coauthor of over 80 books and more than 200 published articles on a variety of coaching- and health-related subjects, and one of those people who make me feel positively slothful in comparison! Thank you, Jim, for always taking time out of your busy schedule to share your wisdom with me. Without you, this book would not exist.

Forewords

"You got a minute?"

Dr. George Selleck has probably posed that question to people more than any other! And if you say "yes," you'd better have more than several minutes, because you will be riveted by the stories based on his nearly 80 years in sports—stories interspersed with names like Bill Russell, John Wooden, Kobe Bryant, and others. And if you want a quick read on his philosophy of life, it's, "Everybody plays—everybody wins."

As a student-athlete at Stanford, George excelled in both basketball and baseball. Bill Russell, the legendary USF and Boston Celtics basketball star, called him "the biggest little man in basketball." Russell's coach at USF, Phil Woolpert, proclaimed George, "the Bob Cousy of the West," after the Celtics' play-making wizard.

When George was inducted into the Pac-12 Hall of Honor recently, he was introduced along with 11 other former conference college players during the conference championship game in Los Angeles. As the inductees lined up on the court, the 5'8" Selleck was dwarfed by the other players, commenting, "I felt like the ball boy."

It was an appropriate comment, considering that when Selleck played at Stanford, he owned the ball. One of the finest point guards to ever play for Stanford, he was famous for his leadership and cross-over dribble. He played in 71 games over a three-year span, averaging 14 points and six rebounds a game. In his senior season in 1955-56, he led Stanford to an 18-6 record. Only a two-point loss to UCLA kept the underdogs from winning the conference. George earned All-American accolades for his efforts.

As graduation approached, he had a choice of playing basketball for the Philadelphia Warriors in the NBA or baseball in the Pittsburgh Pirates system, or both. He chose to do neither. Deciding it was time to turn to other interests, he went back to school—earning a master's in educational psychology at Stanford, a master's in theology at Princeton, and a doctorate in counseling psychology at USC.

In his career, he has reached out to boys and girls, young athletes, college athletes transitioning to the NBA, coaches, school teachers and administrators, parents, and community leaders—in short, anyone and everyone who needed to learn that winning in life is more important than winning on the playing field.

He coached Brentwood High School to two Los Angeles City Championships. As a Presbyterian minister, he led a series of Southwestern congregations. He is sought after as a lecturer and symposia leader. He is widely published on the topic of sportsmanship. He has established several organizations, such as *Sports for Life* and *Parents for Good Sports*. He has also served as a goodwill ambassador for the State Department and has been honored as one of the most accomplished sports educators in the country by the Institute for International Sport.

Currently, Dr. Selleck is taking on his biggest challenge—getting every young person in the country on the playing field, through a dynamic program called Leading2Play. As Selleck observes, "Schools no longer make physical education mandatory. Exercise has given way to sloth. Play is a concept that needs to be reintroduced into our culture. I believe sports and recreation might be the only activities in which kids learn to be team players—on the field or playground and in life." Leading2Play is student-driven and designed to address the health and behavioral issues facing children of all ages. Field trials are in progress to provide each child an opportunity to combine fitness with fun.

Changing the Game is George's eighth and perhaps most important book. Written in memoir form, it recounts many of his experiences—the good and the bad— and (just as he used to do on the basketball court) invites the reader to learn, as well as be entertained.

Russ Wilks
Stanford Sports Scribe '55

George Selleck's life, it seems, is one long fast break. He doesn't know how to slow down, either with a basketball in his capable hands or a vision in his cerebral mind. He's pushing 80, but still acting 20.

My first memory of Selleck is in a rickety-old gym on the Stanford campus, watching him control the game with crisp passes, a wicked crossover dribble, a clutch shooting eye, and the disposition of a burglar on defense. He was 5-foot-8, but played a foot taller.

Fast forward 60 years and Selleck still can't wait to get on a basketball court. But there's so much more to him than a three-point shot. Hoops may have been the impetus to his young world, but that world has exploded in so many directions.

How to describe Selleck? Where to begin? How about counselor, psychologist, educator, coach, referee, Jewish Christian minister—that's right—consultant, public speaker, visiting scholar, entrepreneur, workshop lecturer, author, visionary. And, oh, yes, two master's degrees and a doctorate.

There's no telling how much more he'll add to his resume by the time he turns 90. The man is ageless. Retirement isn't in his vocabulary.

His pride and joy at the moment, besides his family, is his unique Leading2Play program, where kids who might not make their school's varsity can still have fun with sports and other fitness-oriented activities. Selleck already has made progress in implementing innovative noontime, recess, after-school and PE programs at various grade levels.

The Leading2Play program is non-judgmental. The focus is on teaching mutual respect, and the emphasis of the program is designed to help youngsters find their own competitiveness. Selleck says this best when he states, "We want every kid to feel like a winner, so that there are "no forgotten kids."

While it may have appeared that sports came easily to Selleck, he worked tirelessly to develop his skills in football, basketball, and baseball. As a senior at Compton High School, he was named California Basketball Player of the Year in 1952. He wowed even the legends. "George Selleck is the best basketball player I have ever seen, pound for pound and inch for inch," said Stanford basketball icon Hank Luisetti.

"Selleck is a great little player," said UCLA coach John Wooden. "He caused us no end of trouble. Any of us would be glad to have him." After a stellar career at Stanford, he was talented enough to make the school's Basketball Hall of Fame and the Pac-12 Conference Hall of Honor.

Selleck had an opportunity to play in the National Basketball Association, but education was his main game. Yet, he continued to impact the sport's landscape. He looked after baseball great Ty Cobb. Bill Walsh attended a Selleck coaching workshop and took "copious notes." Selleck instructed NBA rookies, including Kobe Bryant, at the NBA's Rookie Transition program.

Selleck has merged these anecdotes and his Leading2Play program's philosophy with his own life story in a well-written, compelling style. While striving to improve the lives of others, he's finally learned to embrace his own achievements rather than focus on his perceived limitations. Like any true teacher, what he's teaching has taught him as well.

Dave Newhouse
Oakland Tribune

Contents

Introduction

In a way, you could say this book has multiple personalities, which I suppose is fitting for a project written by someone who spent over 30 years as a psychologist.

It is, first and foremost, the story of my life. Or rather, stories *from* my life. A lot of people have told me these stories are interesting, and I've gotten tired of arguing the point. Maybe the only people who will end up reading this will be my children and grandchildren, but still there are worse legacies to leave.

This book is for anyone who likes an underdog story—especially an underdog sports story. In reality, it doesn't get much more underdog than a short Jewish kid who ends up becoming a basketball star.

This book is also for anyone who is interested in some of the life lessons I've learned in my almost 80 years as a competitive athlete, coach, referee, Christian minister, psychologist, entrepreneur, consultant, educator, etc. It's been an interesting life, playing with athletes like Bill Russell and working with everyone from Ty Cobb and Kobe Bryant to prisoners on Terminal Island. I've learned a lot—about myself, about others, about the world we live in. Hopefully, you will find what I've learned interesting, entertaining, and applicable to your own life. Or, it may end up being a cautionary tale of what *not* to do. At the end of the day, as long as you get something from it, we're golden.

Finally, this book is for anyone who is, will be, or ever was involved with Leading2Play. It is my hope this book will play at least a small role in helping Leading2Play create what Malcom Gladwell in his book, *The Tipping Point*, calls a "social epidemic." The tipping point is that magic moment when an idea, trend, or social behavior crosses a threshold, tips, and spreads like wildfire. The idea we want to spread is that a youth-driven, sports, and health and fitness program *can* change our kids, change our world, and *change the game*.

How to Read This Book

This book is divided into five sections: 1st Quarter, 2nd Quarter, 3rd Quarter, 4th Quarter, and Overtime. These sports analogies roughly correspond with the different periods of my life. Every now and then, I might throw something out of sequence, but only when it makes sense for the flow of the book. Otherwise, I tried to more or less stick to the chronological order of the noteworthy occurrences in my life.

Prologue
Beginnings … and Endings

In my mid-seventies, when most people my age were enjoying the fruits of retirement, I found myself commuting between Washington, D.C. and my home in Pinole, California, working a consulting job for Professional and Scientific Associates (PSA) and putting the final touches on my eighth book, *Kid Sense: Advice to Coaches and Parents from Kids in Sport.*

I was in a reflective mood. My daughter, Alison, a doctor, had been diagnosed with an inoperable brain tumor and was under the care of the National Institute of Cancer. She and her husband, Keith, a former Stanford basketball player, like myself, had one child—my grandson, Spencer, who was just seven years old. I did not know it at the time, but patients were only accepted at the NIC if they were terminal. All I knew was that Alison was a fighter, and if anyone could overcome brain cancer, it would be her.

So my thoughts were with Alison, as they always were during that terrible, tender time, but they were also on the book I was in the process of finishing. Almost all the books and articles I had previously written had, at their center, the same core value: sports could provide kids with so much more than trophies on the shelf. In *Court Sense: The Invisible Edge in Basketball and Life,* I argued that if kids could learn to think on the basketball court, they could transfer those skills to the classroom, relationships, career choices, and other decision-making situations. In *From the Bleachers with Love* and *Beyond the Bleachers*, which I co-wrote with my friend and Stanford teammate, Dr. David Epperson, we talked about ways families could get the most out of their family's sports experiences—using sport as a way to heal many of the fractures that modern life had created.

Regrettably, however, it seemed the years I spent trying to get parents and coaches to see that sport was more about developing good people than it was about winning hadn't really made much of an impact. Professional and collegiate sports continued to become more entertainment-oriented and less sports-oriented, and youth sports appeared to be following along the same lines.

That's why I thought *Kid Sense* would be an opportunity for kids to give their side of the story. They could talk about how frustrating it is when your coach yells at you to do one thing, and then your parents yell at you to do another. They could talk about the embarrassment of sitting on the bench, only getting to play once the game was well in hand. They could explain why the majority of them quit playing any kind of organized sports by the time they're 13.

On the other hand, as I sat on that 5½ hour flight, burdened by my daughter's illness and questions about the future, it occurred to me that *Kid Sense* was void of integrity. In other words, it was my voice that was speaking, not the kids themselves. Granted, it was a voice that had more than 50 years' experience working with kids in sports, but still—it was like the difference between margarine and butter.

I realized if I was going to do the book right, it needed to feature actual kids' voices. And doing that would involve more work than I could undertake by myself. So I made an appointment to meet with the good people of the John Gardner Center at Stanford. (The John W. Gardner Center for Youth and Their Communities partners with communities to develop leadership, conduct research, and effect change to improve the lives of youth.) They were excited by the idea. They had wanted to do some research on this subject several years prior, but it hadn't worked out. "Give us a month, and we will be ready to go," they said.

Unfortunately, I found my enthusiasm for the project diminishing even as theirs grew. Clearly, there was a lot on my mind—mostly the deteriorating condition of my daughter. The project the Gardner Center envisioned began to feel like more than I wanted to or was able to take on at that moment.

Still, I felt I needed to do *something*. As I have moved through adulthood and maturity, I have found myself not just looking for things to do, but looking for something that makes meaning of my life and makes my life mean something. And since most of my life has revolved around sports, it makes sense I would find that meaning in something that revolved around sport and physical activity. As a young child in a dysfunctional family, I found my solace in sport. And yet it has taken almost 80 years and more than five decades as an athlete, coach, referee, pastor, psychologist, author, parent, and grandparent to understand how much more I could have gotten out of sport and how much better my life could have been if only I had been more aware of what sport was trying to teach me.

To gain some outside perspective on my inner turmoil, I made an appointment with Dr. Alan Gregerman, President and Chief Innovation Officer of VENTURE WORKS Inc., a consulting firm, based in the Washington, D.C. area, that helps leading companies develop winning strategies and create successful new products, services, ventures, and ways of doing business. I had met Alan on two other occasions, but this was our first lengthy conversation.

After listening to me talk about the struggles I was going through personally and professionally, Alan looked at me and asked, "George, what do you want to do with the next 10 years of your life?"

I said, "Alan, don't you mean the next five years?" After all, I was no spring chicken and I thought five years was a pretty optimistic outlook on my part!

But Alan is a long-term perspective kind of guy, and I decided he was right—I didn't want to do a book that a few people would read and that would be it. I wanted to do something with long-term impact. So, we thought about what that "something" might be.

We talked about the idea of trying to interest Nike® in having kids as their spokespersons. After all, Tiger Woods had just fallen from his pedestal, and other adult athletes weren't looking so hot, either. But, then, we concluded that we would walk into Nike's sanctuary, and they would say "thank you" and the conversation would be over— they with the idea (if they liked it), we with nothing.

Next, Alan suggested I put together a portfolio of all the work I had done over the years with athletes, coaches, and parents and send it out to see what might happen. Again, the conclusion was the same. The corporate world would say, "So what?" and the educational world, "That's nice, but..."

Finally, Alan said, "What about working with after-school programs?" After all, I did have a lot of experience in that area, having spent more than 10 years as a consultant with the Anaheim Union High School District, working with their co-curricular staff (music, dance, debate, and athletic coaches), as well as developing their after-school athletic program.

I said, "Hmm. Let me think about that." And that was the genesis of something incredible—something I feel has the potential to change not just the world of youth sports, but the world of youth, *period*. I have found myself able to use my experience to give back to kids and sports in a way that makes a real difference. And along the way, I have found myself.

A year after that first meeting with Alan Gregerman, my daughter passed away. It didn't seem fair that she, with so much to live for and so much to give to the world, was gone, while I was still here. But that is something sport teaches. Life isn't fair. Sometimes, you get a bad call. Sometimes, you don't make the team. Sometimes, parents outlive their children. The challenge is to make every setback, every obstacle, every loss mean something. That is what I learned from sport. And from Alison.

1st Quarter

In May of 2012—despite my reluctance to write another book—I met with a book coach at the suggestion of an associate who thought I should write about the result of my meeting with Alan Gregerman. The uniqueness of the program I was developing was something my associate was sure everyone would be interested in hearing about.

"Forget it," the book coach said. "You're talking about a message. People aren't interested in messages; they're only interested in stories." I left her office feeling depressed and defeated.

Seeking encouragement, I turned to my longtime writing consultant, who has been with me through 20 years, several books, and hundreds of articles. She has never hesitated to let me know when my love of quotes is getting annoying, when I'm using 10 words if two will do, and when she thinks an idea has merit or should be consigned to the trash can and ignited with a blow torch.

Initially, she totally shot me down. I was starting to have issues. But then, she tossed me a caveat. "You know, George," she said, "the book coach is right. People like a good story. And you have a great one! I mean, how many other short, Jewish kids grow up in Compton, become an All-American point guard, get drafted professionally and give it all up to become a Presbyterian minister for a small congregation in New Mexico, made up of World War II draft dodgers and an embezzler from Philadelphia?"

"The way I see it," she continued, "Everything you've done and everything you've been in your life has led you to what you're doing now. So let's tell THAT story—the story of how you got from there to here."

That story begins in my childhood. It is where sport first made its mark on me. It's where I learned lessons that helped me survive and overlooked lessons that would have helped me survive even better. It's where I made relationships that last to this day, and where I failed miserably at others. It's where my life could have been so very different if I had had the right tools and skill set—tools and skills that are critical to what I'm doing now. Thank goodness it's never too late to learn.

Gym Rat

Growing up, I was eager to get out of the house and away from the tension, struggles, and worries of my dysfunctional family. When I was seven, we moved to Compton, right across the street from Roosevelt Junior High School. If ever there was a little piece of heaven on earth, Roosevelt was it. There, I reveled in playing hoops in the gym every opportunity I got.

The gym was open Saturdays and Sundays during the school year and every day during the summer. I was always the first one there, waiting anxiously for the coaches to arrive. I played all day, every day, always with older, bigger, and stronger kids. I was still playing when they closed the gym for the day. It was not uncommon for the last, straggling coach to say, "Look, George, I gotta go."

In that home away from home, I exercised my mind, learned skills, tested them, made friends, created dreams, learned how to compete, developed curiosity, and began to learn about the world outside my home. The days, hours, and years at the Roosevelt Junior High gym shaped my love of play and sport, as well as the way I continue to see and explore my world as an adult.

When I think of those experiences, I think of learning, exploring, experimenting, self-expression, spontaneity, connecting, competition, and lost-in-the moment, rough and tumble, joyful play that created a mood of bliss, flow, and timelessness.

For me, play and participation in sports was a way to express and stretch myself. It was (and still is) an intrinsically pleasurable activity, free of the anxiety that accompanied me in everything else I undertook, without any other goal other than what we were doing at the moment.

Basketball was such a part of me that one of my Stanford teammates, who stayed with my family during the summer between our sophomore and junior year at college to work in the nearby oil fields, remembers how he and my father would spend the evenings after work enjoying a glass of beer, while I would immediately leave the dinner table to find a game of hoops somewhere.

James Naismith invented the game of basketball so kids like me could have fun playing it. I don't think for a moment he had a vision of professional leagues, March Madness, and coaches making millions of dollars. Nor do I think he invented the game so parents and coaches could freak out when a player committed a costly turnover. Nor did he, I'm sure, want parents to put pressure on their kids to excel so that they could obtain a basketball scholarship to college. And yet, that is what we see happening in the world of youth, school, and professional sports.

Basketball gave me the chance to be in the gym, leave all my worries and problems aside, forget about life for a while, and just be a kid and have fun. That was a big part of my decision to take up senior basketball at the age of 55, and it's why I still wander down to the gym when I tire of the treadmill or other fitness activities.

We know that kids and adults alike need play time. Play enables us to achieve a number of positive things, including:
- Learn how our bodies and minds work
- Communicate and socialize
- Exercise our bodies and minds
- Imagine possibilities and opportunities
- See problems in a new and more revealing light
- Create a common language for working together and developing friendships
- See others—teammates and opponents—as human beings
- Relieve the stress of our day-to-day lives and activities

- Gain energy and enthusiasm for other things
- Learn to laugh at ourselves and our mistakes and applaud our accomplishments

Increasingly, however, play is being squeezed out of our lives today—especially in those of kids. Physical education classes are being cut or reduced in the schools. Youth sports programs and school sports teams cater more to elite athletes than to the average kid who just wants to have fun. The problem is, if we don't provide kids with fun and meaningful play, they will surely seek it in other places. And those places might not be as safe or encouraging as a basketball gym. But where can they go? If they're not involved in an organized sports program—which most kids aren't—what options are available to them?

Kids need their own, personal Roosevelt Junior High.

I know I did.

Family Matters

Although I had done a great dealing of counseling as a pastor and followed that by entering private practice as a psychologist, I was unaware of just how many issues I had until I started seeing a therapist in my thirties. Even then, I was only there because outward circumstances had crumbled so badly that I had no choice.

I wasn't a good patient, probably for the same reasons that I was failing on several relationship fronts. But slowly, over time, I started to learn things about myself that have impacted me to this day.

I learned that for a person who counseled other people on their relationships, I didn't have a clue as to how to manage my own. My family moved to Compton in 1941 because my dad, a German Jew during the early years of World War II, wanted to disassociate himself from his German and Jewish background. We were anything but a model family. My mother was a heavy drinker and probably suffered from depression, as did (I suspect) my father. My sister flunked out of college (although she did go on to become a well-regarded nurse) and my twin brother failed to graduate from high school.

When I first married, I could spell the word "family," but I had no idea what a family was and what it took to make a group of people a family. When you couple this with the Puritan ethic I was raised on, it meant I never sat around with my wife and kids. I was always working. When my kids were young, I worked 10 hours a day, refereed basketball games at night, and studied for my Ph.D. in my spare time. Not surprisingly, this approach didn't make me a very good father or husband. It led to two divorces and strained relationships with my children.

Gradually (and much too slowly), I learned family is the unit that shapes our personalities and plays a major role in the people we become. I now put a lot more time, effort, and thought into the relationships I have with my children, grandchildren, and wife.

Effective families provide the members of the family with support and encouragement. Families give each other opportunities to develop important life skills. Families provide children and adolescents with a sense of belonging and a special identity. They are a source of emotional support, comfort, warmth, and nurturing.

It took me too long to learn these vital relationship skills. Fortunately, I'm also discovering it's not too late to help others learn them.

My Brother's Keeper

Harold ("Butch") Selleck—my twin brother—was born right after me. He got off to a rough start—including a life-threatening stomach surgery when he was just a few days old. I guess he never overcame that difficult beginning. I well remember my pain as a young intern in psychology reading from the very first DSM (*Diagnostic Manual of Mental Disorders*) about what was then labeled "Inadequate Personality Disorder" (later manuals eliminated this diagnosis due to its insensitivity). Persons with inadequate personality disorders were described as often having a chronic inability to meet ordinary life demands in the absence of intellectual disabilities. The diagnosis went on to describe such persons as having a severe dependency on others. This description fit my brother perfectly. I believe my parents tried their best to get him the help he needed, but this was the mid-30s, and psychology was still in its infancy. Consequently, Butch's life was anything but easy.

I worried about Butch constantly. I was what you would call an "enabler." I did his chores for him and gave him my allowance so he could spend extra time at the movies he loved. I remember in the 3rd grade, facing him across the room in a spelling contest. I felt obligated to misspell a word so Butch could last longer than I in the contest. On the other hand, I had to not be so obvious in my misspelling that the teacher knew what I was doing. It was tremendously stressful for me.

The need to protect my brother was a challenge that followed me throughout my athletic career. Every time I succeeded, guilt would whisper in my ear, "What about your brother? How is this impacting him?" When I was chosen California Player of Year, Butch actually verbalized my struggle: "One brother's a success, the other's a failure."

As I have learned from books, and more from my own experience, our own unfinished psychological and emotional issues either interfere with our ability to meet the needs of others or contribute to words, actions, and attitudes that are not helpful. Negative childhood experiences contribute to our growing up differently from other children, missing some of what good parenting can offer to help our growth toward adulthood and maturity. While I did not turn to alcohol or drug use as my parents did, my childhood played a significant role in the inner anxiety and other feelings that are seemingly unexplained in my life, i.e., insecurity, self-doubt, self-criticism, painful feelings of inadequacy and guilt, feelings of isolation, and difficulty with relationships.

Inclusion and acceptance are so important to kids. One study revealed a child's biggest fear upon entering junior high was not that of getting lost or being unable to open his or her locker. It was the fear of not having anyone to sit by at lunch. Kids need a place where everyone is welcome, and no one is turned away. They need a place where they are their "brother's keeper," but in a natural way—not a way that causes stress and anxiety. It is challenging, because it takes knowledge and skills and, more importantly, a willingness to reach out to others. This situation can be difficult for youth who are—naturally—wrapped up in themselves. But I am getting to see it happen, and the results are wondrous.

The Boxing Lesson

When Butch and I were in elementary school, there was a lot of buzz about boxing. Joe Louis was about halfway into his string of 12 heavyweight championships at the time, so my father thought it would be a good idea for my brother and me to learn "the gentleman's sport."

Unfortunately, my father was anything but gentle in the way he went about this situation. His boxing instruction consisted of purchasing some gloves for my brother and me and insisting we fight each other. I'm not sure how my brother felt about it, but this was horrible for me. The thought of me hitting him was torment for me.

When I wouldn't engage in fighting my brother, my dad yelled at me, and he yelled even louder when I did fight but didn't try very hard. After a few minutes of this, we were finally allowed to stop.

I was always trying to compensate for my brother's physical and mental limitations, and every achievement I experienced just added to the guilt I felt over the differences between us. In the long run, I don't know if my actions were helpful or harmful. Did they help my brother understand I cared about him? Or did they make him feel less than competent to successfully run his own life?

Thinking of my brother reminds me of how important competence is to our development. Feeling competent is the first step in feeling confident. When you help kids find and develop their *competencies*, it, in turn, increases their self-confidence. Some kids may have a flair for organization, others for motivation, others for promotion, and still others for sports or physical activities. When given the chance to develop those competencies, you end up with some pretty confident kids. Even better is when kids get to help other kids develop their competencies. As a result, the confidence levels are off the charts! This is something I am witnessing right now, as you will learn at the end of this book.

Trees, Airports, and Loss

Even though Butch and I were twins, I only have a few stories I really remember about him.

When my dad was in his late 60s (he was 55 when he married my mother), he took my brother and me to Mt. Baldy to experience snow for the first time. This was my dad's first time in the snow, too. So, what did he do but put Butch and me on a toboggan and push us down a hill—straight toward a tree. When the impending disaster became clear, I pushed my brother off just before we crashed. My dad rushed to us, saw the bone pushing through the skin on my arm, and—using his medical training as a dentist—avoided a compound fracture by pushing the bone back in. Yeah. Ouch!

My last memory of Butch is equally painful. I remember running into him unexpectedly in the Portland, Oregon airport. He was in the military at the time, and I was on my way to officiate a basketball game at the University of Oregon. Instead of a joyous reunion spent catching up on all that had been going on in our lives, my own brother ditched me. One minute he was there, and the next, he was gone. After that experience, I think I only saw Butch twice—at my daughter's wedding and at the wedding of one of my nephews. He spent the last 10 years or so of his life working as a security guard on the grounds of the San Jose County fairgrounds and died alone at the VA hospital in Napa. No one had even known he was there. Days after his passing, I was finally called by the police, who were trying to notify Butch's family and thought they would try my name.

It would be safe to say I shared closer relationships with my teammates on the basketball court. While not every kid comes from this kind of dysfunctional background, many do. Some come from even worse situations, which is why it is so important that kids have a place where they can find refuge from whatever may be going on at home or in other parts of their lives. They need a place they can feel safe, comfortable, and welcome. They need a place where they can feel like they are part of a family. In reality, family isn't always the one we are born into. On occasion, it's the one we make for ourselves.

First Hoops

Lafayette Elementary School is more than 135 years old and is located in the outer Richmond District of San Francisco. I attended kindergarten through 2nd grade there before our family moved to Compton.

The school surrounded a large, asphalt area where I shot my first baskets at a cylinder hoop, attached to a single pole that had no backboard. That strange but beautiful hoop was the love of my life—and one that got me firmly started on the road to basketball success.

What was so special about it? Well, no backboard meant you had to focus squarely on the rim, against a background of vastness and sky as you attempted to shoot the ball into a small space. As a consequence, it taught me concentration and precision from the very first time I attempted to throw the ball.

To this day, when coaching young or experienced players who are having trouble making shots, I suggest they pick a spot on the rim to shoot at. Doing this not only narrows their focus, it also expands their concentration.

I spent a lot of time with that basketball hoop as I waited for my mother to pick me up from school. I learned to be alone and at home with a basketball as my companion.

While I have no clear remembrance of when I began to transfer the skills of focus and concentration to the larger game of life, I feel very fortunate that I've come to a place where I'm able to model and share the value of those two skills I first mastered on a desolate playground over 70 years ago.

George "Shorty" Kellogg

I was a skinny sixth-grader at Colin P. Kelly grammar school in the fall of 1945, making the 40-minute (one-way) bus ride from Compton to the Long Beach YMCA, where my parents had enrolled my brother and me in tumbling and swimming. I hated tumbling and swimming. I wanted to play basketball. First, however, I had to find a team.

George (Shorty) Kellogg was the fitness instructor at the Y. He had just returned to Long Beach after completing three years of service with the U.S. Coast Guard. I didn't know it at the time, but before joining the Coast Guard, Shorty had spent about 20 years coaching basketball. One day, I approached Shorty about coaching a Class D team. He told me he would coach if I rounded up enough boys to play. "It's a deal," I said. And that was how my basketball career began.

I learned a lot from Shorty, and most of it wasn't even about basketball. Shorty was a devout Quaker. He talked very little, and when he did, his voice was quiet. One of the things I remember him telling us was that a champion does not lose control when a call goes against him or he's the subject of some overlooked roughness or foul.

I knew a little bit about getting roughed up. Because I was usually the highest scoring player on my team—as well as the smallest, I got pushed around a lot. In high school, there were a couple of games in particular where I was knocked flat to the floor with no foul called. Part of me wanted to jump up and get in the ref's face, while another part of me wanted to jump up and get in my opponent's face. On the other hand, the part of me that could hear Shorty's voice in my head say, "Let it go; be a champion," prevailed. So, I jumped up, shook it off, and proceeded to play my game.

Shorty wasn't particularly knowledgeable or skilled as a basketball coach, but as a role model, he was superlative. From Shorty, I learned the power of a caring adult.

Shorty was an encourager. He was genuinely interested in me and the other players—in the dreams we had and the problems with which we struggled. He attended my high school games when he could, and even a few of my college ones.

There was a time when I thought the world was made up of people like Shorty, influencing and empowering lives like he did. As the years passed, however, I have come to realize that people of that caliber are rare.

Every kid should have a Shorty in their lives—a mentor who models a positive, caring attitude at all times and shows what true leadership is all about. Unfortunately, not every kid does—at least, not yet. On the other hand, a way to fix that exists. How? Well, we'll talk more about that later.

Words Matter

As a kid growing up Jewish during the time of World War II, I heard a lot of comments—directly and indirectly—about "that little Jew." My mother, trying to provide me with a snappy comeback, shared the old saying, "Sticks and stones may break my bones, but names will never hurt me."

Well, Mom was wrong. Those names hurt plenty.

Words are powerful. Long after bones have mended and bruises have healed, the sting of an unkind word can stay with us. Words carry enormous weight and power. They can be uplifting, comforting, healing, encouraging, depressing, antagonistic, damaging, discouraging, or condescending.

According to a study conducted by a professor at Penn State University, there are more words in our vocabulary that express negative emotions than there are words that express positive ones.

A lifetime of trying to make a difference has taught me many lessons, perhaps none more important than to be more careful with my words, for example:
- Instead of the word "problem," I like to use "challenge." By looking at a situation as a challenge, it is perceived as temporary and solvable.
- I try to change "I can't" to "I can" or "I will." For example, "I can't do the dishes" becomes "I will do the dishes as soon as I finish this e-mail."
- When I say "could have" instead of "should have," it removes guilt and shame and puts no one down.
- I make a huge effort to change "always" to "often" and "never" to "seldom." "Always" and "never" are absolutes and are usually exaggerated words. They do not convey an accurate meaning. They cause others to become defensive and prevent you from getting the results you need.
- I prefer "life lesson" versus "mistake." This verbiage allows us to learn from the past.

- I use "I want to" or "I am going to" instead of "I need to" or "I have to." This approach implies choosing to do something—that I am my own boss.

Along those same lines, everyone can be a leader when you de-emphasize the noun *leader* and emphasize the verb to *lead*. Leadership is an action you take, not a position you hold. Leadership is about taking responsibility—both personal and social—for working with others on shared goals. Often, I find kids who are a little intimidated at the thought of being a leader, because they're shy or nervous about putting themselves "out there." Watching them become leaders through the process of implementing leadership actions is a beautiful thing.

I guess you could say there really aren't words for it.

Best Friends and Broken Bones

Al Waner was my first and best friend. We regularly traveled together on the bus to the Long Beach YMCA to play basketball. We were always the two guards on any team—first at the Y, then at Roosevelt Junior High, and later at Compton High, where we won the CIF championship two years in a row.

We didn't get along, however. I would say we probably had at least one fight a day for years. I specifically remember one time when we got in a disagreement about something, and before you knew it, both of us were taking a swing at each other. Our fists collided at the same time, and I screamed in pain. My wrist had been broken. Al was horrified, and immediately apologetic. In fact, his mental pain over the incident probably outweighed my physical pain.

Al's dad, a scoutmaster, was so concerned about our constant fighting that he had us each braid a bracelet. Then, we had to trade bracelets and wear the other person's bracelet to remind us of our friendship. I don't know how well it worked, but we are still friends to this day.

Al was always—and still is—an exceptional person. Always the most popular kid in school, he was elected 11th and 12th grade class president. He went on to become a minister, a school principal, and then an assistant superintendent. Today, after several retirements, he is a volunteer member of the school board in Big Bear, California, where he and his childhood sweetheart live most of the year.

For someone like me, who spent most of my childhood feeling disenfranchised and different, having a friend like Al was nothing short of a miracle. Broken wrists notwithstanding, we took care of each other in countless ways. Any fight we had was almost immediately made up with a handshake or an "I'm sorry."

I will say it many times in this book, but the value of friendship to young people is incalculable. In adolescence, especially, youth use their friends to help shape their own sense of self. Instead of pitting youth against each other, adults need to give kids the opportunity to learn the value and meaning of friendship. We need to give them the opportunity to find their own Al Waners.

The Little Engine That Could

I don't remember a lot about my early childhood. I do, however, vividly remember the book *The Little Engine That Could*. I remember first seeing the book at a friend's house. I was fascinated by its bright red cover, with the picture of the little engine pulling railroad cars up a hill, past trees, telephone poles, and wires.

A few weeks later, my mother gave me a copy of the book, and I began reading it myself. In the tale (which you are all probably familiar with), a train needs to get over a high mountain to deliver toys and food to the good children on the other side. Its engine, however, stalls out before it can get across. The toys try to flag down passing engines to take them the rest of the way, but the engines all refuse for various reasons. Finally, a little blue engine agrees to try, even though she has never pulled such a heavy load. Chugging away, the little engine makes it over the mountain, with the train cars full of toys and goodies, all the while repeating the words: "I think I can, I think I can."

I have always identified with that little blue engine. Even before performance-enhancing drugs had been invented and athletes ballooned to twice their normal size, I was considered too small and too skinny to excel at sports. And yet, excel I did. I was the smallest starter in the nation on a major college basketball team. Subsequently, I was a collegiate All-Star. I was drafted by a professional basketball team.

Furthermore, I have absolutely no doubt that my athletic and career efforts have been greatly influenced by the mantra of the little engine as she chants, "I think I can. I think I can. I think I can." Accordingly, it is important to remember, always to try as hard as you can; never give up.

Achievements come from effort, and effort requires energy—the emotional fuel to get moving and get it done. As I reflect back on personal and organizational experiences where I have seen excellence, energy has always been involved.

I have seen athletes who had little promise of success become successful because they worked harder than anyone—because they corralled the emotional fuel within themselves to push on to their goals and dreams. I have seen young people who had doubts about their ability to lead or inspire others accomplish marvelous things.

Whatever I've achieved has been because of my desire and willingness to work hard, to dig deep for this energy. At my age, it is harder to find that energy, but whenever I feel myself slacking, I just think of the little engine that thought she could—and did. That's when "I think I can" becomes "I know I can!"

It Takes More Than a Whistle to Make a Coach

When I was growing up in Compton, the school system consisted of six years of elementary school, four years of junior high, and then four years of a combined high school/junior college experience. As a result, there was a tremendous junior high sports program. We had a six-team conference, and it was not unusual to have 3,000 or more people show up at football games. When the basketball season rolled around, the bleachers were packed.

As I entered eighth grade at Roosevelt Junior High, I had already established a considerable reputation on the basketball court, and I fully expected the trend to continue. In our first game of the season, however, our opponents surprised us with a box-and-one (a four-man zone defense, with one player playing me man-to-man). It was a new and innovative system and one with which we were not very familiar. It meant that I always had two players (and sometimes more) guarding me. It was an extremely challenging situation. Accordingly, at the first opportunity, I called a time-out. In the huddle, I turned to my coach and said, "Coach, what should I do?"

His disconcerting reply was, "I don't know!" That's when I realized it takes more than a whistle to make a coach.

I have spent many years playing for coaches, working with coaches, and doing some coaching myself. What I learned from that experience is that the field of coaching is constantly changing. Teams change, rules change, kids change, society changes. Coaches need to change, too. Just as there is no "one-size-fits-all" defense, there is no "one-size-fits-all" coaching style. As a coach, if you are not continually evolving, progressing, and trying new things, you may find yourself with a revolution on your hands, as players bolt for other teams, parents challenge your decisions, and administrators question your methods.

One long-time college coach noted that when he first started out, all he had to do was tell his players to do something, and they would do it. "If I told those teams to go through a brick wall, no question—the wall was in trouble." The next generation of players, however, was different. "That was the MTV generation," the coach explained. "They were used to having information in sound bites; I could no longer hold their attention on just the strength of my personality. They were also more analytical; they'd ask why they had to go through a brick wall. With those kids, I had to find a halfway point between command and explanation." ("Field of Changes," Martin Stillion, Online Response, Winter 2002)

I think the aforementioned is a great analogy for life. As the commercial says, "Life comes at you fast." Adaptability is crucial to being successful. Just as computers need to be continually upgraded to meet the demands of the latest software, we need to make sure the programs we create to help kids be successful in life are constantly upgraded to meet the needs and demands of today's world. This is a lesson I have taken to heart, as you will see later.

Late Bloomer

Compton was a wonderful place to grow up, especially if you love playing sports as I did. The 6-4-4 system of education offered a highly competitive inter-school sports program that challenged and tested our skills with exceptional athletes from schools in the Lynwood, Paramount, Roosevelt, Willowbrook, and Enterprise districts of Compton.

I was a quiet kid whose struggles for acceptance and belonging were even more difficult as one of only two Jewish kids in the school (the other being my brother). I was shy and withdrawn (except when there was a ball in my hands); a sensitive kid whose feelings were easily hurt.

As a junior high school student, I lacked self-confidence in social situations. I was looked upon as being "way too serious," making it difficult for people to feel at ease around me (a barrier to intimacy that threatens my ability to connect with people even today).

Sports, however, offered me a pathway out of my personal and social ghetto. As such, I was really looking forward to playing "big-boy" football (tackle) in the 9th grade. Unfortunately, a broken arm caused me to miss that opportunity. In 10th grade, however, I made the team and quickly became the star receiver.

Football was a big thing—a real opportunity to be accepted and to belong. There was a Friday night party after every game, which was my chance to be one of the "cool" kids. It was not to be, however. My parents decided my brother and I should be confirmed in the synagogue in Long Beach (there was no synagogue in Compton), and that meant attending Friday night services for the entire year. No Friday night parties for this football "star!"

Consequently, my interpersonal and social skills were not on a par with my classmates. Even though I got good grades, it was always fast-food learning to rid myself of the anxiety of not doing well. It was never the thoughtful reflection necessary to real learning. I was a classic late bloomer. It has taken me a lifetime to approach comfortableness in my own skin, and more importantly, evolve as a unique personality/individual.

The challenges that faced my adolescent self are the same ones many kids face today:

An identity crisis: *Who Am I?*

Lack of self-confidence and low self-esteem: *I am worthless*

Self-trust: *Am I credible?*

A sense of hopelessness: *Where am I going?*

Confusion and ambiguity concerning moral issues: *What is right and wrong?*

How do we provide opportunities for kids who may be struggling with these issues to find themselves, to be themselves, to gain self-confidence, and to come out of their shells in a fun, friendly, supportive environment? How do we contribute to a kid's understanding that it is okay to be different, because we all are different in one way or another? How do we help kids discover and focus on skills, talents, and abilities they might not otherwise have recognized until much later in life?

I think I have discovered the way to do just that. While nothing is wrong with being a late bloomer, and our struggles are a huge part of whom we become, there is a way to equip kids to better handle those struggles and turn them into opportunities—to help them bloom. That, however, is a story for later.

The Third-Place Lesson

When I was in high school, I volunteered to coach the 7th and 8th grade boys' team at the Long Beach YMCA—the same place where I learned to play basketball as a kid. My team was not particularly talented, but they loved to play basketball, and they grew to become great friends with each other. By the end of the season, they had worked and improved enough to make it to the semi-finals of the Southern California YMCA tournament.

We played hard and well, but lost the game. It was a long, quiet trip back to Long Beach, and I wondered how I would get the boys ready to play in the consolation game after such a difficult loss.

We decided that we would hold a practice the next morning before our game. The next day on my way to the gym, I was trying desperately to think of which motivational speech I could fall back on to pump up the team, but my efforts proved to be unnecessary. As I walked into the gym, I was immediately struck by the spirit and energy that was present. The entire team was present, working hard, giving each other high-fives, and concentrating on their drills with incredible enthusiasm. The fact that they weren't playing for the championship didn't seem to matter at all. That's when I realized what motivated these kids wasn't the desire to win that first-place trophy—it was the friendships they had made and the joy they got from playing a game they loved.

They played that afternoon with a lot of pride and intensity against a very good team and won. They so enjoyed the experience and didn't want it to end that they wore their sweaty, dirty uniforms all the way home.

I learned a lot from those kids about motivation—lessons I have used with other athletes, with people with whom I've worked, with family members, and with many others. Some of these lessons include:

- Learn what motivates people. Some individuals are motivated by their drive to succeed. Others are motivated more by their fear of failure. The success-motivated individual welcomes and even thrives under pressure, while the person driven by fear dreads critical situations and the possibility of failure and disapproval. Fear-driven individuals need extra encouragement, understanding, and patience to overcome or successfully manage their fears and perform to the best of their abilities.

- Motivate by challenges. If you really want people to get to that next level, challenge them. A challenge is positive and motivational. A threat, on the other hand, is negative and gets the person preoccupied with the consequences of failing.
- Be positive. Nothing good comes from negativity. Be positive *no matter what*, and you will be a successful motivator.
- Use recognition. Recognition is one of the most powerful motivators that exist. Every day, let your employees, your athletes, and your kids know that *you* know they're there and giving an effort.
- Model motivation. If you want to be a better motivator, *you* have to be motivated! If you can't get excited about something and always seem to "go through the motions," you can forget about motivating anyone else.
- Become a salesperson. Good motivators are good sales people. You have to sell people on hard work and the pursuit of excellence. You have to get them to buy the fact that their sacrifices and sweat are worth the price of the goal. In other words, you have to explain to them the necessity of their efforts. For example, simply telling an athlete to do something is nowhere near as effective as explaining to them how a particular exercise or drill will help them get closer to where they want to go.

Someone once wrote that you cannot motivate others for the long run; you can only create an environment for self-motivation. I have taken that principle with me into the work I do with youth, and I feel it has made an incredible difference.

No Knee? No Problem!

When I was growing up, Compton was one of about 100 communities that made up the greater-Los Angeles area. At the time, Compton's population was around 40,000, and it was considered the sports capital of the West, if not the nation.

Five junior high schools—Roosevelt, Willowbrook, Enterprise, Lynwood, and Paramount—fed into the two-year high school. We played inter-school competition from 7th to 10th grades, with league standings and championships in all major sports, plus tennis and swimming. Tackle football started in 9th grade and was played in 10th grade, as well. The 9th and 10th grade tackle football program was extremely strong—probably unmatched in the nation—making the high school team they supplied truly outstanding.

My early sports years were marked by numerous injuries, probably due to the fact I only stood about 5'5" in the 10th grade and weighed no more than 120 pounds. Nevertheless, I was always a starter on any basketball team I played on, and usually the best player.

Since I had a broken arm in 9th grade when football season rolled around, I couldn't play tackle football until 10th grade. I started out playing both offense (wide receiver) and defense (safety). Midway through the season, I broke my thumb (it's still crooked to this day), and the doctor suggested I give up defense and just stick to offense. As a result, I continued as a starter on offense, scoring the only touchdowns in our 19-18 championship loss to Enterprise Junior High.

I managed to avoid further serious injury until about halfway through basketball season. I was driving for the basket when an opponent tripped me from behind (I later learned that the players had been instructed to "knock Selleck off his feet every chance you get"). In those days, the mats behind the basket were pretty skimpy. My right knee missed the mat and pounded directly into the wall.

My best friend, Al Waner, rushed over to where I was writhing on the floor. "Al," I said, "I think it's serious."

It was. Everything that connects the knee to the tibia was shattered—due in part to the force with which I hit the wall, and also due to something called Osgood-Schlatter, disease, which causes weakness in the joint area.

That was the end of my season. The doctors informed me that it was also the end of my playing days. After surgery to insert a pin in my leg, I wore a cast for almost six months. I didn't give up on basketball, however. In the fall, I entered 11th grade at Compton High School and despite the fact they had several returning players (not to mention all the excellent players coming in from the district's junior high system), I made the starting lineup for the first game of the season. Right in the middle of our pre-game warm-up, however, my knee locked up. I couldn't bend it. I couldn't run a step to save my life.

Fortunately, my dad had many friends in the medical profession. I began making the rounds of several physicians who basically agreed that I had the leg of a 60-year-old, and I should start looking for other activities (chess, perhaps?) with which to entertain myself.

Unwilling to accept this prognosis, my parents put me on a train from Los Angeles to San Francisco to visit my godfather, an orthopedic surgeon who had been head of the U.S. Army orthopedic team during World War II. He examined my leg, and reported that I had a bone spur on my kneecap. If I returned to San Francisco during Christmas break, he would remove it.

As soon as school let out for Christmas, I headed back to San Francisco. The surgery went well, but I didn't realize how well until I noticed what seemed like an endless parade of doctors entering my room to hover over my knee, examine it thoroughly, and then leave.

I finally asked my godfather what was going on, and he replied that when he opened up the knee to remove the bone spur, he discovered the entire kneecap had been shattered. So, instead of removing a bone spur, he removed my kneecap!

It should be noted that in those days, no kneecap meant you would have a stiff knee for the rest of your life. Fortunately for me, however, my godfather had learned from a Swedish doctor in the war how to remove the kneecap (in those instances, usually because of shrapnel wounds) and still leave mobility in the knee. The surgery that he performed on me was the first of its kind ever done in this country and was written up in various medical journals.

Of course, I didn't care about all that—I just wanted to know if I could play basketball again. My godfather said yes, I would be able to play. I don't know if he really believed that or if he just said it to make me feel better, and since he died not long afterwards, I never got to ask him.

I left the hospital to stay with my grandmother in her apartment, while a special cast was made for me. Again, my godfather was way ahead of his time. The cast was constructed out of a corset-like material, similar to the walking casts of today. It was designed to give me much more freedom than I would have otherwise had.

Not content to sit around waiting for the cast, I talked my grandmother, on my first day out of the hospital, into letting me go to a nearby park to watch kids play basketball. One thing led to another and just a few hours later, I was back in the hospital. Amazingly, all I had done was rupture some blood vessels. The delicate surgery my godfather had performed was undamaged.

I returned to school after Christmas break. Since we were on the same campus as the junior college, our high school schedule was similar to that of the college students. We took classes and had various free periods that we could use for whatever we wanted. My coach suggested that I spend one of my free hours in the gym, shooting baskets. He would provide someone to chase the ball down for me, given that I had one leg in a cast, while the other one was weak from the effects of Osgood-Schlatter.

Subsequently, that's what I did—hobble around on my thin, shaky little legs and shoot the basketball over and over. As the season wound down and we came to our final league game, the coach came to me and told me he wanted me to suit up that night. "But, Coach," I said, "I can't run."

He responded, "I'm the coach, and you do what I say."

So I suited up and sat on the bench until the last 10 seconds of the game. Then, the coach pointed at me and said, "Selleck, go in and just stand at half-court." Those 10 seconds of standing meant I was now eligible for the CIF (California Interscholastic Federation) playoffs.

We entered the playoff semi-finals with 25 wins and 8 losses, preparing to face Alhambra High School, which was 32-0 at the time and had two players who were going to be starting at UCLA and USC the following season. At practice on Monday, the coach told me I was going to be the starting point guard for that Friday's game. My mouth dropped. I had yet to actually play a single high school game, I had both knees in braces, I could hardly run, and he wanted me to start against a team that was heavily favored to beat us?

When Friday came, I ran the team as its point guard for the entire game. In the final seconds, I was wide open for the game-winning shot. As the Alhambra defense panicked and converged on me, I passed the ball to a teammate under the basket. He laid the ball in for the upset and the win.

The next night's game against Pasadena High School was anticlimactic in comparison. Because they were not the same caliber of team as Alhambra, the coach did not need me to play. I sat on the bench and watched as my teammates built an insurmountable lead. With three minutes to go and the game safely in hand, the coach sent me into the game. I hit three long shots and the game was over—our coach's first CIF championship.

As soon as the gun went off, the coach came over to me and said, "George, next year you will be the most outstanding player in the state of California." He turned out to be right. When the next year rolled around, I was voted the Outstanding Basketball Player of the Year by *California Magazine*.

To this day, it is an abiding mystery what the coach saw in me in light of my numerous injuries. I think he must have had an extraordinary sense of perception. I have tried to do the same for the players I've coached—and indeed, for anyone who's been a part of my life. I have found that when you try to see past the surface to the potential within, more often than not, people will live up to that potential.

I think it's interesting that most kids start life full of physical activity. They love to play, move, climb mile-high bookcases, and engage in other death-defying activities—usually before the age of three. Somewhere along the way, though, this mindset changes. Adolescents become self-conscious about any number of things, including their bodies, trying new things, and embarrassing themselves in front of others. At the same time, sports become more competitive and more demanding. This "perfect storm" results in 80 percent of kids dropping out of youth sports between the ages of 13 and 15.

Many kids would decline to call themselves athletes, because they think of athletes as the jocks who are on all the sports teams. In reality, however, what is an athlete, really? *Webster's Dictionary* defines an athlete as "one who engages or competes in exercises, or games of physical agility, strength, endurance, etc." That definition applies to just about everybody.

Compared to most of the kids I played with when I was young, I didn't look like your typical athlete. But I kept playing for two reasons: I loved to play, and I had people who believed in me. If we can build a program that provides kids with those two factors, then I believe we can reverse that 80 percent number and create a new definition of what it really means to be an athlete.

Discovering My Kryptonite

My senior season was rapidly winding down, and our team would continue on through the playoffs and championship game, as we had throughout the season—undefeated. I was the leading scorer in the conference and would eventually receive CIF Southern Section and State Player of the Year honors.

None of this mattered on this particular afternoon, however. Shortly after I arrived at practice, our coach announced we were going to play some one-on-one. As we began to pair up, Woody Sauldsberry shouted, "I want to guard George."

Woodrow "Woody" Sauldsberry would later become the NBA's Rookie of Year in his first professional season with the Philadelphia Warriors (now the Golden State Warriors), and a future NBA All-Star. For the purpose of this story, however, the really significant factor was that Woody was 6′5″, strong, and fast, with very long arms and legs. I stood 5′8″, if that. Up to this point and throughout the remainder of my basketball career, every team I played against would put their smallest and quickest player on me, hoping to match my quickness and variety of offensive moves. Nobody—and I mean nobody—ever thought of putting a bigger person on me. They just assumed a big guy would not match up. Boy, were they wrong! Woody's long arms and legs shut me down completely. I had to take three steps to his one. He stopped me cold from doing what had always come easily to me, which was beating my man one-on-one.

Needless to say, I never told a soul that Woody was my kryptonite. And nobody ever figured it out.

That experience taught me to never think I had "arrived." No matter how much I knew or how good I might be, I could always improve. For example, I was a counseling psychologist for over 20 years. You would think that would make me an expert (or at least pretty good) at knowing how to relate to people. And yet, given that I am on my third marriage—somewhere along the line, I definitely had room for improvement.

A need exists to help kids recognize how to take things they learn from playing sports or participating in different types of exercise and apply these lessons to other aspects of their life. Leadership, perseverance, teamwork, and organization, for example, are all qualities and skills that are equally valuable, whether you're part of a sports team, a debate team, or a family. Not everyone recognizes or teaches that point, however. In reality, I firmly believe that when we teach kids how to make connections between what they do when they're playing a game of soccer and what they do when they're sitting in their math class trying to stay awake, we'll strengthen their ability to be successful in both.

In the Zone

In my senior year of high school, in the midst of what would become a 32-game winning streak, my Compton High basketball team went up against Ventura High. During that game, I took 16 shots outside the key (equivalent to today's three-pointer) and made 15 of them.

Sports psychologists have a term for how I performed against Ventura. It's called being "in the zone." When athletes are "in the zone," their mind and body work together in perfect harmony to achieve success. It is not uncommon for athletes to pay a lot of money to individuals whose job it is to help get them "in the zone."

If you're a parent with a child in sports, maybe you've been fortunate enough to experience those heady times when your child is in the zone. More likely than not, however, you've experienced many more times when your child hasn't been in the zone, and you've wished you knew what to say or do to help him or her get there.

What would you think if I said I knew a way for kids *and* parents to regularly—not just once in a rare while—experience the kind of sports satisfaction that comes from being "in the zone?"

Before I inform you to achieve the aforementioned, I'd like to provide a little background into the history of sports psychology. Sports psychology is actually a fairly new field. In the beginning (what I call the "first wave"), its focus was primarily on the physical—what the body needed to do to more successfully perform sport-specific skills. For example, baseball players would be told to visualize their swing, the premise being that if they could mentally "see" themselves using correct form, they would then follow through physically.

Then the "second wave" of sports psychology came along. This wave focused on helping athletes improve the mental aspects of their performance. Athletes were taught techniques that could help them concentrate better, stay calm under pressure, and effectively manage the stress of competition. Still, the primary goal was performance enhancement.

The first two waves contributed a lot to the sports experience in helping athletes improve their performance. On the other hand, they do have a drawback, given that they both revolve around the goal of increasing an athlete's satisfaction through improving their performance. While performing well is a critical ingredient of a successful sports experience, it's not the only thing that makes sport and other fitness activities fun and rewarding.

That's why I believe a "third wave" of sports psychology—or way of looking at and experiencing sport—needs to occur. This wave needs to be one that moves beyond focusing on performance enhancement and the mental game to exploring the meaning, value, and contribution of the sports/fitness experience to individuals, families, and communities. This third wave would follow a similar movement in traditional psychology, which began with Freud and the focus on the subconscious mind (we are all a bundle of neuroses), and then moved on through behaviorism (we are primarily shaped by our environment), and up through humanism (we each have unique inherent capabilities that can be fully realized only when we are valued, supported, and provided with meaningful life activity).

In the third wave of sports psychology, I believe that the focus should turn toward using sport and fitness as a tool to develop the whole person—not just the physical part of a person. Beyond that, sport and fitness could be seen as a way to develop families and, by extension, entire communities. (This is not exactly a new idea I'm proposing. Pierre de Coubertin, the founder of the modern Olympic movement, continually preached the potential of sport to reform humanity, even in his later days when he became disillusioned by the growing corruption of organized sports.)

How would this work? To begin with, kids would need to be trained to open their minds to a more expansive view of sports. Along with teaching them how to visualize themselves connecting with the ball or replacing negative thoughts with positive self-talk, kids need to be taught to look at their peers, competitors, and fans as partners in the shared sports experience. In addition, as youth learn new skills and techniques, they need to get in the habit of asking themselves, "How can what I've learned benefit me as a whole person? How can it benefit my family? My community?"

Finally, kids need to learn how to view the pinnacle of sport as more than just performing well. In reality, a zone exists beyond the zone to which we can aspire. Today's "zone" is the connection of mind and body to achieve athletic success. Tomorrow's zone is the connection of physical self to inner self, as well as to others, in order to realize the full potential of sports and fitness to provide meaning and value to life.

The Foul Shot I Didn't Want to Make

It was my senior year of high school, and our basketball team was having a great season. Our team was good—really, really good. It was so good that Woody Sauldsberry played second string for most of the year.

We had been invited to play in the Beverly Hills Invitational Tournament. It was the final day of the tournament, and we were tired. Two of our starters were out with the flu, we'd played two games the day before and one that afternoon, and now we were preparing to go up against Long Beach Wilson for the championship.

Later in the season, we would play Wilson twice and beat them by 20 or more points each time, but on this night they were a tough opponent. The score was tied, as the clock ticked down to eight seconds remaining. I took a shot and missed it. A Wilson player grabbed the rebound and his teammates immediately began shouting "Time-out!"

There was just one small problem. Wilson didn't have a time-out to use. The referee tried to let them know they would be assessed a technical foul if given a time-out, but in the noise and confusion, his warning was overlooked.

The expression on the players' faces as they realized their mistake was painful. I felt bad for them, especially since many of the Wilson players were good friends of mine from the Long Beach YMCA.

As I joined my teammates in our huddle, I couldn't share in their elation at being presented with this golden opportunity to win the game. I was even more depressed when our coach immediately designated me as the one who would shoot the technical foul.

I thought I knew what I had to do. "Coach," I blurted out. "These are my friends. I am going to miss the shot, and we will beat them fair and square in overtime."

In reality, I had a pretty good relationship with our coach and fully expected him to be awestruck by my incredibly noble offer. What I didn't expect was that he would grab my wrist—hard—and snarl, "You miss this shot, and you won't play another minute this season."

Okaaay. I climbed up out of the huddle (the Beverly Hills gym was a "swim gym," which meant it had a pool beneath the removable gym floor, and the players sat along the sidelines in dugouts). I then stalked over to the free-throw line. In front of the packed house, I hurled the ball toward the basket, almost without looking. The shot went in, I was named player of the tournament, and we went on to an undefeated season.

It was only later after much reflection that I realized my grand gesture had actually been rather insensitive and immature on my part. I was thinking of my buddies on the other team and how wonderful it would be if I could do this for them. I wasn't, however, thinking of how it would affect my current teammates and coach. My coach's job was to win games, or at least give his team the best chance to win. My teammates' job was to play their best—and as part of the team, that was my job, too. I wasn't, however, thinking about that. I was in my own little world—a rather narrow world, at that.

I learned from that experience that right and wrong and what is "fair" are not always as simple as some people think they are. Very few of our decisions are made in a vacuum, which is why it's important to take into consideration the context of the decision and who else might be affected by it. When I am faced with difficult decisions today, I try to ask myself not only, "How will this affect me?" but also, "How will this affect others?" I think back to that day in Beverly Hills and try to remember that it's not always a question of, "What is the right thing to do?" but rather, "What is the best thing to do?"*

---

* An interesting sequel exists to this story. Some 45 years later when I was consulting with a large restaurant chain in Southern California, I met the niece of the captain of that Wilson team, who as a boy had been one of my very best friends from the Long Beach YMCA. She recognized my name from all the stories her uncle used to tell, and put me in touch with my former teammate. We met for lunch, and I told him the story of what had gone on in the huddle that day. Tom responded with a smile. "Well, let me tell you what was going on in our huddle. All the other guys were saying things like, 'No problem, he'll miss it,' and stuff like that. When they were all finished, I just said, 'No, he won't.'" Tom's recollection just goes to point out another important lesson—sometimes others know us better than we know ourselves!

The ability to make good decisions is an extremely valuable skill. Equally valuable is the ability to learn from poor decisions. A program that puts kids in charge of making decisions, as well as allows them to make mistakes and learn and grow from those mistakes, will help kids develop a skill that will serve them well all their lives.

Don't Call Me a Natural Shooter!

From the *Los Angeles Times*:

GEORGE SELLECK, COMPTON HIGH SCHOOL FLASH, IS NAMED CIF BASKETBALL PLAYER OF THE YEAR FOR 1952 SEASON

Seldom, in this day of towering basketball players, will you find a "little man" heading the list of all-star ballots.

This was the case, however, in this year's All-C.I.F. basketball team voting as George Selleck, Compton High School's diminutive guard, was voted C.I.F. Basketball Player of the Year. It took the Helms Athletic Foundation's All-Southern California Board of Basketball only a few minutes to single out Selleck as the top player in C.I.F. high school ranks for 1952. Only two teams, Compton High School and Loyola High School, placed more than one man on the 1952 All-C.I.F. first and second teams. Compton High, under the capable coaching of Kenny Fagans who directed his team to the Coast League Championship, placed George Selleck, guard, on the first team and Al Waner and Delbert Johnston, both guards, on the second team. Loyola placed Jack Dunne, center, on the first team and Fernando Neri, forward, on the second. Seventeen schools have men on the honor teams.

"He gets more out of his slight physical build—5'8" and 135 pounds—than any player I have seen in the past 25 years," said Coach Fagans of his star basketeer. Fagans calls Selleck the best natural shot he has ever coached, and George's 511 points in 28 games, an average of 18.8 points per game, attest to this statement.

Selleck's performance this year is all the more phenomenal when you learn that he played minus one knee cap. He played only slightly last year, because of the operation, but despite this handicap, came back strong in the 1952 campaign. Selleck was named the outstanding player in both the Compton and Beverly Hills Tournaments.

The aforementioned article has always bothered me, along with statements people have made over the years: "You were such a natural." "You were born with talent." On one hand, it is truly nice to be remembered. On the other hand, I wish people understood that none of my success on the court came to me easily.

The truth is I spent hours upon hours before school, during recess, after school, and on weekends practicing shooting, day after day, for many, many years to become a good shooter and player.

When it comes to the ability to do something, two schools of thought exist. The first line of thinking is a by-product of the traditional model of reasoning that "you either have it (ability), or you don't," and if you don't have it, there isn't much hope for you to become competent. The second school of thought—the "efficacy model"—argues that self-confidence plus effective effort leads to development.

Carol Dweck, author of *Mindset: The New Psychology of Success*, has identified these two different mindsets. The first she calls the "fixed mindset," in which individuals see their ability as set. Either you are talented musically, academically, athletically or you aren't. Either you are smart, or you aren't. This mindset is a dead-end, because whether you succeed or not is determined by something totally outside your control.

The other mindset is the "growth mindset." You believe in your ability to grow and improve, regardless of where you start. Which one sounds more appealing to you?

I believe the message of the "growth mindset" is a wonderful, positive attitude to pass on to our kids: "I can get better at math or improve my fitness or be able to play a sport competently if I just work hard at it."

The teen years are a time of tremendous growth and transformation for those involved. Not only are kids are quite different, they tend to experience a unique level of evolvement—in physical size and capability, emotional maturity, and interests. The value of effort is an important message that can help them navigate through this period, as well as encourage them to improve and learn.

Accordingly, individuals should feel free to call me anything—"short" (I am), "slow on the uptake" (sometimes I'm that, too)—but don't call me a natural shooter. Call me a hard worker. Because that's a compliment I'm more than willing to take.

A Wise Decision

A couple days after I'd been named C.I.F. player of the year, the phone rang in our Poinsettia Street home. "It's some man named Rupp who wants to talk with George," my sister shouted. And indeed, it was.

Adolph Rupp—the legendary coach at the University of Kentucky—was one of the most intimidating and colorful figures in sports. For decades, Rupp was the winningest coach in basketball, a holder of four national titles, and well-known for his off-the-cuff quips, usually laced with both sarcasm and profanity.

I immediately recognized the name, though as a 17-year-old kid, I was not familiar with his reputation. In what was probably one of the wiser decisions of my young life,

I politely declined Mr. Rupp's invitation to consider playing basketball for him and the Kentucky Wildcats. I had always dreamed of going to Stanford and was not open to other considerations.

From a basketball perspective, though, Kentucky might have been a good choice for me. Rupp was an early innovator of the fast break and set offense—strong aspects of my game. Furthermore, Rupp preferred a tight man-to-man defense, which again was something at which I was quite good. Another significant early basketball innovation of Rupp's was the "guard-around" play, which allowed players like me to be more creative and free on offense.

On the other hand, Rupp had the reputation of being an arrogant, gruff, "my-way-or-the-highway" coach. He was an early and forceful advocate of the winning-is-everything philosophy, often making statements such as, "We want to win. We just have to win. Lord knows, no one wants to win more than we do." He is also quoted as saying, "If it doesn't matter who wins or loses, then what in the hell is that scoreboard doing up there?" And finally, "Basketball without victory has little meaning."

No, I don't think I would have been happy playing for Coach Rupp.

Later, when I began working with young athletes, their parents, and their coaches, I saw the damage that could be done when such a high premium was put on winning. I also firmly believe this attitude is part of what has led to the incredibly high drop-out rates in youth sports.

The aforementioned is why I believe it's so important to put kids in charge of running their own games, and recognize that the rewards of effort and progress are even more valuable than the rewards of winning. Because basketball—or football or baseball or soccer—even without victory, still has plenty of meaning. Hopefully, even Coach Rupp would agree with that philosophy at this point.

In My Humble Opinion

When I was named CIF player of year, it was a pretty heady thing for a skinny, 5'8" kid playing his first full year of high school basketball. Not long afterwards, my mother and I were walking the family dog around the block when she remarked, "George, the thing that has impressed me most through all that has happened with your sports this year is how humble you have been!"

While I now know that my mother meant this as a compliment, for some reason, at the time, I interpreted it to mean that I should be careful not to get too full of myself. My head literally dropped down several notches (all the way to my chest, actually), and to this day, I still struggle to take any kind of pride in the successes I've had in life. It is interesting to note that *Webster's Dictionary* partially describes humility as "having or showing awareness of one's defects." In reality, I had that in spades.

In my day, humility was viewed as a positive attribute. You did not spike the football when you made a touchdown, fist-pump after you scored a basket, or rip your shirt off and wave it around after making a goal. If we had tried any of these things, I'm sure our parents would have risen up *en masse* and marched us all off the playing field by our ears.

In today's world, I think humility is often viewed (at least in the sports world) as a negative. Unfortunately, some individuals associate it with words like spineless, spiritless, and boring. When I coached, I liked players with a lot of spirit—but I also needed my players to be humble enough to be open to learning what they needed to learn and to playing their role on the team, even if that role consisted primarily of sitting on the bench.

I think humility is not about making individuals feel small, but is about helping them understand how much they still have to learn, grow, and develop. Humility allows people to keep their minds open and to see another person's point of view. It is about having a correct estimate of yourself—not thinking less of yourself, but thinking about yourself less. It doesn't mean being weak, reticent, or self-effacing. It means recognizing values and principles and putting them in front of oneself. One of the qualities of a good leader is humility—the right kind of humility. I have seen that kind of humility—and that kind of leadership—in the kids with whom I work.

And Mom? It's a little late, but thanks for the compliment!

Retiring My Jersey

One day, I was going through some old, wooden scrapbooks from my childhood and found the following article from *The Roosevelt Lionews*—my junior high school newsletter:

George Selleck's Jersey to be Retired

In an awards assembly, the Athletic Commission bestowed a great honor upon an outstanding sportsman, George Selleck. George has excelled in sports during his four years at Roosevelt. He was deeply honored to receive such an outstanding award for his favorite life of sports.

As the students in the future years walk the halls of Roosevelt, they will see in the trophy case, along with the many honors Roosevelt has won in the various fields, the basketball shirt of George Selleck, with the big red "3," resting in its place of honor. Roosevelt is delighted to bestow this honor upon him with the hope that the future years will be eventful ones for an all-round athlete, the Lion who held the key position, George Selleck.

To be honest, I had forgotten all about this event until I came across the article. I certainly don't make an annual trek back to Roosevelt to gaze at my jersey—if it's even still there. Part of me wonders if the honor had less to do with my athletic prowess and more to do with the numerous injuries I sustained over my playing days (two broken arms, a broken thumb, a dislocated elbow, and five surgeries on my knee). I think the school probably thought, "This kid's playing days are over—let's give him some positive memories."

On the other hand, I have learned over the years that it is impossible to be completely objective about yourself and how you perform in any area of life. As a consequence, feedback from others is essential to gain an accurate perception and self-estimate of our knowledge, skills, and attitudes. Learning how to give appropriate feedback to others is a critical leadership skill. Maybe the people who bestowed this honor on me were simply being nice. If so, it was much appreciated. Maybe, however, they saw something in my athletic abilities and determination that I didn't quite recognize myself at that point. If that was the case, then it was even more appreciated. I felt like someone believed in me, and that is something every kid needs to have—someone who believes.

Lead On

When I was a short, skinny 10-year-old, my mother would drive me to the bus stop at the intersection of Greenleaf Street and Long Beach Boulevard so that I could take the 30-minute bus ride to the Long Beach YMCA. I initially began my "Y" experience in the tumbling class—which I hated and wasn't very good at—and swimming, which I also hated because, as the culture of the time dictated, we swam naked. It didn't take me long to learn that the basketball court was where I wanted to be.

I was blessed from that point on to have coaches who were excellent role models and who helped me build the strong desire I have today to give back to kids. In that regard, when I say that I was "blessed," I mean that in every sense of the word. We've all heard of or experienced coaches who think the experience is all about them, individuals who brow-beat their players, throw chairs at them, or worse. I, on the other hand, had coaches who helped me develop my skills as a player and a person.

Shorty Kellogg was my first coach. Even though he knew more about tumbling than basketball, he was a wonderful example of how to pay attention to kids, take them seriously, and support them.

My junior high school coach became a lifelong friend and encourager. He loved basketball, and had played in college and for the military during World War II. He taught individual, as well team, skills and approaches, something you don't always see in today's coaches.

My high school coach, Ken Fagans, who went on to serve as CIF Southern Section commissioner from 1954-1975, might not always have been warm and fuzzy, but he knew basketball and he knew how to coach it. He saw in me ability and potential that were way beyond my personal understanding.

Finally, there was Howie Dallmar, my coach at Stanford. Howie, like me, played for Stanford, became a collegiate All-American, and was drafted by the Philadelphia Warriors of the Basketball Association of America (a forerunner to today's NBA). He was the third leading scorer on the team that won the 1947 BAA Championship. After coaching at the University of Pennsylvania for several years, Howie came back to Stanford and coached for 21 seasons. Howie's gift to me was his confidence in my ability to lead the team and his appreciation for what I brought to the game.

I believe that my success and, in particular, my passion for developing leadership skills in others is rooted in the experiences I had with these coaches. They helped me recognize that:

- Leadership is a process in which many can participate—not just a few.
- Leadership is about taking responsibility for working with others (teammates, fellow students, co-workers, etc.) to achieve common goals.
- Leadership involves identifying and utilizing the skills, abilities, passions, and desires of your teammates and potential teammates.
- Leadership is about connecting across boundaries—cultural, racial, religious, and so on.
- Leadership is about continuously learning and improving.
- Finally, leadership is about being accountable to those with whom you are working and those you are seeking to serve.

These qualities and traits—so important to me in my life—are ones every kid deserves to learn—sooner rather than later.

I have four college degrees: A bachelor's and master's from Stanford, an MDIV in theology from Princeton, and a Ph.D. in counseling psychology from USC. You would think I would have come out of all that a lot smarter than I did. Sure, I learned—but many of the lessons went unrecognized until I was much older and more self-aware. Some of them didn't even occur to me until I was writing this book.

In addition to being able to attend school at some of the finest universities in the country, I had other experiences during this period that shaped me into the person I am today and strengthened my resolve to help youth go into their college years prepared to get more out of it than I did. I was able to play basketball against and with the great Bill Russell. I was Ty Cobb's live-in caretaker near the end of his life. I made friendships that I keep to this day. But ...

I am old enough now to recognize the futility of regrets and human enough to still have them. I wish I had understood the purpose of school better. I wish I had struggled less with issues of identity and insecurity. I wish I had put more effort into relationships instead of being so focused on myself. But if I had, would I be where I am—who I am—today? And would I be doing what I'm doing?

If changing the past means changing the present, I don't know that I would do it. I feel that what I'm doing now is too important—not for me, but for the hundreds of kids I work with and for the hundreds upon hundreds I hope will be positively impacted in the future. When you finish reading this book, you'll have to let me know if you feel the same way.

But for now, it's off to college we go!

Stan the Man

A few months before my freshman year at Stanford, I received an invitation to a party at the home of Horace Heidt in the exclusive Brentwood area of West Los Angeles. Horace Heidt was a famous musician and radio and television personality, whose 1941 hit, "The Hut-Sut Song," is heard in the movie *A Christmas Story*.

My invitation had come from Jack Heidt, Horace's son, on behalf of his Phi Gamma Delta fraternity brothers, who were illegally rushing me. It was pretty heady stuff for a kid from Compton who had never seen such a mansion—let alone been inside one—and who did not know it was against the rules for fraternities to have contact with freshmen until after their first quarter at school.

At the party, I made friends with a guy named Stan, who was about to begin his senior year at Stanford. Stan suggested he catch a ride with me to school when it started. Honored, I readily accepted.

Five weeks later, in my old beat-up Plymouth, with our stuff in the back seat, we drove the old Highway 101 from Los Angeles to Palo Alto. As we were approaching

Salinas, just before the turnoff to Fort Ord (at the height of the Korean War), we entered a construction zone, with a sign instructing cars to slow to 15 miles per hour. It was after 4 p.m., and the workers had all gone home for the day. As a result, instead of slowing down, I cruised through the area at about 45 mph.

Suddenly, a flashing red light appeared in my rearview mirror. The officer who approached my window was almost apoplectic with rage. "Where are you going in such a hurry?" he demanded. Scared, I was about to answer, but before I could, a calm, cool, and very collected Stan leaned across the seat and said, "Officer, we've just been drafted, and are reporting to Fort Ord for duty." Oh!" the startled officer replied. "Well, uh, good luck, boys." And off we went with no speeding ticket!

The point of my story is that I am not advocating breaking rules—especially traffic rules. The lesson I want to get across in this instance is about keeping your cool when those around you are in danger of losing theirs. As a counselor, I know that any time you are in a situation in which one person is scared, angry, traumatized, or upset in any way, it is critical that you remain calm. If you let your emotions spiral out of control, you can't help the other person.

I think learning how to plan for and handle unexpected situations is an important factor for all kids to have. Hopefully, it doesn't mean that they'll grow up knowing how to talk their way out of traffic tickets, but that they *will* be better at handling those curve balls that life likes to throw at us.

Freshman Year

In the fall of 1952, I arrived on the campus of Stanford University to begin my college education. I was anxious and apprehensive. My high school experience had consisted of only the 11th and 12th grades, because of the 6-4-4 system I've mentioned previously. Because most of my college requirements had been completed by the end of my junior year, my senior year of high school was made up primarily of free periods and electives.

I was somewhat aware of Stanford's academic reputation, but I was on the Palo Alto campus more as a jock than a student. When I got to my first class in the Western civilization course—the bane of every freshman's existence—I thought it would be the end of me. All of my classmates were nervous about that subject—even the really smart ones. I think I must have studied at least twice the number of hours of anyone else just to pull Bs in the class. It really made me wonder if I was going to be a successful college student. That fear is something that stayed with me throughout my undergraduate and graduate studies.

It wasn't until I began writing books that I realized I had gone through 12 years of college and obtained four degrees, with the mistaken notion that whatever school I was attending at the time was responsible for my education. Once I started to write—to put my ideas, thoughts and feelings out there—I began to realize *I* was responsible for what I learned and until I accepted that responsibility, learning was not going to take place and certainly wasn't going to be any fun!

I've finally developed several strategies that have helped me to not only enjoy my intellectual efforts, but have also allowed me to feel more capable and competent in my efforts. First, I take time to think and reflect. I do my best work on walks or in the shower. The more I think on a subject and note my thoughts, the better the product becomes. Whenever possible, I give myself as much time as I can to revise underdeveloped ideas.

Second, I try not to compare myself to others as I have done in the past. I embrace the importance of determining where *I* am and working from there.

Third, I am less afraid and more inclined to seek out advice. This factor includes input from friends, classmates, and whomever I think may bring fresh eyes and perspectives to the situation.

Finally, I am having fun! Life is too short (especially at my age) to stress over things that don't need to be stressed over. Okay, while I still stress more than I should, I don't stress as much as I used to.

As I work with youth, I try to help them employ these principles as well. For example, asking kids to spend time reflecting on the skills and qualities that make a good leader, or stressing the importance of having fun—because that's when some of a person's best learning takes place.

I just wish it hadn't taken almost 80 years for ME to learn these things.

Dumb Jock

I was the first kid from Compton High School to attend Stanford University. You would think that would have been a self-esteem booster, but it wasn't. Because I was at Stanford on an athletic scholarship, and because I don't remember having a single intellectual discussion in my family as I was growing up, and because one of the first things they did when I registered was to place me in a course set aside for those who entered the university deficient in English, I felt like the epitome of a "dumb jock."

This issue is one that I've struggled with my whole life. As I stated in my book, *How to Play the Game of Your Life*, "When athletic identity is too large a part of your total identity, it fosters immaturity and naïveté. Focusing so much attention on the athletic self allows the other areas of your life to go underdeveloped. You may fail to see the consequences of your actions. You may lack sophistication, perception, and common sense." That, my friends, was me in a nutshell.

Even as I got older and stopped identifying myself as [only] a basketball player, I still struggled with knowing exactly who I was and where I fit into the world. Once, while I was single between marriages, I decided to put a couple of restrictions on myself when I went on a first date. During the date, I would not tell: one, my profession (psychologist); or two, whether or not I had children. It was revealing how short-lived my mission was. I was uncomfortable and unable to connect without mentioning my work and my kids. It was clear to me that I was continuing to define myself by what I did, how well I was doing professionally, and how much my children were achieving. In other words, while it wasn't about sport, it was still about producing. It was not enough simply to be someone, but I also had to *do* a great deal to be accepted.

It is normal for kids to struggle with issues of identity and to "try on" different identities—nerd, Goth, jock, etc.—on their way to determining who they are. Trying on and shedding different identities is how they learn what suits them. Putting their own twist on these identities is how they learn what makes them unique. What kids need is an accepting, all-inclusive environment for them to discover who they are and who they want to be. Finding that environment can be a different story … until now, that is.

Dave and Ben and Me

David Epperson and I met during my very first days on the Stanford campus in 1952. I was a lowly freshman on a basketball scholarship, even though the varsity coach had never seen me play. Dave was a junior and a member of the varsity squad. We met during an informal pre-season scrimmage in the old Encina gym on campus. When Dave reported on me to the varsity coach, "He can play!" a friendship began that has existed to this day.

In the more than 60 years since that first meeting, Dave and I have co-authored two books, co-founded a non-profit, conducted dozens of workshops and trainings together, written joint articles, gone on retreats, and shared a common perspective and commitment to help all participants—athletes, coaches, administrators, parents, and fans—get the most out of their sports experience.

I am indebted to Dave. In many ways, he has been my intellectual mentor. When we first started to collaborate more than 30 years ago, I was a psychologist seeking to improve the lives of people through counseling and psychotherapy—the individual approach. Dave, a sociologist, introduced me to the concept of making a better world by focusing on groups, systems, norms, and organizations. My condo and garage are filled with boxes of white papers, articles, and trainings that Dave, a prolific writer if ever there was one, has put together.

Recently, I rediscovered an article in which Dave begins a discussion of Benjamin Franklin's famous "seven virtues" by sharing Franklin's quote: "We must all hang together, or we will hang separately." That article got me thinking about how Franklin's seven virtues have a lot to say about my present efforts, for example:

❏ Franklin had an aversion to tyranny. Throughout his life, Franklin was willing to compromise on many matters but not on this one. In sports, we've seen a lot of tyranny. Fortunate is the athlete who hasn't experienced at least one command-and-control coach whose favorite phrase is *"Drop and give me fifty,"* when kids fail to fulfill their expectations. My response? Let's put kids in charge of creating fun and meaningful sports and fitness experiences that are open and inviting to all individuals regardless of athletic ability.

❏ Franklin valued free expression. He believed the surest guard against tyranny and arbitrary power was free expression, the free flow of ideas and a free press. No tyrannical society can long exist, he felt, when it cannot control the flow of information and ideas. *"Listen up! Let me do the talking"* is an injunction we hear from coaches in gyms and playing fields everywhere. However, I believe a good youth program is one in which the voice of the kids is heard first and foremost—their ideas, their thoughts, their feelings.

❏ Franklin understood the value of humor and lightheartedness for living the good life. He invented what became the quintessential genre of American folksy humor—a style adopted by several humorists, such as Mark Twain and Will Rogers. *"Quit horsing around"* is a common command given by youth and school coaches that is aimed at making sport a very serious undertaking. On the other hand, isn't it better in the long run to put the joy back into sports and play? Aren't kids more likely to make a habit of something they *like?*

❏ Franklin understood the importance of humility in establishing effective relationships in a community. When Franklin made the list of virtues he wanted to acquire, he very proudly showed it to his friends, one of whom, a Quaker, pointed out he had left one off. Franklin was often guilty of pride, the friend said. As a consequence, Franklin added humility to his list. *"Show some pride"* is a statement often used to appeal to an athlete's need for recognition. In reality, a big difference exists between humbly receiving recognition and being cocky. In the current sports culture, a virtue has been made of what Franklin considered a violation of a basic virtue. Kids need to know that being humble does not mean being weak, reticent, or self-effacing. It means putting others ahead of self. It means standing firm for your values, even in the face of opposition. It means being a team player.

❏ Franklin embraced the ideals of liberty and democracy. More than most diplomats in our history, Franklin understood that America's strength in world affairs would come from a mix of idealism and realism. When woven together, as they would be in policies, ranging from the Monroe Doctrine to the Marshall Plan, they were the warp and woof of a sturdy foreign policy. *"We can't let the inmates run the asylum"* coaches often say when it is suggested that athletes be given a voice in how their lives in sports are to be managed. I believe, however, that the kids should be put in charge. Every kid should play. Every kid should make a contribution. Decision-making should be collaborative and participatory.

❑ Franklin understood the value of compromise. He was not America's most profound political theorist. On the other hand, when it came to working on the Declaration of Independence, he embodied one crucial virtue that was central to the gathering's success: a belief in the nobility of compromise. *"It's my way or the highway"* is an approach to leadership that is often practiced in school and youth sport that runs counter to the American way. Compromising and working out differences is not only a virtue, it's an essential skill for surviving in today's world.

❑ Finally, Franklin appreciated the importance of tolerance in promoting the common good. The great struggles of the 20th century were initially against fascism and then against communism. As was made clear on Sept. 11, 2001, the great struggle of the 21st century will be between the forces of fanatic fundamentalism and those of tolerance. It is important to remember that America was not born with the virtue of religious tolerance, but had to acquire it. Team-building is critical. Kids have to learn to think and work together—not as a bunch of robots with the same opinions, but as part of a team that celebrates the diversity and uniqueness of each participant.

I do not consider myself to be anywhere near as smart as Benjamin Franklin or even Dave Epperson. On the other hand, I am smart enough to know good ideas and good people when I see them. So thank you, Dave, and thank you, Ben, for both.

Searching for Meaning at the "Mem"

Stanford Memorial Church, which stands at the center of Stanford's campus, is the university's architectural crown jewel. It was one of the earliest, and is still among the most prominent, interdenominational churches in the West. It was probably a strange choice of location for a short, Jewish basketball player to spend a lot of his hours, but I liked it there.

The "Mem"—as it was affectionately called by Stanford students—was a quiet place to hang out and think. After long days of classes, studying, and practice, I would often head for the Mem, where I could be alone without feeling alone, if that makes sense. I didn't really understand it at the time, but I was searching for a sense of who I was—intellectually, emotionally, and spiritually. Weeks and months passed, and I continued to visit the church often.

I would sit by myself and wonder what did I want to do with my life? What kind of person did I want to be? Was I taking the right path educationally? What did I really believe about religion and spirituality? How should I balance the interior and exterior aspects of my life? In what ways could I contribute to society?

The need to feel that life has meaning is as central to our well-being as is the need for food and water. It doesn't matter what type of religion or spirituality you embrace— or whether you embrace any at all. Everyone wants to feel that sense of meaning. A well-known psychiatrist tells the story of when he was a harried young medical resident, working with a patient who was dying of cancer. This series of events was in the days before hospice care and the judicious use of medications to ease a patient's last days. The woman was in a lot of pain. Despite her predicament, she would greet the doctor every day with a smile and a gentle, "How are you doing?" One day the doctor was feeling particularly stressed, and it must have showed, because the woman didn't give him her customary smile. Instead, she looked at him with concern and said, "Doctor— are you okay?"

This doctor was amazed and a little ashamed. He was the one who was supposed to be asking *her* that question. It made him wonder how this woman, who was in excruciating pain and who knew she didn't have long to live, could look beyond what she was experiencing and express her concern about him. He also noticed that even though she was in pain and dying, she still appeared to be *happy*. How could this be? He finally decided that one key to the woman's attitude was her ability to find meaning in her suffering. No, she didn't enjoy being in pain, and given a choice, she probably would have preferred not to be, but she didn't have any control over that. What she did have control over was how she chose to react to what she was going through—and she chose to enjoy her last days to the best of her ability. If that meant cheering up the doctor who was taking care of her, then even better! It meant her life still had meaning.

Helping young people address questions that add meaning to their lives is extremely critical. Telling students they need to do well to be able to pass their classes, graduate high school, get into college so they can get a good job, buy a house, etc. falls way short of satisfying their need for meaning and purpose. Each stage of life should not be mere preparation for the next stage. Each level should be purposeful—an end in itself, a meaningful experience for all. If we want kids to buy into the process, then at least some portion of their time needs to deal with issues that concern them. They need to be free to enjoy the moment; free to enjoy the feel of the sun on their face, the smell of grass that has just been mowed, the sounds of their friends around them. They need to be free to find meaning in those very small things, which will eventually help them find meaning in the much bigger things that are still to come. And sometimes, they need programs that help them experience these things.

Avoiding Icebergs

Learning athletics was pretty easy for me. Balls seemed to magically love my hands and fingertips, whether it was catching a baseball or football or learning how to shoot a basketball. My hands and fingers always did their job, and did it splendidly. In other areas of my life, however, it was different.

Stanford was on the quarter system. On the first day of class, most of my professors would hand out a syllabus, which usually included a term paper due at the end of the quarter. Upon receiving the syllabus, I would head for the library almost immediately and begin reading, outlining, and writing the term paper. I usually would have it completed by midterm.

You might ask, "What's wrong with that, George?" What's wrong is my purpose was to get the paper done, not to learn. I did not stop and reflect on the material I gathered. I did not include in the paper information that was discussed in class. I just had to get it done and out of the way.

Why did I do this? In a word: ANXIETY!

Those who know me best would not say I'm a laid-back kind of guy. I have struggled with anxiety for as long as I can remember—not the clinical kind, but the everyday variety that makes me a bit of a workaholic and (just ask my family) the last person you'd want to be at the airport with while waiting for a delayed flight. Anxiety, or the feelings that arise from uncertainty about what lies ahead, has interfered with relationships, negatively impacted my decision-making, and robbed me of learning how to relax and enjoy leisure time.

All of us like to find shortcuts to our destinations—like when I wanted to get my term papers finished so I wouldn't have that anxious feeling about them eating away at me. On the other hand, as a result of hurrying to get every project done, I did not gain from reflecting on my readings or my class experience. I didn't understand I was easing my anxiety at the expense of having real learning take place.

Preparation is the most important key to success. By that, I mean complete preparation—not rushing ahead, not overlooking steps in the learning process. Without proper preparation, individuals can develop some very bad habits.

Back then, I thought I was doing what I needed to in order to be a good student. Fortunately, I understand myself much better now. Because the physical aspect of being an athlete came easily to me, it was the foundation I worked at with determination on a regular basis. I could spend hours working on one aspect of my shot, until I felt I was as knowledgeable about that particular fundamental as I could be. In the meantime, I was overlooking a weakness in building my foundation for my life. I was like an iceberg, working on the part that was visible—the top third—and ignoring the two-thirds that were still underwater.

That's what I'm working hard to help kids avoid today. Because no kid is an island— or an iceberg.

The Importance of Belonging

I always felt like an outsider growing up. More than anything, I wanted to belong. I wanted to be part of the "in" crowd. I wanted to be part of ANY crowd.

At Stanford, I was invited to join the Delta Tau Delta fraternity. There was just one catch, however. The national Delta Tau Delta fraternity did not accept Jews or other minorities, which meant that I couldn't attend the monthly house meetings or pay dues to the national organization.* That was okay by me, though. I had no money, was at Stanford on a full-ride scholarship (which included tuition, room, and a "hashing" job for my meals), and my social conscience at the time was pretty weak. To be part of the Delts on any terms was better than not being part of the Delts at all. Still, that sense of feeling different was an issue for me.

Three years later, still searching for that sense of belonging, I decided to convert to Christianity. That effort brought a new set of challenges. First, my mother's family all lived in the San Francisco area and had been taking a lot of pride in my basketball success at Stanford. Our games were televised on the local stations and my name—my *Jewish* name—appeared regularly in the papers. The announcement that I was a Christian and headed to Princeton Theological Seminary went over like a lead matzo ball. Second, I began to learn that how much I was accepted within the Christian church depended on the position I took on various issues within the faith community. It took me a number of years to catch on, but it gradually became clear that while I had entered the church because I believed its teachings could provide myself and others with the strength and courage to face and overcome problems, there were a significant number of people who placed just as much (if not more) importance on what your views were on social reform or whether cookies or brownies should be served at the next board meeting. This schism played a key role in my decision to leave the ministry several years later.

Because a part of me still sometimes feels like that little boy (and young man) who didn't belong, I feel it is critical to create a place where kids feel safe and welcome, as well as a part of a community. When kids feel significant—when they feel that they count—then they have the sense of security, self-esteem, and self-confidence to make a difference in the world around them. Wouldn't you agree?

Tickets

It was a warm and delightful Sunday, and tired of the stuffy Stanford library, I headed for the Frosh Amphitheater, with books and class notes in hand, to study for my sophomore finals. I'd only been there a few minutes when several elementary-aged kids from Palo Alto descended upon me, recognizing me as "that basketball player" and wanting me to play some hoops. Somewhat panicked over my need to study, I instead organized a scavenger hunt and offered two tickets to Friday night's game for the winning team. When they returned almost two hours later, I told the winners that the tickets would be left at the "will call" window under my name.

After the game on Friday, I met up with my girlfriend to whom I had entrusted the tickets. I asked her if everything had gone okay, and in a barely audible voice she

---

* I would like to note that two of my fraternity brothers and good friends—Harold "Hap" Wagner, former CEO and chairman of the board of Air Products, a Fortune 500 company, and Peter Likins, past president of Lehigh University and the University of Arizona—led a delegation of Stanford Delts to the Delta Tau Delta conference in 1958 and successfully challenged the discrimination that kept me and others out of the national Delta Tau Delta Society. I was inducted into the house as a full member in the 80s.

---

replied she had arrived too late—the kids had already been there and left, extremely disappointed. I felt horrible! As a consequence, I wasn't going to be "that basketball player"—I was going to be THAT basketball player. The basketball player who broke two little boys' hearts!

Thinking quickly, I drove to the office of Walt Gamage, the sports editor for the *Palo Alto Times*, who wrote a daily column called "Sports Shots." My impression of Mr. Gamage was that he was a nice person and maybe he'd be willing to help. So I explained the situation to him.

Gamage shared my problem in his column the very next day, telling his readers I wanted to correct this oversight, but I didn't know the boys' names or how to get in touch with them. He communicated how terrible I felt about letting the kids down, and offered to give them my phone number so I could make things right.

Amazingly, the boys (or someone they knew) ended up reading Walt's column and calling me. That afternoon I drove to their home and delivered two tickets for that night's game.

I have never agreed with athletes who say they aren't role models. Of course, they're role models—just like parents and teachers and custodians and presidents are role models. We all have the responsibility to be role models. It's part of having integrity as a human being.

The Cow Palace

It was my junior year of college, and we were playing the eventual NCAA National Champions (the San Francisco Dons) in the Cow Palace before a sold-out crowd of over 13,000 fans—the largest crowd to attend a college game in the West at that time.

The star player for the Dons was future NBA great Bill Russell. We would later be roommates and teammates at the NCAA All-Star game, but at the moment, we were nothing but fierce competitors.

I had the ball in the left corner along the baseline. I managed to dribble past my defender but waiting for me under the basket was Bill. What to do? Given that the guy was at least a foot taller than me, there was no way I was going to jump over him without suddenly growing a pair of wings. No, what was needed here was *strategy*.

Using the step-and-a-half you are permitted on drives to the hoop, I did two things: one, I used my left hand to fake a drive for a reverse lay-up, and two, I used my right hand to place the ball on the ground. Bill stayed right with me as I soared (as much as a short guy *can* soar) through the air to the other side of the basket. Meanwhile, my teammate Russ Lawler, who had learned to expect the unexpected from me, calmly reached down, picked up the ball, and laid it in for two much-needed points.

It was one of those "and-the-crowd-went-wild" plays. Had I planned or practiced it? No. It was creativity and innovation way beyond what I thought I was capable of. However, I know now that for years, I had been developing the skills that brought me to that particular moment.

It started with the openness to try new things on the basketball court. This kind of openness comes naturally to little kids, but the older we get, the more self-conscious and inhibited we become. This situation was certainly true for me off the court, but not on the court. I learned to shoot a jump shot in the 7th grade, when jump shots were first making their presence in the game. Subsequently, driving to the left side of the court came next for me, then the crossover dribble, and more. Those new skills, combined with a predisposition for action, fueled my growth on the court. But beyond that, I had the ability to see patterns and make logical connections. (I talk about this factor in depth in my book, *Court Sense: The Invisible Edge in Basketball and Life*.)

While it took many years for me to identify and transfer these lessons from the court to my life and work, the effort is finally paying off as I work with kids today. More than ever before, I've needed to use innovation and creativity not only to successfully reach a generation of kids who are so very different from any I've previously experienced, but also to come up with tools and approaches to market my program in a world besieged by others competing for the same dollars. When you think about it, it makes going up against Bill Russell look like a cakewalk.

Overlooked

In my first year as a varsity player at Stanford, our leading scorer, Ron Tomsic (eventually a member of the 1956 U.S. Olympic basketball team) went down with a severe knee injury. Ron's loss led to me becoming second in the conference in scoring, behind the league's top scorer (our center, Russ Lawler). I was also named honorable mention All-American and first-team all-league selection.

When Ron returned the next year, I did what any good point guard is supposed to do—which was to make sure Russ and Ron got their shots and to also get the ball to as many of my other teammates as possible. I took less than six shots a game, but we had a winning season and took second in the conference.

When the All-Star votes came at the end of the season, my name was absent from the lists. I didn't think much about it at the time. In those days, we just played. The awards and accolades weren't as meaningful as they seem to be now.

The local sports editor, Walt Gamage, however, was outraged that I was overlooked and wrote, "We note yesterday that in the announcement of the annual all-star teams selected by the Basketball Writers and Sportscaster Association that the name of George Selleck didn't appear. This failure to recognize real basketball talent has caused us to draw this conclusion: The voting members ... must have exceeding poor eyesight or during the

Stanford games, had their eyes on the pompom girls instead of the court. We could have said that perhaps the All-Star selection might have been rigged, but were afraid some of the more sensitive members of the group might resent such an accusation. But how they could fail to recognize a genuine article like Selleck is way beyond our reasoning." Gamage went on to quote my coach, Howie Dallmar, who said, "I sincerely believe that George is good enough to play with any college team in the nation."

Gamage's observations were followed by this comment from former Stanford basketball coach, Bob Burnett: "Look, I'm prejudiced, but I think that little guy is one of the greatest players we've ever had around here. These past two seasons I've seen him make plays I thought before impossible. I don't think of George as a little man … To me he is a great basketball player, and you can forget about his size. Above all, he's smart out there on the court. He's always setting up a teammate for a shot with a clever feint and a pass. And talk about clutch players! I've never seen anyone like George for taking command when the chips are down."

Gamage concluded his article by calling up Hank Luisetti—who had been the Michael Jordan of his time—to get his opinion. Luisetti said, "George Selleck is the best basketball player I have ever seen, pound for pound and inch for inch. He is a throwback to the day when a player had to be an all-round performer. He can dribble, pass, and shoot with the best of 'em. I saw him make a pass over his shoulder down in the Cal game Saturday, which I thought was one of the greatest plays I've ever seen. I just think he is tremendous!"

I'm not sure when I first read Walt's article (my mother kept my scrapbooks and not until my sons became interested did I dig into them), but as the sun sets on my life, this praise and recognition—especially from one of the very best who ever played the game—is quite rewarding.

It has made me realize how much every kid needs to be recognized and praised for their efforts—regardless of whether or not those efforts result in any kind of tangible rewards. That's exactly what we're trying to do now—give kids opportunities to have fun, put effort into what they do, and be recognized for it.

My Best Play

There was a little less than three minutes to go approaching halftime against the University of Oregon. We were playing before our customary enthusiastic, packed house at the old Pavilion on the Stanford University campus. The score was tied.

An Oregon pass was deflected and bouncing toward midcourt between the two Oregon guards. I dove toward the ball, as the Oregon players were a step away from retrieving it. As I hit the ground, I somehow managed to flip the ball with my right hand over my right shoulder to a teammate running parallel about 10 feet away. He immediately let fly a beautiful pass to another teammate racing toward our basket on the left side and that teammate scored an easy basket. The roaring crowd came to their feet as our team quickly scored two more buckets before the halftime buzzer.

Monday, at the Northern California Sport Writers' weekend luncheon, where I was honored as player of the week, Howie Dallmar told the audience it was the first time in his long coaching career that he had forgotten he was the coach. As a result, he found himself standing and cheering the play with the rest of the fans.

It's exciting to be able to teach kids how to make great plays—not necessarily great plays on the basketball court, but great plays in life. Youth sports have become an adult-driven enterprise. Far too often, it is guided by a perspective that is modeled after college and professional sports and supported by many coaches and parents "stuck" in the elite sports paradigm that today's entertainment sports industry requires. Nearly all sports for kids are conducted by adults who create, incorporate, administer, outfit, coach, and officiate programs and leagues. This virtual adult monopoly means that most boys and girls seeking athlete competition or experience have little choice but to depend on whatever the community sports system offers.

Watch what happens, however, when you put tools in kids' hands to create and administer their own sports, health, and fitness program. It helps them become the playmakers. Accompanying that set of circumstances will be the same kind of joy and excitement that my coach, teammates, and crowd enjoyed as a result of an extraordinary effort that sparked a win over Oregon on a long-ago day in 1956.

The Cigarette Lighter

Toward the end of my final year of basketball at Stanford, I received a phone call from Pete Newell, who coached Stanford's arch rival, the University of California's Golden Bears. The call from Mr. Newell was an invitation to play in the East-West college All-Star game at the famed Madison Square Garden in New York City. He also mentioned that I would be rooming with Bill Russell, considered to be one of the best players in the history of college and (later) the NBA.

Soon, I was flying across the country to play in the game, which we (the West) won, 85-65. It was all very exciting, but this story isn't about the game. It's about the cigarette lighter that was presented to each All-Star on behalf of The Fresh Air Fund. It should be noted that I have never had a cigarette in my mouth and always thought it was a little odd that a group called "The Fresh Air Fund" would be giving out cigarette lighters, considering that cigarette smoke tends to make the air the opposite of fresh. Nevertheless, the lighter was a thing of beauty, with a 17-jewel Swiss watch embedded in it. My mother was especially charmed by the lighter and proudly showed it to all her friends until the day she died.

It wasn't until later that I learned that The Fresh Air Fund was actually a not-for-profit agency that was founded in 1877 to provide free, healthy summer vacations for thousands of kids from disadvantaged communities in New York City. The proceeds from our game went to help support that effort.

What I learned from this situation is that you can never assume your own theories are the correct ones. It is always helpful and important to look a little deeper. Throughout my career, I have used something called the null hypothesis to keep me from believing and acting on my own assumptions. With the null hypothesis, you don't use data or evidence to prove that you're correct—you use it to eliminate other possibilities. By doing that, you increase the probability that your theory is correct. You never actually prove your theory—you just improve its probability.

This approach is a scientific research model that I have used in human behavior activity. For example, if a coach sees a kid who's not motivated to practice hard, they might think, "Oh, that kid is lazy." Well, maybe they are. Or maybe the kid is sick, hurt, uninterested in that particular sport, or experiencing family or personal problems. As you gradually eliminate some of these theories, you gain a higher probability that your own theory is correct. While a margin for error still exists, that procedure will help keep you on your toes and help you maintain an open mind, as you work to provide kids with the kind of understanding that keeps them engaged and involved.

A Week With Bill Russell

When I arrived in New York City to play in the college All-Star game, I was quite nervous. I had broken my wrist a few weeks earlier in the National AAU tournament, and I was about to be on the hardwood with the best of the best in the world of college basketball.

When I checked in at the hotel, the front desk informed me that my roommate for the week would be Bill Russell. Winner of two NCAA championships and NCAA Player of the Year as a collegiate player and 11 championships as a player and coach of the Boston Celtics. Five-time NBA Most Valuable Player. The greatest team player of the 20th century. Of course, he hadn't earned all of these honors yet, but everyone knew it was just a matter of time.

I had played against Bill twice. The first time, my freshman team beat his freshman team. The second time, his national championship team downed us before the largest crowd in West Coast basketball history to that point—13,874 spectators at the San Francisco Cow Palace. Our paths had also crossed briefly at the weekly Northern California Sportswriters luncheon, when we shared player of the week honors three times during the 1955-56 season. Sportswriters frequently referred to me as "the little man's Bill Russell" or "the best little man in the game," while Bill was universally called "the best big man in the game."

I'm sorry to say I don't remember having any deep, meaningful conversations with Bill. We were just a couple of kids in the big city, and I think we were both a little overwhelmed by it. What I do remember very well, however, was the example that Bill set for all of us with his teamwork, leadership, and focus.

Late in the fourth quarter of the game, with the West leading by almost 30 points over a strong East team that featured future NBA star Tom Heinsohn, among others, a time-out was called to allow some of our bench players to get into the game. It would have been easy to slack off a little. Bill, however, was telling everyone, "Okay guys, let's not slow down now. Let's hang together and play together. There's work yet to be done."

Bill and I may have been separated by over a foot in height, but when it came to teamwork we were on the same page. We both recognized that successful teamwork requires a number of factors, including:

- Getting people to view success in terms of group—not individual—performance. I first learned this factor on the basketball courts of the Long Beach YMCA—a lesson that was reinforced through junior and senior high school championships. In order to win, my teammates and I would have to subordinate our individual goals in favor of group success.

- Involving all teammates in the process. To this day, when I show up at my local 24-hour fitness center and work my way into a pick-up game, I make a point of returning *every* pass to the player who threw me the ball, telegraphing: one, I'm a team player; two, you don't need to worry about giving the ball to me, because if you are open I will get it back to you; and three, if we want to stay on the court we're going to have to play together. Otherwise, we'll lose and have to sit down.

- Being unselfish. Whether as a point guard on the court or a consultant in the business world, the only way I've achieved success is to play to the talent and needs of my teammates. As a sophomore at Stanford, I was second in the conference in scoring. Subsequently, I decided that it was necessary to increase my point production when Ron Tomsic, our best scorer, went out with a season-ending injury in our 12th game. The following year, however, Ron was back. As a result, I concentrated on setting up Ron, Russ Lawyer (our high scoring center), and my other teammates. To me, it was never about how many points I scored—it was about how well the team did. In my consulting work, I have seen how destructive it is to an organization when individuals put their egos ahead of the well-being of the group. It not only limits progress, but threatens the very existence of the organization itself.

Because teamwork is such an important life skill for all of us, it's vital for kids to learn there will be no success unless they all work together. Unfortunately, on occasion, there's not much fun, either.

Praying on the Free Throw Line

The score was tied, with precious little time on the clock. I was part of a team called "Venture for Victory."* Our team of All-Stars, from various faith-based colleges (with the exception of me, from Stanford), was playing the Brazilian Olympic team. Brazil's best player was on the free throw line, about to shoot, when suddenly one of my teammates blurted out loud enough for me to hear, "Lord, help this player miss this free throw." I responded, equally loudly, "Lord, help him make this free throw." The player made the free throw, and once again I was the outsider. My teammates, who had been suspicious of my religious credentials from the beginning, now knew they had made a mistake in inviting me on the trip.

The story illustrates my lifetime struggle between religion and spirituality. I like what Bobby Knight—the well-known and highly controversial, retired basketball coach—said on the subject. An interviewer asked Knight what he thought of athletes "pointing to the heavens" after hitting a homerun. Knight responded critically, "Well it seems to me that God is siding with the batter, and screwing the pitcher."

To some individuals, the term *religion* conveys an exclusive faith—one that draws a circle that keeps others out. In contrast, spirituality (to me) is a faith of inclusion—one that draws its circle in a way that invites the whole world in. Spirituality provides meaning for life and gives us the depth to capture and hold a broad, clear picture of reality—one in which we can see that we are called to a higher purpose than self-service and self-satisfaction. In this sense, I am reminded of the first book I read as a young Christian, *Your God Is Too Small*, by J.B. Phillips. In his book, Phillips argued that, in varying degrees, we suffer from a limited idea of God. I don't know if God is definable. I do know that my childhood, teenage, and early adult definitions are probably quite out of date.

Even though I am approaching my 80s, I still feel I am learning about spirituality and sincere faith. My wife likes to tease me by saying things like, "I thought when I married an ex-minister, you'd be more religious!"

I hope my program's message of acceptance and inclusion is something all kids who participate in the program will take away with them. I guess you could say that is our "religion."

Ty Cobb

It was February of 1957. I had spent the previous summer touring Latin America with the "Venture for Victory" team. Although I had been drafted by the Philadelphia Warriors

---

* The team was part of a Christian outreach program that had sent basketball teams to Asia for more than 10 years, and in the summer of 1956 decided to go to South America. While it was made up of players from exclusively Christian colleges, my recent conversion and high profile at Stanford prompted them to invite me. I was a babe among lifelong Christians, who took my spiritual temperature almost hourly. I didn't do well. I didn't know the jargon, use the proper buzz words, and simply was not "spiritual" enough.

(as they were known then), I had decided professional basketball was not where my future lay. In other words, my career as a hotshot athlete was officially over.

Originally, I had planned on attending Princeton Theological Seminary in the fall, but I was experiencing some pressure from a conservative religious group that had me quite confused as a young person in the faith. As a result, I postponed my decision to attend Princeton and instead signed on for graduate studies at Stanford.

One Sunday afternoon, I received a phone call from a physician in nearby Santa Rosa. I had never met the man, but apparently he had spoken to someone at the church where I worked and that person had given him my name.

He told me he had this patient, a former star athlete, who was trying to get his life in order after a long bout with the bottle. This doctor thought the companionship of someone who'd lived the sports life and could relate to the patient's glory days might be therapeutic. Would I agree to meet with him?

When he gave me the man's name, I realized that "star athlete" was an understatement. The struggling alcoholic the doctor was talking about was none other than Ty Cobb.

Cobb had played—epitomized—Major League baseball for 24 years, before retiring in 1928. His career totals in hits and stolen bases ranked him No. 1 on both all-time lists until well after his death. Cobb won the American League batting title every year from 1907 to 1919 (except for a 1916 "slump," when he batted a mere .371). To this day, his lifetime batting average of .367 stands as the Major League record. Cobb wasn't just a star. He was a legend.

He was not a happy man, however. While he may have had the adulation of millions, he had no friends and loved ones to share the final years of his life. His aggressive, pugnacious attitude and uncontrollable temper had led to three divorces. His two sons died at an early age, leaving Cobb completely alone.

I met with Cobb at his large, rambling house in an exclusive area of Menlo-Atherton. Cobb had not only been an outstanding baseball player, he was also a savvy businessman who had made a fortune through shrewd investments. His home was well-kept, and decorated in a clean, masculine style.

During our conversation, Cobb explained he had a problem with staying sober and that he needed someone to keep him company so that he wouldn't "turn to the booze." I must have passed muster, because a few days later, I packed my bags and moved in.

For the next few months, the two of us ate breakfast together every morning. At night, we would occasionally go out to dinner. People would sometimes stop by our table, and Cobb would be civil to them, but distant. At home, I would read to him, mostly from the *Reader's Digest* and sometimes from the Bible. We also spent hours pouring over applications for the Cobb Educational Fund, which awarded scholarships to needy students in his home state of Georgia. I wasn't paid for my time and didn't expect to be—it was all done in the context of helping out a fellow member of the Christian community.

In the hours and hours we spent talking about his career and disappointments, what stuck with me (even more so as the years have turned to decades in my own life) was how Ty Cobb wrestled, at age 70, to make sense out of his life. Baseball had given him fame, notoriety, and money, but it hadn't brought happiness, sense, or meaning to the life he struggled through after his last at-bat.

Today, it seems as if everywhere you look, the lives of those who live in the sports world are unraveling. College coaches are losing their jobs because of improprieties. Schools are facing recruiting violations. Athletes' reputations are tainted because of drug use, violence, immorality, and more.

No wonder an increasing number of people decry the role that athletes and sports play in American life. Some individuals simply issue a blanket condemnation of sports for the failed lives behind the headlines. Such a view, however, is too simplistic. Having been around sports all my life, first as a player, then as a coach, referee, parent, and educator, I know the athletic experience can enrich a person's life in ways nothing else can.

So, why do so many athletes screw up?

I have finally decided that they just don't get it. Too many athletes, either through ignorance or selfishness, fail to see and take advantage of the many opportunities sport offers to educate, inspire, and link them to other members of their communities.

Sport, though it taught me a lot about teamwork, discipline, and hard work, could have taught me much more had I a better awareness of the balance between the life-long game we play and the games measured in quarters, periods, innings or rounds. Any individual who fails to grow and develop through their sport's experience will miss the wonderful lessons that only sport can provide.

Ty Cobb flunked those lessons. His character development never equaled his tremendous athletic growth. Life isn't about whether you can reverse dunk or pitch a no-hitter. It's a celebration of who you are and what you have done with your given time. Unfortunately, Cobb never understood that point—or if he did, the understanding came too late to make a difference in his life.

Cobb died in 1961 at the age of 74. I had long since moved out of his home. I don't remember why, although it probably had to do with needing to focus on my master's thesis and other responsibilities and not being able to be there for him 24 hours a day. I later read that only four people from the baseball world attended his funeral.

When I think of Cobb, it is with sadness at the terrible waste of potential. My experience with Cobb is one reason why I have devoted so many hours to working with young athletes and developing programs for youth. I want to ensure their lives don't follow the same path as Cobb's. I want to encourage them to use sport to make friends, to test and challenge themselves, to have fun, to grow and develop. I want to encourage them to use sport to learn *about* life, but never to substitute *for* life. Life is the main course; sport is merely the dessert. The latter is meant to enhance the former, not to take its place, and individuals who try to do otherwise will find themselves like Ty Cobb—empty, alone, and hungering for something they can't even name.

Mini Me

While working on my master's degree in counseling at Stanford, I also assisted with the freshmen and varsity basketball teams. As an assistant coach, I was involved in recruiting high school basketball players for our program. On one particular Friday night, I went to Menlo-Atherton High School to evaluate their star player, Bob Wendell. Bob was a good player, who went on to captain the 1959-60 national championship Cal Bears basketball team.

Nevertheless, it only took me a few minutes of watching Bob play to decide that I did not like how he ran the team. He was directing their activity, involved in all aspects of the game, and—to be honest—kind of bossy.

Then, it hit me like a thunderbolt! Bob looked and acted on the court the same way I did. Sure, my teammates and our fans seemed to love the "take-charge" nature of my play, but to others, I probably appeared quite obnoxious. Looking at Bob was like unexpectedly catching a glimpse of myself in a mirror—and not liking the result one bit. That experience has served as a powerful reminder to me over the years of the importance of being introspective—of taking a good look at ourselves and being able to honestly assess our strengths and weaknesses.

Self-concept is an accumulation of thoughts and beliefs that we have about ourselves. It is an attribute that is manifested in our various behaviors. We know that behaviors can be modified and changed. On the other hand, when you are working with kids, they must be active role-players in improvement of their self-concept. Not only must they recognize that a problem exists that needs to be resolved; they must also make the decision to change.

Self-discovery through being introspective is a reward unto itself. On the other hand, self-honesty can yield even greater inner strength and peace of mind—less strife within and less strife with others—given its potential to have a more positive and more practical affect on an individual.

While introspection is not a cure-all for all problems, it is a valuable tool for growing up and becoming a better and happier person. It is a lifelong learning tool that helps guide us in identifying what our personal strengths and weaknesses are. Taking the time to reflect on what we've learned and what we still need to learn is essential for our growth and development.

That being said, did I change my style of playing basketball? Not really. On the other hand, I have changed a lot of other things about myself—hopefully for the better. I know I feel better about the person I am now, versus the person I was 60 years ago—or even 10 years ago. Furthermore, I plan to keep the process going for as long as I can. Because thanks to the value of introspection, you can teach an old dog new tricks.

The Bad Tooth

My desperate longing for a close relationship with my father—or at the very least, some kind of positive father-son interaction—led me to do something rather foolish when I was in college. It started with a toothache that wouldn't go away. Instead of going to a local dentist, I decided it would make more sense to return home to Compton and have my father remove the tooth for free. Not only would I not have to pay for the extraction, but it could be a father-son moment for us.

At the time, my dad was in his 70s, but he still ran a small dental practice. When I arrived at his office, I settled into the dental chair, anticipating the quick and successful removal of my tooth. Subsequently, then, I hoped maybe some manly conversation between the two of us might occur or perhaps the two of us might go out for ice cream.

To numb my mouth, my dad used ethyl chloride. I don't know if our more modern painkillers hadn't been invented yet or if my dad just wasn't current in his techniques. Either way, I felt the pain of all his efforts. To make things worse, he unintentionally broke the tooth on which he was working. At that point, he told me I needed to go to a specialist to complete the extraction. I refused, insisting he could do the job himself. I wasn't trying to be mean or insensitive or even cheap. I just had a stubborn desire for this situation to be a successful activity between my dad and me. As a result, with his ancient instruments, my 70-something father worked for hours to remove all of my tooth and its roots.

Looking back, it was probably insensitive on my part to make him do that. On the other hand, I was determined that we would succeed together. I don't know if you'd call the end result a success, but it was the most time I'd spent with my dad in a long time.

I think this scenario just proves, once again, how important the relationships in our lives are and how much we are willing to go through for those relationships. It also helps point out that we don't always make the best decisions, when it comes to developing or strengthening our relationships. If I'd had more empathy for my dad, I might have realized how uncomfortable it was for him at his age to have to work on my tooth as long as he did—and how unpleasant it must have been for him to see the pain he was inflicting on me. I was a little short-sighted then, but I'm grateful for the chance to make up for it now in the work that I do. I'm also really grateful for Novocain.

Coaching at the Hun

In December of 2012, I was surprised to receive a letter informing me that I had been selected for induction into the Hun School Athletic Hall of Fame. The "Hun," as we called it, is a private school in New Jersey, located near the Princeton campus. I hadn't been in contact with them since the late 1950s.

At the time, I was attending Princeton Theological Seminary and was hard-pressed to meet my financial obligations. I was waiting tables in the Seminary dining facilities to pay for my meals, teaching a class for a small stipend, working with a youth group on the weekends, and getting paid $100 a game for playing with the Trenton Colonials, a minor league professional basketball team. I also received some tuition assistance from a kindly gentleman in Medford, Oregon, at whose cannery I had once worked for two summers. As a result, when the president of the Hun School contacted me about directing their basketball program, I jumped at the opportunity. Of course, I would have accepted the position under any circumstances, considering my love of basketball.

I had gotten the bug for coaching as a graduate student at Stanford, when I coached the freshmen and assisted with the varsity team. Coaching at the Hun was a delightful experience. Tom Horwich, one of my players from back then, was kind enough to share some of his memories of that time with me:

> *George: You were a wonderful fresh light in an environment that was not always so uplifting …. You knew the game backward and forward. You showed us things that were simple, easy to understand, and most importantly even at our level we could execute … And yes, you tried to teach me to shoot simple, one-handed set shots with both feet on the floor. I had come from an era of the right knee up when shooting that simple shot. I never was very good with both feet down. Funny, the things one can remember from over 50 years ago. It is hard to remember what happened yesterday.*

> *When you first started coaching us, I was on the bench, and you were playing fellows whom I knew were not in my league or at least didn't have my experience and talent. After a couple of games, I said something to you, and you listened, and in the next game, you put me in and that was a permanent change. You were approachable, you listened, and you made a decision one way or the other to try and make the team work cohesively … Most importantly, you made the practices, the games, and the down time fun and entertaining, and everyone felt that they belonged and enjoyed the experience. Everyone respected not only your talents, but your approach and your mutual respect. What more can a coach do?*

While it is a privilege to be honored for something I did so long ago, I also like to think that over the years, my attitudes and behaviors toward the young athletes I was fortunate enough to coach, as well as the coaches I have trained, have continued to evolve and develop—just as athletes and coaches themselves have evolved and developed. It's that experience I bring to the work that I do now, and in addition, hopefully, the end results will be as rewarding as the work I was able to do at the Hun so many years ago.

Harsh Critic

In my last year at Princeton Theological Seminary, I was required to take senior homiletics—a class designed to help would-be preachers give sermons that didn't put their congregations to sleep. Our class of seven met regularly in the Princeton University chapel with our professor, Ernest Gordon, who also served as the dean of the Princeton University chapel.

Dean Gordon was a Presbyterian minister, as well as a native of Scotland, who had been a company commander with the 2nd Battalion, Argyll and Sutherland Highlanders. He spent three years in a Japanese prisoner of war camp during World War II and was one of the prisoners who helped build the legendary "Bridge on the River Kwai."

At Princeton, Dean Gordon developed the reputation of someone who was decidedly unmoved by social nicety or convention, as his verse in the faculty song noted:

All hail to Gordon, Earnest [sic] Dean
Of Heaven and Hell he paints the scene.
If you can take his brimstone brew,
You'll get your Scotch on Sunday too.

When spring came, it was my turn to step up to the podium with my diligently prepared sermon. While I was very nervous and knew it wasn't my best performance, I was still unprepared for Dean Gordon's blunt criticism. In his Scottish brogue, he looked at me and said, "Most of the students in your seminary have something to say, but they just can't say it very well. You, my young friend, have nothing to say, and you sure as hell can't say it."

With a review like that, it's a wonder I became a minister at all. We all have times in our lives when we are hit with criticism. If we are lucky, it is constructive criticism that is put to us in such a way that we recognize it as such and learn from it. More often than not, however, criticism is meant to wound. There are far too many cases of young people who have been criticized and harassed to the point of taking their own lives.

My experience with Dean Gordon illustrates just how much times have changed and how much we, as a society, need to change with them. Dean Gordon was undoubtedly what we would call "old school." Many of the coaches I used to know were also "old school." They ran their teams like drill sergeants—yelling, screaming, insulting, and punishing. At the time, most players didn't think twice about this kind of abuse, because it was the standard.

Kids today, however, are different. In turn, sport needs to be different. Sport needs to be about providing young people with an accepting, nurturing environment where they can feel safe to be themselves. It needs to be about teaching them how to work with each other in a positive way, and how to recognize and bring out each other's strengths—not point out each other's weaknesses.

I like to think that, despite his gruff ways, Dean Gordon would agree.

Warm Things of the Heart

In graduate school at Princeton and later at the University of Southern California, I was exposed to some pretty bleak theories on the nature of humankind. At Princeton, it seemed to me as if the "warm things" of the heart—such as the parables and miracles of the New Testament—were placed on a table for a cold, analytical evaluation. Subsequently, at USC, the more I studied counseling and psychology, the more it seemed we ALL fell under the category of abnormal psychology.

Over the course of my career, however, first as a pastor and later as a psychologist, the longer I observed and talked to people, the more I became convinced that human nature was a lot better than the books made it out to be. Even though I sometimes saw the worst part of people, I steadily grew in my belief that the human spirit held more possibility than most of us knew.

Of course, it helped that my work allowed me to see sides of people to which not everyone was privy. One day, I might be in my office with a parishioner who was struggling with thoughts (or actions) of adultery, and the next day, I would see them at a church picnic, gently rounding up a group of children for a game of "Simon Says." Or, as a counselor, I might meet with a person whose family members viewed them as lazy and unmotivated, while I saw someone whose depression was so crippling that every day was a struggle just to stay alive. Their courage in not giving up was incredible to me.

I have learned we seldom see the totality of another person in our everyday interactions. When we judge a person as lazy or rude or ignorant, we are only seeing part of the person—the part that has been triggered by a particular set of circumstances on a particular occasion.

No matter how frustrated, troubled, or dispirited a person may appear on the surface, deep down they want to do better. They want to succeed. Such an attitude is an intrinsic part of the human spirit. What we need are more programs that encourage the discovery and development of that spirit, especially for children.

3rd Quarter

Finally, I found myself in the real world … and feeling about as prepared for it as I did for my college career. This next section covers the early years of my varied careers—from pastor to psychologist to consultant.

This section covers some of the challenges that came with raising a young family when I really didn't have any idea what a typical family unit was supposed to look like.

It covers the end of one marriage and the beginning of another.

These were the years when my work took me from running a parish in New Mexico to teaching coaching seminars for people like Bill Walsh. In fact, if there was one constant in my life, it was sport. If I wasn't playing, I was officiating, coaching, or teaching other coaches how to do their jobs better. Through it all, I was subconsciously putting together pieces of the puzzle that I would be presented with many years later. I was learning about relationships and how they worked. I was learning how to run organizations. I was learning how to help people help themselves.

During the process, I was learning about sports and fitness and the value they provided to people's lives. I knew this was something important, but how important I wouldn't know until much later.

What's a Nice Jew Like You Doing in a Place Like This?

Following my conversion to Christianity and my graduation from Princeton Theological Seminary, I headed to Reserve, New Mexico, a town of less than a hundred people, to become pastor of five very small congregations (Reserve had 25 members, Glenwood 12, Apache Creek 15, Quemado 13, and Fence Lake a dozen or so). I preached at three of churches on Sunday and two on Monday night. I was the first pastor these churches had had in almost 10 years.

The congregation in Reserve consisted mainly of draft dodgers from World War II and an embezzler from Philadelphia. The rest of the congregation throughout the five-point parish was made up of people working on road crews, cattle ranchers from throughout the area, and local school teachers (many of whom worked in one-room schools). I called monthly on every parishioner (there weren't that many, and I wasn't that busy). In time, my knowledge and understanding of people grew as they progressively shared their stories and struggles with me. While I wonder how empathic and helpful I was to these people, they taught me a lot about the uniqueness and commonality that we all share with each other as humans.

At Reserve, I learned one of the most important lessons of my life—that behind every face is a story. I have tried to keep this factor in mind in my efforts to serve others and make a difference. As such, I try to keep in mind that helping always needs to start with an appreciation of the other person's context rather than your own.

After Reserve, I moved to Bell Gardens, California and became pastor and director of the Westminster Church and Community Center. Bell Gardens has always been an underserved and under-resourced community with traditional urban problems, including significant poverty and educational concerns. During the time I was there, the community of Bell Gardens was home to multiple generations of welfare families. As the person charged with ministering to the complex needs of the community members, I learned that for every person who was on welfare who shouldn't have been, there were at least two people who were so dysfunctional that they either did not know how to or were incapable of accessing the system.

I also learned that people do not want to be "fixed," especially from the outside. Some of strongest church communities in Los Angeles would send canned goods, food packages, and volunteers into Bell Gardens, only to find their efforts poorly received and unappreciated. The people who were able to make a real difference in the community were individuals like Laura Leonard, a wonderful woman who had no formal training or education, but who spent an average of 20 hours a week calling on shut-ins, working with elementary school children at the Community Center, and serving on the boards of both the Center and the Church.

In the meantime, conflict was brewing between the Social Services arm of the Los Angeles Presbytery, which included all of the Presbyterian churches from San Diego to Santa Barbara, as well as my fellow inner-city pastors. It centered around the "patronage" model of service, which involved having the more affluent and upper-class congregations and communities sending food and money through the Social Services ministry to their less-affluent brethren, rather than assisting and equipping inner-city churches to become more self-sufficient. In reality, this tradition of "giving to the poor and unfortunate" was more to make the suburban and wealthy churches feel good than to develop leadership and social activism in the inner-city communities.

The inner-city pastors, feeling that my minor athletic celebrity gave me easier access to "important" people, anointed me as their spokesperson. In actuality, I was way too young and inexperienced for the job, and the resulting battle left me with significant emotional scars. I have never forgotten my discomfort in debating on the floor of the Presbytery (with a man who later became the head of the United Presbyterian Church throughout America) the issue of the role of the local congregation in serving its community versus the well-meaning, but less effective, methods employed by the suburban churches. Despite my inadequacies, changes were made, and the first Urban Presbyterian ministry—a collaboration between Social Services and the local inner-city churches—was created.

Following several years of additional work in Bell Gardens, I was asked to become pastor of the St. John's Presbyterian Church in West Los Angeles. St. John's was a typical suburban church, serving a middle- and upper-middle class population, a relatively short distance from the campus of the University of California at Los Angeles. St. John's was also home to many graduate students from UCLA who lived within walking distance of the church. The church had experienced rapid growth in the late 1950s and early 1960s, and the construction of a new sanctuary was underway to serve its members and the community. I was 31 years old at the time I became pastor, and still far too immature to truly meet the challenges of a growing, dynamic congregation.

St. John's was my first real introduction to dealing with the social and self-esteem needs of people. In Bell Gardens, people were too worried about putting food on the table to spend much time thinking about "what Fred meant by that comment he made last Sunday after church." Within weeks of being in my new position at St. John's, a steady stream of people started filling my schedule, looking for help and support with their relationship and self-esteem issues. Considering that I was still struggling with my own issues in that area, I felt less than qualified to advise others on what they should be doing. It was then I decided I'd better get qualified—the sooner the better. As a result, I applied to and was accepted into a Ph.D. program for counseling psychology at the University of Southern California.

The experiences I had as a pastor were very different from those I would have had had I gone on to play professional basketball after college. In reality, however, they were just as critical to shaping my philosophy as any experience I had on the playing field. Whether kids are from small towns or large cities, whether they have parents who struggle to put food on the table or who drive the latest model sedan, they all have a need to be seen for whom they are and to be respected for what they can contribute. They need to have opportunities to lead and serve within their own communities, as opposed to having outsiders come in and tell them how to run things. They need to be able to learn that it is relationships, not programs, that change lives. They also need to have access to programs that give them the opportunity to form relationships and connect in rich and meaningful ways.

Not Ready to Get Down

It was a Saturday morning, and the lead elder of the congregation I was pastor of at the time was in our home to discuss an issue. As the elder was droning on, my son John, who was around three years old, came through the front door with tears streaming down his face. He had apparently failed to be included in the activities of the older kids across the street, and the rejection had hurt him terribly.

I picked John up, held him in my arms, and comforted him with words of love and reassurance. Then—because I was in the middle of something—I made a *huge* mistake. I put him down and said to him, "Okay, John, stop crying. It will be okay. You can handle it. Now, off you go!" The elder looked at me and said, "George, your son wasn't ready to get down and return to the other kids." Without question, he was absolutely correct.

That incident was a perfect metaphor for my life. My father was 55 when he married for the first time. My mother, a kind and generous person at heart, was burdened with an old-school, insensitive husband, an adolescent daughter struggling to find her place in the world, and my twin brother who, after life-threatening surgery within a week of being born, never seemed to catch up. She turned to alcohol for her support.

Since I seemed to be the most capable of meeting the challenges of everyday life, I was released from the comfort and support of my parents and told to "handle it" myself.

As a shy, small boy with the added challenge of being one of the only Jewish kids in town, I needed to belong, feel connected, feel capable, and feel significant. At the time, I thought, as many individuals do, the way to meet those needs was to be popular and gain status through athletics, good grades, and whatever other achievements I could muster up. I didn't understand these factors were only external measures of success and had more to do with what I could do and achieve, rather than who I was as a person.

As the years have passed, I learned that the most meaningful definition of success is internal. It's not about what happens to us, but rather the choices we make that determine our sense of enjoyment, fulfillment, effectiveness, self-esteem, happiness, and success.

We need to encourage kids to focus on their potential, rather than on their limitations. Healthy self-esteem is like a child's armor against the challenges of the world. Kids who know their strengths and weaknesses and feel good about themselves seem to have an easier time handling conflicts and resisting negative pressures. They tend to smile more readily and enjoy life.

If I had been more secure with myself, more aware of my son's needs and less concerned about what the elder might have been thinking about the interruption, I, too, would have known that John wasn't ready to leave the safety of my lap and go rejoin the other kids. Fortunately, I've grown up a lot since then, and even more fortunately, John managed to grow up even better than I did.

Laugh It Off

In the fall of 1960, I received a call from Ken Fagans, my former high school basketball coach. Ken was now the CIF Southern Section Commissioner of Athletics, which meant he oversaw all of Southern California's high school sports. Ken wanted to know if I'd be interested in refereeing some games.

At the time, I had eight years of college, three college degrees, and was making less than $5000 a year. Furthermore, I was about to start a family. Did I want to make some extra money? Heck, yeah! Within a year, I was working freshman games at the highest collegiate levels; within two years, I was refereeing varsity level games for schools like UCLA, USC, the University of California, the University of Kansas, and others.

My considerable background as a player helped, but the job was not as easy as I initially thought it would be. Maybe you haven't noticed, but refs are not necessarily the most beloved individuals in sport. Also, it is one thing to ref a high school game and another thing entirely to ref a game for UCLA, with its million-dollar program and long history of basketball championships. To say that pressure exists on the referees is an understatement. In fact, probably one of the most important qualities a ref can develop is a sense of humor. I remember one game between Seattle University and Santa Clara University at the San Jose Civic Auditorium. I was working the game with my friend and fellow official, Bob Herrold. The coach of the Seattle team was "Bucky" Buckwalter, who went on to become a coach and executive in the NBA. The first half was winding down, when Bob called a foul on Seattle. Bucky was livid. He jumped up from his seat on the bench and screamed, "How come we have EIGHT fouls, and they only have ONE?"

Without blinking an eye, Bob turned to him and said, "You're wrong, coach. You have NINE." At that point, he then promptly gave Bucky a technical. Fortunately, Bucky had a sense of humor, too, because he just started laughing.

We go through many tough times in life. We lose jobs, we lose loved ones, we have health challenges—the list goes on. Having a sense of humor makes these tough times easier to get through.

Kids today face a lot of pressure—much like a referee in a basketball game. Their lives are moving practically at the speed of sound. From their parents, there is pressure to get good grades, to get into advanced academic programs, to make the team, to get a scholarship. From their peers, there is the pressure to fit in, to wear the right clothes, to listen to the right music. From themselves, there is the pressure to be part of the crowd, while trying to maintain their individuality and decide who they want to be and what they want to do with their lives.

Kids need the opportunity to experience sports and other fitness activities in a pressure-free environment. In such a setting, the goal isn't to decimate your opponent or be the top achiever—it's to have fun. Because it doesn't matter whether you're a kid, a coach, or a top-level basketball official, if you can't laugh about life's ups and downs, then you're guaranteed to have more downs than ups. And where's the fun in that?

Go Solve the Problem

When I first started officiating games, I was always assigned the lowly role of umpire. In contrast, the individual designated as the referee got to be the lead official—the person who communicated with administrators and the press, talked to the captains at half-court prior to the game, etc. During this time, I was often paired with Bob Herrold, who was excellent at mentoring me in my role as an umpire.

As time went on, I began to kid around with Bob. "Hey, Bob!" I would say, "Don't you think it's time I got to be the lead official?" He would just laugh and brush me off.

Finally, one Saturday, Bob and I were in the official's room at the San Jose Civic Auditorium. The game was between Santa Clara University and St. Mary's College, and we were just waiting for the signal to enter the arena floor and meet the coaches and captains.

There was a knock at the door. We opened it, and the athletic director from Santa Clara informed us that the St. Mary's team was in their locker room, refusing to take the floor as support for the student protest that was currently underway on their campus. This particular period was a time when demonstrations and sit-ins protesting the Vietnam War were prevalent.

Bob turned to me with a gleam in his eye and said, "George, tonight you are the lead official. Go solve the problem."

Problem-solving. They don't really have a class in it at school, and yet, it's one of the most valuable skills we can learn. As I have worked with and watched top athletes over the years, I have observed that one of the reasons so many of them get into trouble is they haven't had to solve many problems in their lives. They are surrounded by people whose job is to solve their problems for them. As a result, they don't get much practice at solving their own problems.

In reality, we need something that puts kids in charge of planning, making decisions, and solving problems that might arise—such as what to do when an activity gets rained out, or when a field gets double-booked, or when no one shows up for an important planning meeting. We don't want kids just learning how to run a Frisbee golf tournament. We want them knowing what to do when they're 31, and one of the teams they're refereeing refuses to take the floor, and the other official turns to them and says, "YOU go solve the problem."

No Wonder People Hate the Ref!

I had just been assigned to work an important game between defending national champion UCLA and their perennial powerhouse rival, the University of Kansas. The game was played at Pauley Pavilion before a packed house and a national TV audience. It was an up-an-down, fast-paced game, with UCLA playing a full-court zone defense, forcing the Kansas players to hustle to get the ball across the half-court line in the required 10 seconds (these were the days before a shot clock).

During the game, there were three or four times when Kansas failed to make it across the half-court line in time. In other words, as the official responsible for covering the backcourt, it was my duty to call a backcourt violation.

As I previously noted, it was a fast-paced game. The fans were screaming like crazy, and the players were moving like lightning. Once or twice when I made my backcourt-violation calls, I vaguely noticed the Kansas coaches protesting, but I did as I was being taught, which was to stay with the game and ignore the coaches, unless it was absolutely necessary to talk with them. In retrospect, it might not have been the best advice, but as a young and inexperienced official, I was attempting to follow it.

Imagine my embarrassment when I heard a few days later from the supervisor of officials that I had really screwed up. Before I tell you how, let me ask you a question:

How many seconds does a team have to advance the ball after a basket at their end of the court across the midcourt line and into the frontcourt?

If you answered 10, as most people who read the second paragraph of this story would, you would be wrong. The answer is that you have 10 seconds to get the ball across the midcourt line. On the other hand, you have five seconds to put the ball in play and then 10 seconds to cross the center line—which equals 15 seconds. Having played basketball since the 3rd grade and at all levels, including against professional teams, you would think that I knew that rule. Obviously, I didn't.

It is a wonder I was ever asked to officiate another game. Apparently, the Kansas coach was understanding. After he had viewed the film and detected my horrendous mistake, he commented that my officiating was still the best he had ever gotten on somebody else's home court, and that except for my goofs on the backcourt violation, he would have me referring his games any time.

Ben Franklin once observed about a fellow he had known in Philadelphia: "The man died at 25, but wasn't buried until 75." Mr. Franklin understood the importance of remaining a student all your life. My officiating blunder certainly taught me that even if we think we know it all, we rarely do. I am constantly learning new things—even at my advanced age. I hope this attribute is a quality that will get passed down to the kids with whom I work—and especially to any who grow up to be basketball refs.

Judgment Calls

If you talk to any basketball referee, they will tell you the most difficult calls to make are blocking and charging fouls. The rule book declares that if the offensive player contacts the torso of the defensive player, it is a charging (or offensive) foul, and if the offensive player is blocked by the body of the defensive player with his shoulders, arms, or legs outside of their torso, it is a blocking (or defensive) foul. On the other hand, because of the speed, length, and size of players, other factors can determine your call as an official. For example, was the defensive player stationary? Or, who got there first?

One day, I was working a hard-fought game at the Los Angeles Sports Arena between USC and Syracuse—the latter led by future NBA star Dave Bing. It was a close contest. At one point in the game, Bing drove to the basket, while a USC defender attempted to stop him from scoring. As the two opposing players banged into each other, limbs flailing everywhere, I blew my whistle and, without hesitation, signaled a blocking foul on the USC player. Bob Boyd, the Trojans' coach, screamed (as coaches often do), "George! How can you call that on us?"

I calmly responded, "Bob, who was the best player on that play?" My response stopped him in his tracks. As a basketball person, he was forced to think. He then sat down on the bench and stopped protesting.

Some individuals might wonder what happened in that situation. How did I know for sure which player to call the foul on? The truth is, I didn't know for sure. I made a judgment call. Since it was virtually impossible to tell who had really made the foul, my basic principle was to reward whoever made the best play. In this case, it was Dave Bing (which probably helps to explain why he went on to become such a successful pro player).

Too often, officials try to apply the theoretical aspect of the rule and ignore the athletic reality of the situation. You can also see it happen a lot in football, particularly with a pass interference call. Technically, the players are not supposed to touch each other—either offensively or defensively—but they do. As a result, the officials have to make a judgment call.

Bob Boyd, as proficient a basketball expert as anyone, knew what I was talking about when I asked him who the best player had been. I'm sure he would have preferred the call go in his favor, but he couldn't argue with my rationale for making the call that I did.

Webster defines judgment as: *"The process of forming an opinion or evaluation by discerning and comparing; an opinion or estimate so formed; the capacity for judging; discernment; the exercise of this capacity; a proposition stating something believed or asserted."* The truth is everybody uses judgment every day in their decision-making process. It just gets complicated when other people evaluate that judgment. Whether it was a good judgment or bad judgment depends on whom you ask.

In reality, a number of things in life rely on judgment. We often find ourselves in situations where there are no right or wrong answers. As a consequence, our final decision comes down to a matter of judgment. The ability to make good judgment calls is perhaps one of the most crucial assets required of a leader. As such, it is an important attribute for today's youth to acquire.

Not the "Eye Roll" Again!

It was mid-season, and the NCAA coordinator of officials for basketball had just posted a scathing memo on the referee site ArbiterSports, reminding all refs of the importance of enforcing sportsmanship. He was quite upset that some officials were apparently reluctant to enforce "Rule 10, Section 5," a group of unsporting technical fouls, informally known as the sportsmanship rules.

This person also reinforced our responsibility as game officials to speak directly and forcefully to the team captains in our pre-tip-off meeting at midcourt. The goal behind this lecture was to remind the team captains of their responsibility to communicate and enforce sportsmanship by their team.

Thankfully, it was my partner's turn to be the head referee and talk to the kids. As he began his spiel, the two captains did a synchronized eye roll. It was all I could do not to roll my eyes along with them.

Don't get me wrong—I believe sportsmanship is important. I just don't think lecturing kids on their responsibilities in this area right before tip-off (when their minds and interests are clearly elsewhere) is the best way to get the message across.

I have always felt there has got to be a better way to get the attention of today's youth, whether it is about sportsmanship, academics, their health, or their dreams for the future. I believe it is possible to engage young people in their own development and learning, and that doing so requires involving them in activities and subjects that they find meaningful.

How do you do that? You start by asking the kids what *they* want. By using the kids—their voices and their experiences—to lead, you meet the needs of the kids who want to play, but are embarrassed because they're out of shape or overweight. You meet the needs of the kids who know they don't have the skills to be a great athlete, but who don't want to sign up just to sit on a bench. You even meet the needs of those kids who do have the skills and who *are* uber-competitive and who really, really want to have their face on that Wheaties® box—but who would like to play with their friends who might not be on the team with them.

In the end, it's about using kids to sell other kids on the idea of fun, engaging sports and fitness activities. It's about creating an environment where kids can "let it all hang out." When you do that, not only do you increase the number of kids participating in both recreational and elite sports programs, you also decrease the number of kids suffering from obesity and obesity-related diseases. In addition, you bring people together in a positive way. Even better, you eliminate the lectures … and the subsequent eye-rolling.

Hey, Dad, You Just Forgot!

When my oldest son, John, was about nine years old, some close friends invited our family over for a Saturday night dinner. Saturdays were never a very relaxing day for me, what with two sermons and a class to teach the next day. This Saturday was particularly stressful. I was extra anxious about my sermon and worked on it up until the minute we left for dinner.

The sermon was still on my mind as we visited and ate. Subsequently, as soon as we got home, I decided to dive back into my preparations. Except … where were my notes? They weren't at home. We drove to the church. They were not there, either. We drove back to our friends' place. No notes.

I was close to having a nervous breakdown by the time we headed home again. Then, just a few minutes away from our house, I found my notes in the visor above the steering wheel.

I immediately started to beat myself up, which I'm pretty good at. "What's wrong with me?" I growled. "How could I be so stupid?" That's when John spoke up from the backseat. "Dad, you're not stupid. You just forgot where you put your sermon."

Out of the mouth of babes … or nine-year-olds. We are often too quick to judge ourselves harshly, and reach judgments that can stay with us for a lifetime. That factor points out why kids need a supportive, non-judgmental environment, one in which they can not only have opportunities to succeed, but also have opportunities to mess up and learn it's not the end of the world if it happens.

It's my philosophy that we do better as people, families, and organizations when we are cooperative, good at teamwork, and mindful of the common good. Accordingly, in every way we can, we need to help each other, as well as our children, learn to be cooperative, rather than competitive; to be helpful, rather than hurtful; to look out for the communities of which we are a part, and on which we ultimately depend.

Stuck in Sitka

In the mid-60s, I was invited to Sitka, Alaska to talk to various community groups, make some radio and television appearances, conduct a workshop, speak at their high school's athletic awards banquet and assembly, and give the Sunday sermon in a local church.

The Sitka trip came at a busy time for me. I was pastor/director of the Westminster Presbyterian Church and Center. I was also refereeing major college basketball and working on my doctoral degree. In addition, I was attempting to spend time with my two very young children and my wife. My preparation for the trip consisted of throwing some notes from previous presentations, a few sermons, and several books into my briefcase, as I left for the airport.

I flew from LAX to Seattle, where I awaited the seaplane that would fly me to Sitka. With time to kill, I wandered into the restaurant at the Seattle-Tacoma International Airport. Midway through lunch, I headed to the bathroom—leaving some work on the top of the table and my briefcase in an empty chair. Some minutes later, I returned to the table. My briefcase was gone.

I found security, who promptly educated me to the fact that because Seattle was the major airport between the West and Asia, it was a major hangout for international spies. Apparently, somewhere, a KGB agent was probably poring over the papers in my briefcase, trying to decipher the code behind the 123rd Psalm.

There I was—stuck. I landed in Sitka for a week of meetings and presentations, with only my clothes and whatever my brain brought along. It was a difficult week to say the least. I spent a lot of time in the city library, slept very little, and stumbled through the week with minimal confidence and questionable impact.

That week was a turning point in my life. It occurred to me that while I was very self-assured when it came to my athletic pursuits, I severely lacked confidence in other areas of my life—such as in my ability to just off-the-cuff create and deliver an inspiring message to an audience of church-goers. While I thoroughly believed in what I could do on the court, I did not have a corresponding belief in what I could do once I changed out of that uniform. Furthermore, that lack of belief was hampering my growth significantly.

The judgments we make about being able to perform a particular activity—our belief that "I can" or "I cannot"—is a major determiner of our success in that activity. When you're working with kids, you can't just inject them with the belief that they're going to be successful at the things they try. What we can do, however, is nurture them and provide them with opportunities to try a variety of things—from promoting an activity to organizing or playing in one. As a result, they can come to believe in themselves, and grow because of that belief.

From the Pulpit to the Prison

I was having lunch with a friend of mine, a Baptist minister who had broken away from traditionalists within the church, and was now leading a small congregation that met in one of the local parks to worship and perform community service. During our lunch, he happened to mention that he had been invited to lead a group of inmates at the minimum security prison on Terminal Island, off the coast of Los Angeles. He asked if I would be interested in co-facilitating the group with him.

For the next year, he and I met weekly at the prison with a group of about 12 to 15 inmates. They were real people who had made real mistakes. They were also genuinely interested in changing themselves and each other. It was my first actual introduction to the power of community. These men—all very diverse—helped, supported, and cared about one another despite the pain of their circumstances and the uncertainty of their future.

While I have many great memories of that time, the thing that sticks with me the most were their celebrations whenever someone earned a pass to visit the "outside world" or was released for good. They didn't experience envy or hard feelings, just the hope that whoever was leaving would be successful—because that meant that the individuals left behind had a chance of turning their lives around and making it, too.

That kind of support is very important, whether you're a 40-year-old prisoner or a 14-year-old junior high student. It is a tough world for kids today. Many of them feel marginalized and disconnected from those around them. They need a safe place to go—not just safe physically, but safe emotionally. They need a place where everyone's successes are celebrated, and everyone is given the opportunity to experience success and belonging. If it could happen to prisoners on Terminal Island, it can happen for our children.

Three-on-Three at Jim Brown's

Warren Lee and I have known each other since we were ministers together in the 1960s. We're great friends. Not only do we have a shared ecclesiastical history, but we also have a shared love of basketball. Warren's the guy who officiated at my marriage and who will do the same at my funeral (assuming he outlasts me).

Because stories often sound so much cooler when our friends tell them, I asked Warren if he wouldn't mind sharing a few about our time together. The following is one:

There was a time in the late 1960s when I would go to Jim Brown's house (yes, Jim Brown, the football great, turned actor), which was nestled high above Sunset Boulevard in the Hollywood Hills, to play 3-on-3 basketball in his driveway. There, I met and played with and against famous movie stars and pro athletes, such as Elliot Gould, Fred Williamson, Lynn Swann, Tim Brown, and Robert Hooks. Jim was a gracious host who provided soft drinks for those individuals who came to his house, as well as access to his luxurious home. Not only was Jim perhaps the greatest football player who ever played the game, he was also outstanding at basketball and took pride in being able to compete against and defeat topflight NBA players, such as Jack Marin, and college All-Americans, like Mike Warren.

One Saturday afternoon, I invited George to come along. I had not actually seen George play since watching him on television in the mid-50s against the likes of Bill Russell and Willie Naulls. Since George was approaching his late 30s, I figured he was probably a little out of shape and might even choose to be a spectator rather than play. Wrong! Not only did George play, but he put on quite a show. Jim Brown was dumbfounded. He couldn't believe what he was seeing. This short, not-so-young white guy was destroying everyone who tried to guard him and leading whatever team he played on to victory. Finally, Jim took it upon himself to defend George with the same result. Later, Jim found out from his close friend Bill Russell who George was and that he, Russell, had competed against George, when Russell was college basketball's "best big man" in the country and George was the "best little man."

I took away several important lessons from George's performance that long-ago Saturday afternoon. First, no one should ever judge a book by its cover. The two most impressive and unlikely aspects of George's game that day were his defense and rebounding. To be sure, he scored a lot of points, and his passing, as expected, was brilliant. However, what shocked and astounded Jim about George's play is that George made crucial defensive stops on him and out-fought him for rebounds. Second, George truly out-thought Jim and was always a step ahead of him. Third, in the words of Coach Rudy Tomjanovich, "Never underestimate the heart of a champion." George Selleck has as much heart as any basketball player who ever played the game.

From that story, I think you can see why I want Warren speaking at my funeral. He's going to give me a heck of a eulogy!

In all seriousness, though, I really like Warren's comment about not judging a book by its cover. I think a lot of people often make the mistake of underestimating kids, just like Jim Brown underestimated me. In reality, children (and old basketball players) are a lot smarter than we often give them credit for. Put opportunities for leadership in their hands, and they are going to surprise you with what they can do. Why? Because they have a lot of heart and a strong desire to succeed—just like me in Jim Brown's driveway more than 40 years ago.

What John Wooden Taught Me About Socks

Over the years, I had a number of opportunities to interact with John Wooden, UCLA's famed basketball coach. I remember one day in particular—I'd arrived early for a scheduled afternoon meeting with Coach Wooden at Pauley Pavilion. While I waited, I watched the coach, before the first practice of the new season, teach his players how to put on their socks.

It was a fascinating experience. Wooden started by carefully rolling each sock over his toes, up his foot, and around the heel, pulling it up snug. Then, he went back to his toes and smoothed out the material along the sock's length, being careful that there were no wrinkles or creases.

The coach had two purposes for this ritual. First, wrinkles cause blisters, and blisters can cost a team a victory. Second, he wanted to emphasize to his players how crucial seemingly trivial issues, such as double-tying your shoelaces, making sure your uniform fit properly, and yes, putting your socks on correctly, could be.

"Details create success" were the "habits of success" for a coach who won 10 NCAA championships. I have tried to carry that same philosophy into everything I do. There is no substitute for sound fundamentals, habits, and discipline within an organization. The following is a list of "habits for success" that I feel are critical for a successful youth program:

- Know every kid. Be interested in them, and try to learn as much about them as possible, e.g., academic, social, leisure time needs, learning style, and other factors that might impact their progress and growth.
- Help every kid feel like a winner. The philosophy should be "sports for all" versus "sports for the few." There are no "forgotten" kids. There should not be kids who sit on the sidelines until the game is in the bag, before they are sent in to play.
- Help each kid achieve their goals and dreams. Whether it's a short-term goal, like learning how to play basketball, or a long-term goal, like getting into college, provide them with the basic skills and knowledge to be able to do these things.
- Observe the kids closely to properly evaluate and assess their progress toward their goals, and add significant and meaningful data to the knowledge you have about them.
- Identify and support each kid's strengths and interests, and to use that information to further develop skills and self-esteem.

Like John Wooden, I see sports as a classroom, where even the smallest things matter when it comes to achieving success.

A Little Bit Different

Sometime during the early years of the sensitivity training movement, I attended a gathering of Christian ministers in Los Angeles who were attempting to be more honest and open with each other. With a great deal of apprehension, I decided to share with the group how, since converting from Judaism, I had always felt discomfort in the Christian community. Despite being a minister, I never felt like I fit in. After I had finished speaking, a well-known pastor from a large congregation in Los Angeles immediately countered my statement with, "George, that's silly, you've always been one of us."

At that point, one of the younger pastors immediately contradicted him, saying, "Oh, come on, let's be honest here. You know we've all said that George is a little bit different." While it is not fun to hear you are different than others, it was a wonderful verification that what I had been feeling and sensing was actually true. I wasn't imagining things or wasn't totally out of touch.

I've always been attracted by Socrates' bold statement that "The unexamined life is not worth living." He didn't mince his words. He didn't say the unexamined life is "less meaningful than it could be" or the unexamined life is "one of many possible responses to human existence." He simply and clearly said it's not even worth living.

As a counselor/psychologist and consultant, I have seen far too many tragic examples of the effect of an unexamined life. I remember Harriet, a sensitive, attractive woman in her early 50s who realized that a series of repetitive, doomed-from-the-beginning relationships had used up so many years of her life that it was unlikely that she would ever achieve her dream of having a husband and children of her own. I recall Fred, a caring and hard-working man who had neglected his wife and family emotionally for so long that when he finally realized what had happened, he was divorced, depressed, and living alone in an apartment.

We all have blind spots, which is why Socrates' method of self-examination included an essential element that became known as "Socratic" dialogue. Talking with a close friend, a spouse, a skilled clinician, or a spiritual advisor can help reveal those blind spots we cannot see by ourselves.

I think that if I had been more aware of my blind spots, I might not have jumped so readily into a faith in which I didn't feel comfortable. On the other hand, I didn't really have anyone to talk with about it. That's another reason why I work so hard now to not only try to make sure every kid feels like they "fit in," but also that they have the skills and knowledge to be able to examine their lives and know what they want to get out of it.

I like to think that Socrates would be proud.

Mistakes

In the 12th year of my first marriage, I made a huge mistake. Instead of taking all the problems I was dealing with—questions about my career choice, financial worries, unresolved identity issues—and using it as an opportunity to pause, think, reflect, and make some positive changes in my life, I impulsively left my wife and young family. Neither willing nor able at that time in my life to deal with what should have been a wake-up call, I opted out.

Fortunately, Beth (my ex-wife) was able to look past my shortcomings and, while we were not able to maintain our marriage, we were able to maintain our friendship. She has gone with me and our kids on vacation almost every year since then. She also lives with my son, Peter, whom I visit monthly, and of course, we grieved together when our daughter, Alison, passed away. She has forgiven the mistakes I made in failing to maturely deal with the issues we had.

A friend of mine, Marty, is a retired professor of sociology, as well as a volunteer softball and volleyball coach. On the first day of practice, he likes to wear a t-shirt that reads, "MISTAKES R WUNDERFUL OPPERTUNITEEZ 2 LERN!" It is his favorite shirt, because it captures so well a major premise of how he coaches—his "mistake center" concept.

Marty believes that the only way to teach skills to kids and, at the same time, establish a fun environment is to encourage them to take risks in trying new things. We all learn by attempting, observing our mistakes, considering the correction, and being congratulated for the effort. It is for this reason that Marty emphatically communicates to his athletes and their parents that the practice field and game field are "centers of mistakes," where he doesn't want anyone to worry about goofing up. He wants the kids to be free to learn, and mistakes are how we do that.

Sports, play, and games teach us a lot about learning from our mistakes, if for no other reason, because they provide so many opportunities to make them. A receiver drops a pass, a third baseman lets the ball go between his legs, a tennis player charges the net when she should have dropped back, and so on.

Someone once said that the purpose of obstacles is to instruct, not obstruct. One of the best ways to increase a young person's self-esteem is to allow them to try something, get frustrated, try again, get more frustrated, and then try again and succeed. They can then say to themselves, "I did it all by myself!"

If we want a kid to not be fearful of making mistakes, we must show them that they can be relaxed about those mistakes and can still laugh when nothing much is going right. One way to do this is to learn to talk in a voice that's supportive, projecting the spirit that making corrections is both useful and fun.

By proceeding with patience and a positive approach, we can establish a learning climate in which the young person understands that we have a genuine desire to help.

As a result, corrections will then be welcomed because the kids will recognize that our intention is not to hurt or discourage them, but to offer solutions that make it possible for them to perform better. This factor is very important. Fear spoils the fun that kids should have, and it makes them hide their mistakes, instead of recognizing them and working on solutions. Fear can cause young people to drop out of sports and physical activities, which, in turn, will result in them losing the opportunity to engage in and enjoy lifelong wellness, play, and recreational activities. Fear can even cause adults, who should know better, to do things that throw their lives and their families into chaos.

The problems I had in my first marriage were a huge opportunity for me to learn about myself and my role as a husband and father. Unfortunately, I lacked the courage and confidence to deal with these issues. The result of walking away from my internal issues destined me to have continuing struggles in my career, my relationships and life in general.

Successful youth programs guide kids through the learning process, no matter how painful that process may sometimes be. It's a lesson I wish I had learned a long time ago.

An Interview With My Pastor

I was nervous as the time neared for my appointment with Robert Boyd Munger, my pastor at the First Presbyterian Church of Berkeley (the church that sponsored my pursuit of a theological degree at Princeton Theological Seminary).

Dr. Munger was a highly respected pastor, professor, and author of several best-selling books. Though I knew him as a kind and gracious person, I was nevertheless quite uneasy, as I waited outside his office to discuss where I was headed in my career and my life.

Dr. Munger's words have never left me. "George," he said, "you have a problem with commitment." Clearly, he was disappointed in my decision to leave the ministry and start a private practice in psychology. I also knew he was displeased with my divorce. I was left to wonder, as I do to this day, how much those decisions were rooted, as Dr. Munger said, in a lack of commitment.

Was I comfortable with Dr. Munger's statement? No. I'm not even sure I totally agreed with it. On the other hand, I did appreciate his willingness to be honest with me. This much I do know—honest, accurate feedback is vital to our growth and development as human beings. The philosopher who said, "Know thyself," understood how easy it is for us to pull the wool over our own eyes.

Self-awareness is the ability to objectively see ourselves as others see us. For example, I may think I am assertive, and if others see me as assertive, my self-awareness about my assertiveness is accurate. On the other hand, if others see me as unassertive or as assertive in some situations but not in others, then my self-awareness is lacking.

Much of what we learn about ourselves stems less from our own internal understanding than from input provided by the outside world. In fact, research demonstrates the perceptions of others are better predictors of our actual performance than our own subjective viewpoints.

The obvious question, then, is why aren't we all rushing out to get feedback from others? Truth be known, who wants to hear that their idea lacks creativity or they couldn't sing their way out of a barrel? Eagerness to receive honest feedback is something that needs to be nurtured. In reality, we're naturally defensive about potential criticism. On the other hand, that self-protective mechanism can hinder our efforts in expanding our self-awareness.

One way I try to help kids increase their own level of self-awareness is by teaching them how to give and receive constructive feedback. For example, evaluations are done after activities to look at what worked, what didn't work, and what should be changed or done differently in the future. Kids learn that it's okay to make mistakes, and they learn how to learn from those mistakes. Most importantly of all, I try to create an environment in which nurturing, life-changing relationships can be developed—the kind of relationships in which kids feel comfortable in asking for, receiving, and giving the type of feedback that encourages self-awareness.

Being Present

"There is nothing either good or bad, but thinking makes it so," wrote Shakespeare. From my personal perspective, by the time I was in my 30s, I was thinking things were pretty bad. My marriage had failed, my relationship with my siblings was pretty much non-existent, my self-esteem was in the toilet, and I really wasn't sure what I wanted to do with my life. Although I had done a great deal of counseling as a pastor, I was very resistant to getting therapy myself. Giving up control to another person, the prospect of digging into my past, and the possibility of what I might learn were very scary. On the other hand, my outward circumstances had crumbled so badly that I had no choice.

My therapist turned out to be a very supportive person who listened intently and helped me cope with my struggles by encouraging me to express my thoughts and feelings. His words, "George, remember, just *one step at a time*," allowed me to move forward without pressure. It wasn't until years after my therapy had ended, however, that I began to realize what a great gift this man had given me. He was the individual who started me on my lifelong journey of learning how to live in the present.

The point is not to say that no value exists to our future or our past. If we never look backward at the scope of our life—the choices we've made and where they have led us—then, it's incredibly difficult to identify what we've done right or wrong and how to learn from our mistakes. By the same token, if we never look forward—if we don't think about and plan for where we want to go in life—then it's unlikely we'll end up with the future we want. The present, however, is the place where we live. The enjoyment of life has everything to do with being in the moment.

If you think living in the moment is an easy thing to do, try to go five minutes without thinking about that assignment that's due or what you're going to make for dinner once you get home or what your spouse meant by that remark they made this morning. Go ahead—set the timer. I'll wait.

I've always been a worrier. In that regard, my biggest challenge is that I live in the future too much. I worry about things that haven't happened yet and probably never will happen (although you can't persuade me that a zombie apocalypse is totally outside the realm of possibility). I also have regrets about things in my life. No matter how long ago these events happened, the memories can still be very vivid and real. On the other hand, by failing to forgive things that have happened in my past, I come up short in my efforts to move forward and to be present in the moment.

I try to encourage youth to live in the present as much as possible. Young children are good at this—they can be screaming "I hate you!" one minute, and five minutes later, they're snuggled in your lap squeezing your face, with their little hands and smothering you with kisses. For teens, it can be much harder. They can hold a grudge for months or even years. In those situations, what I do is try to help them be more aware of the joy in the moment—the smell of the grass in summer, the blue of the sky, or even the sound of a volleyball being smacked across a net. By making the effort to recognize these things and to take pleasure in them, hopefully, they are learning a skill that will save them a lot of money in therapy bills when they're older.

Something to Run To

Early in my work as a psychotherapist, I was visited in my Santa Monica office by a couple who announced that their 16-year-old daughter had run away. "We are here because you have studied this kind of thing. and we don't know what to do next," they said.

My first thought was, no, I really *hadn't* learned about this problem in any of my classes or internships—but I wished I had. Secondly, I quickly determined that my model of being a mirror more than an advice-giver was totally inadequate for this situation. These parents wanted advice and they wanted it NOW.

Somehow, I was able to calm them down, provide some suggestions, and lead them to implement some actions that eventually reunited them with their daughter and helped them begin to resolve their issues. It didn't always work out that well with clients, but this time it did.

The takeaway from that experience has stayed with me to this day, and it is this: we need to design programs that kids run *to*, not *from*. We are competing with unsavory people who nurture, buy clothes for, and court kids. We are competing with gangs who protect kids, befriend them, are there for them, and even understand, comfort, and identify with kids who are running away from abuse or uncaring parents. We are competing with bars and the glamour of drugs and alcohol. The "just say no" philosophy doesn't work and never did. We need a variety of attractive alternatives to which kids can say "yes." If we don't, too many parents will find themselves sitting in a counselor's office saying, "You're the expert. Tell us what to do!"

Fed Up!

The young man—a high school junior—sat in my office, brought there by parents who were concerned because their son was thinking of quitting football. He had grown up on the football field, starting at age seven with Pop Warner, and now had a good chance to be a varsity player in the upcoming season.

I asked some routine questions, whereupon the boy started pouring his feelings out. "I hate sports. I hate everything about them—the politics, the commitment, the late practices, the early practices, the hard work, the running, the tryouts, the sprints, the boring drills, the parents, the mascots, the jerseys, the injuries, the repetition and, more than anything, the competition and pressure."

He hadn't always felt this way. As we talked, I learned the young man had once enjoyed competitive football and baseball—he would get up early for workouts, practice in the off-seasons, would walk into class dripping sweat and reeking, and loved it all.

What changed? I think the fact the boy's parents thought he needed therapy because he didn't want to play sports anymore was my first clue. Seriously? *Therapy?*

We have gotten to a point in society where many of us take children's sports too far. Excessive parental involvement, thoughtless coaching polices, and programs centered on winning have created a purely competitive, commitment-based sporting environment, turning kids off from the games they love. In addition, while community sports programs exist for kids ages 6 to 13 in many places, opportunities tend to diminish in middle school and even more so in high school. If kids don't make the school team, they often don't have other options. This situation is incredibly sad. Sport should be for all, not just the few. It should be about fun, friendship, and improving one's skills, rather than trophies, MVPs, and college scholarships.

What I do is, in large part, a response to the pain felt by that long-ago young man. It's for the thousands of kids who either drop out of sports because they no longer enjoy it, or have never had the opportunity to experience how much fun it can be. I've learned kids do much better when they own their own activities—when they're able to participate in sports, games, and general physical activity without unhealthy pressure from adults. When you give them the opportunity to do that, hopefully, you're preventing future athletes from ending up in a therapist's office, simply because they are fed up with the whole thing.

Programs Don't Change Kids—Relationships Do

"I have tried over and over, but I'm just not good with people," said the young, crew-cut engineer. "I've just got to accept it. I'm going to be alone for the rest of my life."

He had come to my office seeking a prescription for anti-depressants (which, as a psychologist, I wasn't qualified to write), but what this young man really needed was help in knowing how to relate to others. With therapy and some courage on his part, he was able to move past the stumbling blocks in his relationship, and his depression disappeared in the process.

The biggest part of happiness (some professionals have estimated as much as 85 percent) is determined by our relationships with other people—how well we get along with others and how well they get along with us. Relationships are not peripheral to a successful life. They are central. If we accomplish all or most of our material goals but do not attend carefully to our relationships, we end up empty, alone, and miserable. On the other hand, if we have solid relationships with people who care about us and whom we care about, then no matter what happens in the outside world, we can still be happy.

My experience as a psychotherapist and human relations consultant to businesses and organizations have given me many opportunities to help people learn the art of establishing and maintaining successful relationships. Of course, the obvious question is, if I was so good at helping others with their relationships, how come I had so much trouble with my own? I think it's partly because it is always easier to give counsel when you are on the outside looking in. When you don't have any emotional attachments, for example, concerning whether a woman says yes or no if someone asks her on a date, it's simple to say, "Look, Joe/Bob/Frank—sometimes you just have to put yourself out there and take a risk."

The other part of the dilemma attendant to relationships stems from the fact that learning about relationships is a lifetime experience—and some of us are slow learners. In reality, perhaps we learn as much about relationships when we fail at them as when we succeed. I have done both.

The years have helped me learn that the relationships children and adolescents have in their lives are far more important to their well-being than their achievements are. In fact, do you know what young people entering junior high listed as their greatest fear? It wasn't forgetting their locker combination or getting lost on the way to class. Their number one fear was not having anyone to sit by at lunch. To kids, relationships are everything.

I like to say that programs don't change kids—relationships do. Build the relationships … and the program follows.

Out of My Comfort Zone

Many years ago, I received a phone call from a head hunter. This was the first time that this situation had ever happened to me. Not unexpectedly, I was very surprised and more than a little flattered. The woman said her client was looking for a behavioral scientist to join their human resources staff. I had been doing some corporate human relations consulting with small and medium-sized companies in addition to my counseling work, and was immediately curious about the opening, which turned out to be with Dow® Chemicals.

After several telephone interviews with Dow executives, I was on a plane to their corporate headquarters in Michigan. Ultimately, I was offered the job. As a result, I had a big decision to make—whether to leave my work and life in California to pursue a new focus in my career and an uncertain destination, or to stay where I was comfortable. Ultimately, my curiosity and desire to expand my horizons led me to venture out of my comfort zone and accept a position with Dow, and it turned out to be a wonderful experience.

I pursued the road less taken—not always an easy thing to do for someone with a naturally anxious personality. From that situation, I learned that letting one's curiosity loose can unlock value, experiences, and knowledge previously unimagined. All that is needed is an open mind, a spirit of adventure, and a desire to make a difference.

Curiosity is about asking questions. It's a process—not an end in itself. It's a solution that is ongoing, and always requiring you to ask what you need to do next. It demands that you continue to dig deep and probe for answers. The challenge is to figure out what is worthy of our curiosity and attention.

I have always been curious about people, an attribute that helped me tremendously on the basketball court ("Why does that player keep going to the right every time he has the ball?"), as a pastor and counselor ("Why do people keep doing things that only seem to bring them pain?") and finally, as the founder or co-founder of several programs for kids. I am more curious about kids than just about anything. I'm curious about what they like to do, what they don't like to do, how technology affects them, what kinds of pressures they face—you name it. By indulging that curiosity and listening to the kids themselves, it gives me a better understanding of what ideas, activities, and experiences have the potential to improve the way we meet their needs. What I'm working on at the present time is such an enterprise, and it just might change the game from a focused journey to an experience—a world beyond our comfort zone.

Tennis, Anyone?

I was fast approaching 40 and all that entails. As a consequence, I thought I'd add tennis to the little I was doing for fitness between basketball refereeing seasons. I had briefly played the sport when I was in junior high school—even winning some matches in various junior tournaments around Southern California. When I learned, however, that tennis season conflicted with basketball season, that brought an end to my tennis playing days—until one spring morning when I showed up at the Tournament Desk at the Santa Monica Open.

There were three divisions in the tournament—A, B, and C—with C being the lowliest. Naturally, I was assigned to the C division and sent to a remote court on the outskirts of the city. My opponent was a much older gentleman (at least, he looked old to me, and he certainly moved like an old person, as we gradually warmed up by lobbing balls back and forth to each other). I was a little nervous. After all, I'd just picked up a racket a few days earlier after a 25-year time-out. Still, it wasn't like I didn't have any athletic skills whatsoever, and this guy was *old*.

My opponent won the toss to determine who would serve first. Subsequently, after a few minutes of his slicing serves, drop shots, and other assorted moves, I knew this scenario was not going to be fun—at least, not for me. The old guy won in straight sets, and I didn't score a single point.

As I headed back to the tournament desk to get my next assignment (in the loser's bracket), I ran into Lynn Shackelford. Lynn had been a starter on UCLA's 1967-1969 national championship basketball teams. He looked as miserable as I felt. Apparently, his nerves and lack of confidence with a racquet had undermined him just as it had me. We contrasted our present situation with our days of playing before thousands in Madison Square Garden, coolly shooting free throws without a second thought. How the mighty had fallen.

It was a good lesson in just what it takes to build confidence. Because when you think about it, what is confidence? It's the knowledge that you will perform up to your capability. It is a positive attitude that is highly dependent on past experience. Confidence is built on competency. You have to have the skills before you can have the confidence. Swinging a racquet a few times before entering a tennis tournament is *not* a way to build confidence. Little wonder the old guy was able to beat me.

On the other hand, I had probably shot thousands—maybe even millions—of free throws on my journey to Madison Square Garden. I felt very competent *and* confident in my ability to put the ball through the net. Playing before a huge crowd didn't change that.

We want our kids to feel confident as we send them out into the adult world. Many of them don't feel confident, though, because they lack real-world skills. That skill set is something the right kind of program can give them. Imagine the high school or college graduate who is able to put on their resume: "I helped plan and implement sports and fitness activities for 300 students." Or, "I was responsible for publicizing a community sports and fitness day that was attended by over 200 people." By giving youth the opportunity to develop their competencies in areas like those examples cited, we can help them develop the confidence they need to succeed in the classroom, on the job, or—as the case may be—on the tennis court with some old guy on the other side of the net.

What Goes Up Must Come Down

In my mid-40s, I was invited by some friends to go skiing at Mammoth Lakes, CA. I had never been skiing before. Once we got to the mountain, I think my friends assumed my athleticism on the basketball court was something that would just naturally transfer to the ski slope. Surprisingly to me, all they did was point me to the chairlift for beginners and then, they headed for the more challenging part of the mountain. There were no instructions, no lessons—no nothing.

As I stumbled off the chairlift, I had no idea what to do next. Accordingly, I followed the crowd and was soon on a bigger lift—one with an enclosed cabin carrying me up, up, up! When I reached the end of the ride, I was at the top of a very tall mountain. Now what? Frightened and unsure of myself, I started heading down the hill. I fell a lot. Sometimes I sat down and scooted on my bottom. Occasionally, I actually skied. I'm sure I provided a good deal of entertainment to the people on the chairlift passing over me. While I would never recommend this experience to anyone, I do take some pride in the fact that I faced my fears and not only got down the mountain on my own, but did it without killing myself.

Sometimes, fear is our best teacher. We all experience fear and uncertainty in our lives. It's how we respond to that uncertainty that makes us who we are. We can choose to let our fears cripple us, or we can move through them and experience all that they have to offer.

Another way of making this point is to note the difference between where we are and where we want to be. To get from here to there usually requires leaving our comfort zone and doing some (often painful) stretching. When we are willing to be uncomfortable for a while—to experiment, to stick to it, to make mistakes—we grow and learn. In fact, growth happens when we are the most uncomfortable.

This factor has certainly been true for me lately. My current project has been the equivalent of standing at the top of that mountain not knowing how to ski. It has required that I do things I have never done before and/or activities I am not comfortable doing (such as promoting myself in order to promote the program).

I couldn't ask the kids I work with to stretch, however, if I wasn't willing to do it first. Hopefully, as we take those steps together, we will all learn, grow, and uncover the potential that lies in all of us.

Barnacles

One weekend, my second wife and I were guests at the Newport Beach home of some longtime friends. Our hosts, Haig and Alice, had a small boat, and, after a cup of early morning coffee, Haig invited me to join him for some work on the boat prior to taking it out.

As a result, off we went to remove barnacles from Haig's boat. As we continued chatting, Haig explained to me that barnacles are little calcified deposits (crustaceans) that attach themselves to boat bottoms for the equivalent of a free ride, robbing boats of much-needed maneuverability, thereby significantly reducing their overall speed. "The little buggers get on a bit at a time," he said, "so you've got to be watching for them constantly, because they'll burn up your fuel and steal your speed."

Sometime later, I ran across an article about barnacles, and, curious from my time spent knocking them off my friend's boat, I decided to learn more. "The barnacle," the author explained, "is confronted with an existential decision about where it's going to live. Once it decides … it spends the rest of its life with its head cemented to a rock."

The barnacle metaphor is one I've used many times over the years. Many of us cruise along, often unaware of the barnacles that attach themselves to us. These "barnacles" can be a bad habit, a certain mindset, or an incorrect perception (such as poor self-esteem) that slow us down and result in the loss of maneuverability needed to survive and/or prosper in a world that places a premium on being fast, flexible, and fluid. To succeed in today's hyper-competitive environment, we need to continually scrape away at the stuff that slows us down.

I am working to provide kids with a safe place to do a little barnacle-scraping. This undertaking will allow them to approach the process of identifying personal barnacles positively, rather than negatively. This way, they avoid the risk of having a productive experience turn into a traumatic one. Furthermore, they end up with nice, shiny boats in the process!

Bonsall Elementary

Some years ago, while living in Fallbrook, I volunteered at Bonsall Elementary School, which was near my home. Twice a week, I met with small groups of 2nd and 3rd graders who were struggling with a new language—English—and subsequently were having difficulty with their other school subjects.

I still recall the satisfaction the kids experienced as they made progress with the various subjects. It was not easy, however. Almost universally, each child would start by saying, "I can't do it." It didn't matter if we were working on reading, math, or whatever.

I would usually respond by saying, "Well, let's see … I'm pretty sure you CAN do it." At that point, we would then start with small steps—sounding out a word or working on the simplest math problem. When things would finally "click" for them, I don't know who was prouder—the child or me. It reminded me of watching my children (and grandchildren) pulling themselves up for the first time in the crib or falling over and over again as they learned to walk or missing the baseball 20 times before finally getting a hit.

Success is a powerful motivator. Each accomplishment, however small, reinforces future efforts and leads to achievement, as a positive cycle is set in motion. When adults can join children and youth in this process, encouraging them with our words and our caring, the experience promotes a general sense of pride and supports the development of perseverance from which the young person can draw as they face each new challenge. In this way, success builds upon success; each new accomplishment reinforces self-esteem.

Flat-out Failure

I had been living and practicing psychology in Fallbrook for five years when I learned that the basketball coach at the local high school was going to retire after more than three decades of coaching. While there were a host of candidates to replace him, my experience gave me a leg up, and a phone call from John Wooden cinched the deal. I was hired and started immediately, working with the team in their summer league program.

Much like the volunteer fire department in a small town, who upon hearing the alarm, immediately and without thought, rushes to the call, I sought and accepted the opportunity to coach the team without really thinking about it. The experience, however, turned out to be a flat-out failure. Oh sure, we won our share of games and were competitive in most, but it was not a fun or meaningful experience for either the players or me.

A number of things went wrong, including the following:

❑ Along with being overly optimistic, I was very naïve about what I was getting into. Looking back on the experience, my first clue should have been the inadequate attendance of players for the summer games. Upon reflection, it's apparent the players were deeply locked into the program and culture that the previous coach had established. Promises had been made, expectations were set and it had been that way for a long, long time. The problem was some of the players that were now automatically starters were not very good, and there were a couple of 10th and 11th graders who showed a lot of promise and who were already equally, if not more, skilled than the varsity players. In addition, several of the seniors had a drug problem, which not only diminished their performance, but was also known by their teammates. I'm not sure it was a perfect storm, but it was close, and I failed to note the storm clouds and provide the required leadership to overcome these significant barriers to our success on and off the court.

❑ I failed to plan. Though I consider myself a very organized and disciplined person, serious planning never got my attention until I started corporate consulting. I have since learned that planning includes anticipating, influencing, and controlling the nature and direction of change. In order to plan, I needed to become knowledgeable about the team, their skills, and their commitment to improvement. Wow! None of which were part of this story.

❑ I failed to communicate and connect. Most of the problems encountered by coaches arise from communication problems. The Fallbrook team did not appear to understand or even care about what I was trying to tell them, and their parents got a distorted version of what I was attempting to do with the team. Did I have the necessary communication skills to circumvent these problems and help relieve the stress? Apparently not!

❑ I failed to successfully manage change. Change is seldom, if ever, easy. In reality, changing the roles and playing time for players on a team (as I tried to do) is as difficult as it gets. I now know that successful implementation and acceptance of change depends on a number of factors, including:

- Good communication from the beginning, as well as multiple updates along the way
- Commitment to the proposed change.
- An understanding of the advantages of the proposed change
- An understanding of the disadvantages of not making the change
- The coach championing and carrying out their responsibilities for making the changes work

Oh, well. Mistakes are the lifeblood of learning. Without the willingness to make mistakes and learn from them, learning shrivels up. On the other hand, if you create a culture of learning and growing, you will develop credibility and trust with whom everyone you work.

Listening

It was not an unfamiliar experience, as I listened to the couple in my counseling office:

"He expects me to listen to his problems, but he's never interested in mine."

"She's always complaining."

"He never talks to me. The only time I find out what's going on in his life is when I overhear him telling someone else. Why doesn't he ever tell me these things?"

"I can't talk to her because she's so critical."

In this incident, the woman felt a violation in their connection—her husband was not listening. He, likewise, didn't trust the connection, and felt strongly that he was not being understood. Being listened to means that we are taken seriously, that our ideas and feelings are known and understood, and ultimately, what we say matters.

The yearning to be listened to and understood is also about a deeper need—the need to escape our separateness and bridge the space that often divides us from others. We attempt this by reaching out and trying to reveal who we are—what's on our minds and in our hearts, hoping and praying for understanding. Being listened to and receiving that understanding should be simple, but it isn't.

Listening is one of the most powerful things we do as human beings—when we do it, that is. Unfortunately, most of us aren't very good at it. We're busy formulating our response to what is being said, or we're preoccupied with our own situations, or we tune out, usually because we don't find the speaker very interesting.

Listening—*real* listening—is difficult. Think back to a time when you were really listening to someone. Maybe it was a job interview. Or a meeting where you had to take notes and report on what was said. Or a first date with someone you liked a lot and wanted to continue dating. By the time the interview or meeting or date was over, you probably felt a little bit exhausted from paying attention so much. In reality, that's what real listening feels like. Listening is not a spectator sport. It requires active participation on our part.

When we choose to listen to others, we give them one of our most cherished resources—our time. This reward alone is a powerful symbol of our intentions toward them. By listening, we affirm their worth and express, in an obvious manner, that they matter. In the process, we meet two of their basic human needs—the need to be understood and the need to feel important.

It hurts not to be listened to. Young people, especially, want to be heard and understood. Yet, that need is frustrated every day by adults, teachers, coaches, and friends, in small ways we don't necessarily remember or realize. That doesn't make it hurt any less, however.

Kids need to be taught about the importance of listening, as well as how to listen well. Most importantly, they need to be listened to. They need programs that provide the opportunity for essential relationships to happen, in which listening and understanding can take place.

Nervous Dad

I talked a lot on the phone with my daughter, Alison, during her undergraduate years at Stanford. I always looked forward to these phone calls, but I have to admit, I was not always sure how I was doing when it came to playing the supportive dad during the many issues a young person away from home struggles with during their college experience.

Back then Stanford had (and I assume still does) a policy that students could decide when they were or were not ready to take a final. Alison had changed her major from English to pre-med midway through college, ultimately graduating with two majors—English and biology. On several occasions, with her heavy course load, softball practice, and games, teaching a class for her peers from her experience working for Planned Parenthood® in the summers, and her growing relationship with her future husband,

Alison determined she was not ready for a final and elected to postpone it. This decision meant getting an incomplete in the class until she took the final. Being the responsible young woman she was, she felt the need to report this situation to her father.

On these occasions, our telephone conversations would usually go something like this:

"Dad, it happened again!"

"What's that, honey?"

"I didn't take my final in [name of class]."

Trying hard, but unsure of the proper response, I would reply, "That's okay, Alison. Really, how many kids get into Stanford and switch their majors to tackle pre-med? I know you will take the final when you can and are ready."

"But Dad, it is costing you a lot of money, and if you tell me I must take the final now, I will go take it!"

"No honey, I'm proud of you. When you are ready, that will be fine. I love you." And we would hang up.

Then, I would literally shake like a leaf. Did I say the right thing? Was my daughter asking me to tell her to go take the final? What did she really need from me? I was so afraid I had failed her.

We all love our kids, but often, we simply do not know the best way to help them. We do the best we can, and sometimes, we get it wrong, and sometimes, fortune favors us, and we get it right. Our world is difficult and is not at all an easy venture for today's youth. Our kids need help—through caring parents, through appropriate programs—to develop the attitudes and skills to strike out on their own, think their own thoughts, ask their own questions, make their own decisions, and draw their own conclusions—which I think Alison successfully did as she moved through her life. When she passed away at age 43, she was a physician who had obviously gotten around to taking those finals.

A Fish Story

I think it was the day before my 50th birthday, when I received the most wonderful card from my oldest son, John. It showed a papa bear and baby bear with fishing lines cast into the water in front of them. Below the picture John had written, "Dad—this card reminded me of you. All the times you took me fishing, when you didn't like fishing, and the fact that you didn't know anything about it showed me you loved me."

John was right. While I really didn't like fishing, I loved being with him. And HE liked fishing. So, fishing we went!

I think every divorced parent worries about the effect of divorce on their children. John was just 11 when his mother and I ended our marriage. I'm sure he must have felt a great deal of anger over the situation, despite the fact that Beth and I developed a very positive relationship and have gone on family vacations together almost every year since we separated in 1972.

Still, I worried my kids would hate me for what happened. I worried they would end up with emotional scars that would never heal. Yet, all three of them managed to turn out to be, in my humble opinion, incredible human beings. John, for example, is the smartest person I know. Not only does he have a master's degree in economics from Columbia University, he also has this incredible ability to take the most complex subjects and explain them in a manner that even the youngest child can easily understand. It's an amazing gift. Certainly not one he inherited from me!

My kids have always been keenly important to me. I hope they have always known that I felt that way. I do know my children are part of the reason I'm so passionate about the work I do at the present time. Every child deserves to know that they have someone in their life who cares about them and is committed to seeing them become successful. To paraphrase the old Chinese proverb, "Give a child a fish, and you feed him for a day. Teach a child to fish (or problem-solve or organize or manage a sports and fitness program), and you feed him for a lifetime."

Sand Traps

When I was in my 50s, I used to play a bit of golf. Once, while on a trip to Kauai, some friends invited me to join them for a round. My wife at the time—who had little interest in golf and no knowledge of the game—asked if she could come along and ride in the golf cart. "Sounds good," I said, and we headed for the local course.

It was a beautiful day as I stood at the first tee, gazing down the fairway to the hole that was a little more than 400 yards away. I hit my opening drive—a rather pretty shot of about 200 yards—straight into a sand trap. It was not a great place to be. In fact, it was a very, very difficult place to be. Grasping my 3-iron and mentally crossing my fingers, I somehow managed to hit the ball squarely. Gleefully, I watched it sail down the fairway another 200 yards or so and land about 12 feet from the cup. It was an excellent shot, except for the fact that the ball had landed in a SECOND sand trap. Not a good thing at all, especially for a less-than-average golfer like myself.

Quietly, everyone got in the golf cart and drove to the green. When my turn came again, I took out my sand wedge, and after a few swings above the sand, I took my shot. Amazingly, I hit the ball perfectly. I watched it land a few feet from the hole and slowly roll to about 10 inches from the cup, where I calmly (but with secret elation) tapped the ball in for par. I then returned to the cart, and my wife who said, rather matter-of-factly, "So, what's so hard about this game?"

I have found that life is a lot like golf—it's harder than it looks. Sometimes, we end up in sand traps and have no idea how we're going to get out. On occasion, it seems we will never get out. We'll just keep chipping away, while everyone around us goes merrily down the fairway.

My current project is a lot like golf, also. Sure, it would be exciting to be one of those hole-in-one success stories, where the program catches the eye of a celebrity sponsor and faster than you can say, "Angelina Jolie's leg," we're in every school in the country. In reality, frankly more frequently than I care to admit, I've felt like I was stuck in that sand trap, chipping away. Then, something marvelous will happen. I will hit the ball perfectly—make an unexpected connection, receive a hoped-for grant—and suddenly I'm out of the sand and back on the green again. I won't lie—those moments are fun. It's the time spent in the sand traps, however, that make them so.

The Big Kiss

Sometime in the late 70s, I decided to take up paddle tennis as a hobby. For those of you unfamiliar with the sport, paddle tennis is adapted from regular tennis, but the court is smaller, there are no double lanes, and the net is lower. It's also played with a solid paddle versus the standard tennis racquet, and a depressurized tennis ball. The smaller court makes for a faster game, which I really enjoyed. I took to it immediately.

I had been playing for about four years at the beach club near my Santa Monica office, when I was invited to team up with an older gentleman for the club's Annual Paddle Tennis Tournament. The Tournament was a big deal at the club, with large crowds following almost every match and a big party to celebrate the presenting of the championship trophy.

My teammate, Ron, was not only a lifetime member of the club but had also been playing the sport since he was nine years old. Nevertheless, we were the decided underdogs as the tournament began. Ron, however, was a marvelous defensive player, and I had picked up several good offensive skills to combine with my defensive strengths—all of which came together, as we marched through our opponents and found ourselves on the last day of the tournament in the semi-finals against a team of young college stars from UCLA.

We managed to defeat them, and before a loud and excited crowd, we squared off against another team of collegiate athletes for the championship. As the crowd roared in approval, we won the final match point—at which point, Ron, in sheer joy, grabbed me and planted a big kiss on my forehead! The experience was wonderful!

To take the victory stand with my teammate, who had spent 50 years watching other people up there, was beyond description. I felt a sense of comradeship and connectedness in our teamwork, the joy of just being able to compete and play well, pride in our individual and team achievement, and the welcome feeling of seeing hard work pay off.

Most of all, however, for this skinny little Jewish kid from Compton, the message and expression of welcome and acceptance communicated by that kiss meant that I was truly part of something. It's a feeling everyone should be so fortunate to experience. As Shakespeare said in Act I of Macbeth, "In his commendation I am fed; it is a banquet to me."

The Best Christmas Present

On Christmas day, 1982, my daughter, Alison (a student at Stanford at the time), gave me a copy of *Stanford Sports*, a book that had been published earlier that year. Although it mostly talked about the university's modern sports era, there was a brief section that mentioned me! As icing on the cake, Alison had also gone to my college basketball coach, Howie Dallmar, and asked for the names and addresses of my old teammates. She then mailed each of them a blank sticker to write their impressions of playing with me "way back when." When she gave me the book, it was covered with little notes from my teammates—like this one from Carlos Bea, who in addition to playing basketball at Stanford, also played for Cuba at the Helsinki Olympics, and who is currently a federal judge in northern California:

> "I remember you best not for your shooting and passing, but for your inspiration and leadership, indicated by being [the] number 2 rebounder on your senior team at 5'8" and 138 pounds!"

While Carlos and others of my former teammates have always been kind in talking about my leadership on the court, I must confess I haven't always felt confident or comfortable in my leadership skills *off* the court. I think that is one reason why helping kids become confident in this area is so important to me.

Leadership means different things to different people. For some it is about ego, power, persuasion, being in charge, and "commanding" people. For others, leadership is about:

- Hope and inspiration
- The art of persuasion
- Understanding followers' perspectives and perceptions
- Developing a team and team spirit
- Self-worth and public image

- Getting the job done or solving problems
- Teaching others
- Having fun with friends and family
- Getting involved in the community
- Serving others

Leadership starts with the attitude that nothing is more important than the commitment we make to those we lead, and ends with the belief that we have done our best on their behalf.

I know that when I played basketball, I left everything I had on the court. I think it was that example that my teammates looked up to and came to depend on. I like to think that with my current program, I am once again leaving everything "on the court." Furthermore, hopefully, I'm helping teach young people how to do the same.

Teaching Bill Walsh

In the early 1980s, I was coaching basketball at The Brentwood School in West Los Angeles and practicing organizational and clinical psychology, when a group of Stanford alumni approached me and asked if I had any interest in becoming the Stanford basketball coach. They anticipated there would be an opening the following season.

I was extremely flattered and quite interested. The group suggested I put together a portfolio that they could use in advocating my consideration for the possible opening. As part of that portfolio, I put together a "game plan" for recruiting student-athletes—borrowing heavily from the experiences I was having in my corporate consulting work.

The opening at Stanford did not materialize. In the meantime, however, I learned a lot about the recruiting process of young athletes and concluded that there was a large, relatively unmet need to train coaches in this area. At that time, the typical athletic department was inviting people from their business schools to lecture coaches on recruiting. The intensity of the competition for the country's best young high school athletes, however, was on the rise, and I determined that coaches not only needed additional skills in recruiting, but also a greater understanding of who the kids were from a personal and psychological perspective.

I approached Andy Geiger, Stanford's athletic director, with my thoughts, and he, too, became excited about addressing the need for greater sensitivity to kids and their families, while providing coaches with a more student-centered approach. He suggested that I explore the idea across the nation with some of his peers and arranged appointments for me at North Carolina, Duke, Texas, and Minnesota.

As a result, the *Sports Recruiting Workshop* was born. An effort that ultimately led to more than 100 presentation student-centered recruiting being made to Ivy League schools, military academies, community colleges, and Division I, II, and III schools including Notre Dame, USC, UCLA, Cal Berkeley, Ohio State, Michigan State, Minnesota, North Carolina, and Stanford (where I had the indomitable Bill Walsh taking copious notes for two days).

My experiences in this area taught me several things, including:
- The overwhelming significance of focusing on the needs, interests, values, objections, and concerns of the student-athlete, rather than pushing your school and program (in other words, creating a customer-oriented program).
- The indispensable value of learning by doing and discovery versus lecture and preaching. During the seminars, I would divide the coaches into groups of five to six individuals, present them with six potential "recruits," and have them compete

with the other groups over the course of the two-day workshop to see who would win over the recruits. This allowed them to experience the challenge and needs of recruiting even as they began to learn the specific skills involved.

This approach served me well then and is serving me well now as I work with youth and youth leaders. It's exciting to think that somewhere among the kids, taking notes in my leadership development course, could be the next Bill Walsh.

The Right Stuff

Tara VanDerveer has been the Stanford University women's basketball coach since 1985. Over the course of her renowned career, she has led the Stanford Cardinals to two NCAA Women's Division I National Basketball Championships. In 1996, she helmed the United States women's basketball team as they won the gold medal at the Atlanta Olympics. Tara was enshrined in the Women's Basketball Hall of Fame in 2002 and inducted into the Naismith Memorial Basketball Hall of Fame in 2011.

Back in 1984, however, Tara was just a young coach at The Ohio State University, taking my two-day sports recruiting seminar with about 50 other Ohio State coaches. The seminar was one I had conducted for numerous NCAA institutions across the country, and Tara was an eager learner.

So eager, in fact, that not long after the workshop, I received a call from her. She had been talking with the best high school player in Ohio, but the young woman was considering going to Michigan. Tara wondered if I had any advice on how to obtain this valuable recruit.

"Tara," I said. "Open your workbook." We then proceeded, point by point, to go through the "How to Turn Around a Lost Prospect" section in my *Sports Recruiting* workbook, with Tara patiently and thoughtfully answering each question. We reviewed what she already knew and briefly discussed what she needed to re-check. A week later Tara informed me, "It worked! We got the player! She's going to be a Buckeye!"

Tara and her Ohio State women's basketball team went on to win the Big Ten title the next spring, with a 20-7 record, and the player she recruited became a two-time All-American, whose jersey has since been retired.

When I think of coaches who have "the right stuff," Tara ranks right up there with the best of them. Many of the qualities she embodies are things that I advocate for in the kids with whom I work now, including:
- Respect for her players
- Patience in developing her players as athletes and persons
- The emotional maturity to realize that her players are young people who need to be given the opportunity and freedom to make mistakes

- Rather than expecting her players to play flawlessly, she teaches them and lets them learn.
- An understanding that it's about the players, not the coach. As one of her players commented, "She's not a yeller … not super in-your-face, but when she wants you to do something, she'll definitely tell you."
- Analytical in her assessment of players and the game; committed to learning, to teaching, and to acting on those insights
- Always energetic and positive in her approach to the players and the game

You may think, after reading this list, that these qualities are obvious. *"Of course* coaches (or any adult who works with young people) should act like this," you say. Obviously, you would be right. It's not that simple, however. Ego, impatience, lack of knowledge of how to work with youth—all of these factors can make what should be a positive, enriching experience for kids turn into anything but, which is why it is so important to have the right kinds of adults working with kids. It doesn't matter whether you're an astronaut preparing for a trip to the moon or a parent who has volunteered to coach your child's Little League team; you need to have the right stuff, because someone else's well-being is depending on you.

AYS—Oh!

It had been a wonderful, yet grueling, three-month stretch. As the invited keynote speaker for the American Youth Soccer Organization (AYSO), I had been traveling throughout the country to kick off their annual regional conferences.

At the conclusion of those efforts, I was invited by the AYSO Board of Directors to a meeting at their national office in Torrance, California. My assignment was to give a report on my experience, including my observations and any suggestions I might have for their continual improvement. Because my tour had left me very impressed with the AYSO's focus and commitment on doing what was good for kids, I was excited to deliver what I thought was a very upbeat report.

As the meeting with the Board progressed, however, it became clear to me that just below the surface was a huge tension between the American soccer elites, who were concerned about America's World Cup aspirations, and the volunteers, who just wanted kids to have fun.

Finally, as the conversation became more heated, one of the attendees turned to me and with considerable exasperation, asked, "Dr. Selleck, what's so great about the AYSO approach? As far as I'm concerned, the 'teamwork-first' ethic has become a national weakness. It's a philosophy that stifles kids' natural talents and enthusiasm for winning championships."

Wow! I was totally unprepared for that attitude. I then took a deep breath and hoped something important might magically come from my mouth. Starting slowly, but picking up steam, I said: "Sport is more than skills. It is also about ideas. It is about the direction in life that kids may take, even more than it is about soccer, basketball, or any other sport."

I don't know if I succeeded in changing that person's perspective, but what I said is something I have always firmly believed. Any youth sports program, like AYSO, is every bit as much about how to live your life as it is about learning how to kick a ball.

We Both Could Have Done Better

As a boy, my son Peter was an exceptional basketball player. The problem was that he didn't realize how good he was or how good he could become. As is often the case, what Dad said didn't count. In reality, however, I knew basketball, and I saw what Peter could do and how far he could go in the game, if he only had more confidence in his abilities and potential.

Subsequently, I asked my friend Stan Morrison, who was coaching at USC one day, if he would attend one of Peter's summer league games and offer his opinion on Peter's skills and possible future in the game. He did, and later told me that Peter could be just as good as he wanted to be.

Peter went on in his senior year at University High School in West Los Angeles to lead his team to a league championship and the Los Angeles city finals, and later played for the University of California San Diego. Do I think he was good enough to have played professionally? Yes, I do. On the other hand, I don't think Peter believed he was good enough. Does it matter anymore? Not at all.

Peter went on to follow his passion—teaching—and is now vice-principal of the very successful Preuss charter school on the University of California San Diego campus. He also thoroughly enjoys playing in various adult basketball leagues in the San Diego area. I couldn't be more proud of him, his family, and what he has accomplished in his life.

When I began writing about and conducting workshops on sports parenting, I thought I had better check in with Peter to get some feedback on what kind of a sports parent I had been. The response was so much who Peter is—always authentic and to the point, but never with the desire to hurt. "Well, to tell you the truth, Dad, we both could have done better."

I hope I am doing better with the kids with whom I currently work—better at instilling them with confidence in their abilities, and better at trusting they will ultimately do what is right for them.

By the 4th quarter of my life—a period of time beginning roughly in the late 1980s and ending with my fateful conversation with Alan Gregerman—I was beginning to recognize certain patterns to what I was doing and where I ultimately wanted to go.

These patterns include my consulting work, which more often than not centered around helping individuals discover and capitalize on their personal strengths.

It includes time spent with my young grandchildren, who provided me with a whole new perspective on what kids today think, feel, want, and need.

It includes my first real efforts at building programs for kids—my successes, failures, and the drive to keep at it until I got it right.

It includes the highs of working with young athletes, like Kobe Bryant, and the lows of losing people I love—Alison, my sister, my brother-in-law, and dear friends.

Through it all, there was sport. Whether I was playing in the Senior Olympics or in casual pick-up games at the local gym, working with young kids or NBA rookies, sport was the compass that kept driving me toward the North Star of where I am and what I'm doing today.

In Search of Community

For years, every Monday, Wednesday, and Friday that I was in town, I was part of a noon pickup game with a somewhat motley assortment of former basketball players and player wannabes. Our group included doctors, lawyers, probation officers, kids who would probably end up needing probation officers, etc. We represented a variety of religions, races, and cultural and economic backgrounds. On the other hand, we were all connected to one another through this weekly sports experience that we shared. When someone didn't show up for a while, we got worried. If someone made a mistake on the court or wasn't playing very well, the others displayed a sensitivity not often found in a group of competitive male adults. We were a community.

As I look back on my life, I realize that I have always been seeking community. I have always wanted to feel that I belonged somewhere—that I was welcomed, wanted, and needed.

When I was growing up, my family was the only Jewish family in our neighborhood during a time of great anti-Semitism. As a child, my parents repeatedly told my siblings and me that our well-being as Jews was dependent on Franklin Delano Roosevelt, who was our president at the time. So heavily had this message been drilled into us that when Roosevelt died suddenly and the news was announced over the school loudspeaker, I jumped up and ran without stopping three miles to the safety of my home.

In our family, Friday night attendance at synagogue (plus weekly Sunday school class) was mandatory. As I grew older and became heavily involved in sports, this stipulation meant missing out on the post-game parties and celebrations that went along with being an athlete. As a result, I ended up resenting my Jewish heritage and disassociating myself from the community I might have discovered there.

At Stanford, I joined a fraternity, but I still had a sense of being different. My fraternity brothers were wonderful, but my Jewish background kept the fraternity's national chapter from recognizing my membership.

When I eventually began exploring Christianity, I was never quite sure how much of the welcome I received from the Christian fellowship on campus was due to me as a person and how much was due to the fact that I was one of Stanford's star basketball players. Nevertheless, I persisted, spending hours upon hours in Memorial Church, searching for meaning, a faith that I felt was true, and, as always, community.

I think that need played a pivotal role in my eventual choice to convert to Christianity and become a pastor. In my parishes in New Mexico and California, I worked mightily to create community among the members of my congregations, and I think I succeeded. As an individual, however, I still struggled. The inclusiveness I worked so hard to help others feel was lacking in my own life.

The only time I really felt accepted and a part of something was when I stepped on to either the basketball court or the playing field. I had a deep desire to connect with and find support from others, and sport was where that desire, more often than not, was met. From the time I was 10, I would spend three, four, and even five afternoons a week riding the bus 25 miles each way to Long Beach and back to play basketball at the YMCA. In junior high and high school, I would be in the gym or on the field every day—summer, winter, weekends, breaks. In sport, I felt safe. I felt secure.

And now, in the twilight years of my life, I find myself turning to sport again. This time, it's not so much to establish my own sense of community, but rather to help others find the community that they are looking for and so desperately need in these unsettled times.

I remember a college buddy of mine talking about moving to Germany with his family in 1946, just after the end of WWII. At that time, there was a lot of tension and fear between the German and American children. "However," he said, "when we started to play ball together, the fear disappeared, and the bonding began."

More than nationalism, and more than religion, sport has the power to bring people together on a global, ongoing basis. Sport has the power to heal. It has the power to teach. It has the power to inspire and uplift. In fact, it has a number of attributes upon which strong, healthy communities can be built.

Of course, many individuals might say, "Excuse me, George, but have you watched a sporting event recently?" To those people who would point to the state of sport today, with its camera-hogging professional athletes, rioting fans, and brawling Little League parents, I would answer that it does not have to be this way. Our sports communities do not need to mirror the ills that are occurring in other areas of society. In reality, our sports bodies can lead the way in addressing many of society's problems and concerns.

In order to create these kinds of communities, however, we need to come up with a new sports paradigm. Until now, sport has primarily been seen as a competitive endeavor. Too often, this competitiveness can lead to divisiveness and strife. To change this situation, we need to start viewing and promoting sport differently.

My good friend and former Stanford teammate, Dave Epperson, has suggested that rather than view sport as a competition, we should see it as a composition. In a sports composition, as in a musical composition or a written composition, there are many layers that contribute to the success of the overall piece, and competition is but one layer.

I love that analogy. I wish someone had shared it with me when I was younger. Had that occurred, I think I would have gotten more out of sport than I did. I know I would have gotten more out of life than I did. Maybe, that's why I'm drawn to the work I'm doing now, which is to share with others the lessons I did learn from sport and the ones I wish I'd learned.

The sense of security that comes from belonging and feeling connected through sport enables young people to reach out and identify with others in a positive and constructive way. Kids who feel accepted, liked, and respected know that they have a support system that can help them deal with the knocks that life sometimes gives them. They are comfortable being who they are and don't have to pretend to be something or someone they are not. They don't need to go searching for community, because they have already found it.

Big Sister

One of the wonderful things about writing this book is that it has given me the opportunity to reflect on the many people who, in their own special ways, have supported and encouraged me throughout my life. One such person was my sister, Jackie. Because she was three years older than I and we lived in a home where people didn't seem to talk and certainly did not share their feelings, I never really knew my sister until relatively late in life.

I do know that she attended Long Beach Poly High School, which was a 45-minute drive from our home. To this day, however, I do not know how she got to and from school. I do not know why she went there instead of Compton High. Perhaps my parents thought she would fit in better at Long Beach, or that it would give her a better chance to get into a good college. She was accepted to Stanford, but dropped out after her first year because of poor grades. She bounced back, however, graduated from nursing school, and became a successful nurse. Her later years were filled with countless hours of volunteer work for local organizations. Of course, there was also her commitment to raising her four boys and her support of their sports activities and educational pursuits.

I remember my sister attending several of my games at Stanford with her eventual husband, Bob. She proudly told me stories of times when she thought I was being roughed up by opposing players and how she would scream from the stands (boy, am I glad I never heard her), "Don't hurt my little brother!"

Jackie passed away on March 28, 2009. A few months earlier, she invited me to join her and the local rabbi to discuss and plan her memorial service. That invitation goes a long way to describe my sister. She was strong, courageous, and a very direct person in her approach to whatever she was involved with, including her own medical care. She had battled breast cancer since her early 30s, as well as leukemia for more than two decades, and she did most of this on her own, since her husband, a surgeon, had died over 20 years earlier.

The death of a sibling is a particularly poignant loss, because they are so much a part of our history. When a brother or sister dies, part of you dies with them. The loss of Jackie meant I had lost someone who knew me as a child and was a link to my past. Unfortunately, I failed to take advantage of that link. Jackie was a connection to my past, and now, it is no longer available to me. I am sad that my relationship with my siblings was not what it should have been. I grieve for what I had and lost and also for what I never had at all.

My history just makes me all the more aware of the need that children have to have supportive, caring relationships in their lives. Hopefully, most of our kids have those already. For the few kids who might not, however, the right program can provide refuge, respite, and an example of how positive relationships work.

Process, Not Product

The parents had brought their 10-year-old son to my counseling office, because they wanted to know what was "wrong" with their child, who no longer wanted to participate in organized sports.

As I sat down to talk with the boy, he broke into tears, saying how he used to love baseball and other sports, but he had now grown sick of them because, "No matter what I do, it'll never be good enough!" After a short pause, I asked him to explain. "My coach is never satisfied. My parents are never satisfied. I'm not as good as the other kids—they're all a lot better than I am."

I ended up working with the boy for a couple of months to provide him with tools to deal with two major obstacles to his having a meaningful and fun sports experience: one, the unrealistic expectations of his coaches and parents, and two, his own unrealistic comparisons between his skills and those of the other kids.

We talked about the need to compete against himself—not others. We talked about how to set realistic goals. We talked about day-to-day improvement as a better way to measure his achievement, as opposed to who beat whom, or who got more playing time. We talked about using his personal best as a guide. Hopefully, he left my office not only with the ability to enjoy sports again, but also with a stronger sense of self, as well as with the tools that would help him get through other competitive moments in his life.

In my work over the years, I have always sought to make the point that kids are more concerned with the *process* of play than with the end product. They enjoy simply participating—running up and down the field, shooting hoops, throwing a ball around, etc. Adults, on the other hand, are preoccupied with the end product—who wins, what the final score is, how many minutes their child played, etc.

All games involve achieving a goal, despite the presence of an obstacle. Nowhere is it written, however, that the obstacle has to be someone else. The purpose of a game can be for each person to make a specified contribution to the goal, or for all of the players to reach a certain score, or for all of the players to work with the other participants against a time limit. When you look at it through this lens, opponents now become partners.

When feelings of self-worth are derived from external sources, such as winning a game or beating someone, your value is defined by what you've done and who you've defeated. That kind of value is fleeting at best, and not the pathway to true self-esteem.

We need to teach kids that progress is movement toward a goal. Even if that movement is very small, it is still progress, and that's what is important. We also need to teach them to focus on the good part of competition—the ways in which it can help them develop self-esteem, create friendships, and serve as a model for positive, assertive, and realistic efforts for whatever they undertake in life. Hopefully, the things these kids learn NOW will help keep THEIR kids out of the counselor's office.

Breakfast With Brad

Prior to my 40-year college reunion, various classmates were given the assignment of connecting with other classmates to encourage their participation at the three-day event. My assignment was to contact Brad Leonard, a classmate and successful lawyer who lived 13 miles away from me in Escondido, CA.

I had never met Brad before. When we decided to get together at a little breakfast joint in Escondido, I was prepared for the usual small talk ("Wasn't Stanford great?" "So, what have you been doing with yourself for the last 40 years, etc.?"). What I wasn't expecting was someone who had practically memorized every moment of my college basketball career.

As it turned out, Brad had been a hoops guy himself. He had played in high school and dreamed of continuing on in college, but was cut from the freshman team at Stanford. At that point, he told me, "I thought my basketball life was over. At that point, I decided to live my dream through you, George, and let me tell you—it has been wonderful." You can imagine how tongued-tied and startled I was. What do you say to something like that?

For the next five years—until he passed away from a sudden illness—Brad and I met at the same place a least once a week, and during that period of time, he gave me the most wonderful and incredible gift—the gift of being able to see and appreciate my basketball experience through someone else's eyes.

It is important to note that I had never seen myself play. This might be hard for today's players to understand, but back then there was no high school film to watch, and the few Stanford films available were shot in jerky, black-and-white 8 millimeter. Even those few films were eventually destroyed in a campus fire. As a result, I had no idea how I really looked on the court.

Brad, however, seemed to remember everything. Every move, every play—he related it all to me. Of course, it helped that he had been the announcer for the campus radio station, which allowed him to see all of our home games and several of the away games as well.

I suppose it sounds a little conceited—"Oh, tell me more about how wonderful I was!"—but it wasn't like that. I don't know if it was due to my rather Puritan upbringing or just an inherent part of my character, but I've never been good at enjoying success. In 1952, when I was named CIF Southern California Player of the Year, as well as State Player of the Year by *California Magazine*, and my mother commented on how impressed she was with my "humility" in handling the recognition, the message I took away from my mom's comments was don't talk about your achievements, keep your head down, and above all, don't express any kind of pride in what you might accomplish.

With Brad, however, I was able to look back on what had been an incredibly important part of my life and start to really appreciate the impact that it had on me and the joy it brought to me and to others. It was that new perspective that spurred me to write *Court Sense: The Invisible Edge in Basketball and Life*—which makes the connection between the skills and behaviors needed to excel on the court and those needed to excel in life.

I learned a valuable lesson from Brad: it is important to be able to enjoy and celebrate the successes for which we work so hard. I'm not talking about bragging or putting others down. Rather, I'm talking about being able to say, "I [or "we"] worked really hard to put this activity together, and it turned out great! High five, everybody!" A good youth program gives everybody, regardless of their ability, the opportunity to experience and enjoy that wonderful feeling that comes with being successful at something. Furthermore, they don't have to wait until they're 70 to figure it out!

The Coach of All Coaches

I first met John Wooden, UCLA's legendary basketball coach, in March of 1952, when I was honored as the year's top CIF player. He approached the table where I was sitting, and after introducing himself said, "George, I understand that you have always wanted to go to Stanford, but should you consider playing for UCLA, we would be delighted!" I could tell that he really hoped I would continue my basketball career at UCLA, but always the gentleman, he did not push.

UCLA was our toughest opponent during my years at Stanford. We took second in the conference during my senior year, losing two close games to a Bruin team led by Willie Naulls—the first game by two points and the second in overtime. Following those two heartbreaking losses, Wooden told the *Los Angeles Times:* "Selleck is a great little player. He kept Stanford in the games, when we figured we had 'em down and all but out. He caused us no end of trouble. Any of us would be glad to have him."

During my years officiating college basketball games, I refereed at least 50 UCLA games, where I was fortunate to witness Coach Wooden working with some of the all-time greats, including Kareem Abdul-Jabbar and Bill Walton.

Some years later, Coach Wooden was kind enough to welcome me several times to his Encino home, where he gave me advice and encouragement in my efforts to help athletes, coaches, and parents get the most out of their sports experiences. In October 2000, my colleague Dave Epperson and I interviewed Coach Wooden the day before his 90th birthday. On that occasion, he generously shared some of the wisdom he had accumulated during his long and illustrious career in sports. He reported that early in his life as a coach, he had "many rules and few suggestions." At the end of his coaching career, however, that had changed to "few rules and many suggestions." His three unbending rules were to be considerate, be on time, and refrain from profanity.

To me, Coach Wooden personified what coaching and sports should be about. He was one of the few coaches in sports history who was able to win championships, while insisting that he and his athletes uphold the highest standards of conduct, both on and off the court. He was able to amass one of the most impressive winning records ever, without resorting to browbeating, intimidation, incivility, or disrespect. He was more concerned with processes than outcomes. His focus was on executing a game plan, confident that if his athletes did all the right things, they would win more than their fair share. Wooden exhibited values and principles that I hope to carry on in my work—because every kid should be fortunate enough to experience the coach of all coaches.

The Most Persuasive Tool

"What did you say?"

I had been sitting beside Kevin, the owner, CEO, and President of a freight forwarding and customs brokerage company in Southern California. Kevin was at his computer, reviewing a draft of his upcoming presentation at his industry's annual convention, and I, as a consultant, was offering my input.

As Kevin, a very intelligent and gifted entrepreneur, was intently focused on his computer screen, I had made a casual comment regarding my first impression of his opening remarks. Startled by whatever I said, Kevin shot back with increased attention, "What did you say, George?"

Basically, my comment had been, "Kevin, all communication begins with the other person." For more than 25 years since that day with Kevin at his computer, I have found this thought to be true and helpful in my efforts to connect with others in business, sports, and life.

George Bernard Shaw once said, "The greatest problem in communication is the illusion that it has been accomplished." How true. One of the biggest reasons we humans fail is our inability to communicate. Most of the time, we unconsciously leave communication to chance. On the other hand, just because we say something doesn't mean we have communicated it. In reality, the area in which we're usually falling short isn't in what we're saying; rather, it's in what we're not hearing.

Listening is one of the most powerful things we do. Unfortunately, most of us aren't very good at it. When we listen to other people, we give away one of our most important resources—our time. This factor conveys a powerful message. By listening, we communicate that the other person has worth and value, and that they are not just a platform for meeting our needs or accomplishing our goals.

Listening well doesn't just happen. It is an acquired skill that demands active participation. How active? Remember what it was like in those college lectures, which your professor prefaced with, "This material will be on the test"? You need to listen to the other person, as if you were going to be taking a test on what they've said once they're finished.

Listening well involves being fully present and staying in the moment. All your attention, your thoughts, your energy—everything!—should be focused on the other person. To be fully present is to:

- Suppress your urge to talk about your needs, opinions, stories, or judgments.
- Let go of any inner conversations you might having.
- Listen for the essence of what the other is saying, while resisting the temptation to immediately categorize, respond, or offer solutions.
- Be open to being changed by what you are hearing.

Listening well involves paying attention to and understanding nonverbal behavior. Former television talk show host Dick Cavett was once asked by an interviewer what was the most awful thing that ever happened on his show? Cavett replied, "The man who dropped dead during the program." Cavett continued, "He was a health expert. No matter how many times I tell it, people laugh, because the black comedy of the fact is that, moments before, he said, 'I'm going to live to be a hundred … I never felt better.'"

Sometimes, people say one thing and do another. On occasion, words come out of the mouth that the rest of the body refutes. The discrepancy is not usually as dramatic as in the story Cavett tells, and the evidence is typically more subtle. On the other hand, there are always non-verbal clues about what is really going on with a person. Facial expressions, body motions, voice quality, and physiological responses can be extremely communicative.

We need to accept the fact that listening well can be painful. Bob Waterman, author of *Renewal Factor*, points out what should be, but seldom is, apparent to anyone who is serious about listening to others: "Listening, really listening, is tough and grinding work, often humbling, sometimes distasteful. It's a fairly sure bet that you won't like the lion's share of what you hear."

We should never underestimate the importance of listening to the kids with whom we interact. Without question, we know that listening well is something that can change the direction of their life.

The Long Arm of Kobe Bryant

For more than 10 years, I was part of a team of facilitators working in the NBA's Rookie Transition Program, which was designed to help new players know what was expected of them and how to handle themselves during their first year in the league. The basic goal of the program was to make the transition to NBA life much easier. In the program, the players learned about every aspect of life as a professional athlete, including money management, dealing with the media, nutrition, making smart decisions socially, and being a role model.

As a member of the staff, I would spend 1 ½ hours each day with 10 of the rookies. We would discuss things like how they would face the pressure of having to prove themselves all over again, the challenge of maintaining their wealth in a professional sports culture where droves of athletes end up bankrupt, and so on. While all the players who attended the program were exceptional athletes, one young man just out of high school was the most memorable—Kobe Byrant.

I remember Kobe as a careful listener, and while he didn't ask a lot of questions about what life as an NBA player was like (his dad had played in the NBA), the ones he did ask were helpful to the group process. He was, for such a young person, surprisingly mature and very aware that the NBA was a business.

Kobe was eager to prove he was more than just another high school flash with potential, which was how some people described him at the time. He seemed to know he had what it took to be able to compete in the league immediately. He also realized he still had a lot to learn and that the current and former players who spoke to the rookies had a great deal to offer.

Kobe's intensity and skills (not to mention his off-court exploits) have made him a "love-him-or-hate-him" kind of guy for many people. The Kobe I remember, however, is the person who stood at the baggage claim with me in Los Angeles, as we waited for our luggage to arrive from our Orlando flight. Putting his long arm around me, he said, "Hey, Doc—thanks for all your work with us this week."

I work with all types of kids. We get the outgoing ones, the quiet ones, the athletic ones, the uncoordinated ones, the smart ones, and the smart-aleck ones. We may even get some potential Kobe Bryants. What they all share is the desire to prove themselves and be recognized for their achievements. We give them the opportunity to do both.

The Wine Cellar Enclave

I had been consulting for one of California's smaller cities for a couple of months, when I was invited to a luncheon meeting by a couple of department heads. They were vague about the purpose of the meeting, but assured me I would find it interesting. The hint of intrigue was … well, *intriguing*. So I went.

The meeting was held in the wine cellar of a local restaurant. I'd been to the restaurant before, but did not know the wine cellar even existed. I was shown to the basement, where 11 people huddled around a long, wooden table.

After some coaxing from the meeting organizers, participants began to share their feelings about their management. It quickly became a gripe session, characterized by a high degree of frustration and anger.

This scenario all occurred in the middle of the organizational downsizing and decentralization of the 90s, when both public and private organizations were experiencing a great deal of business turbulence. Managers were being held accountable for the productivity and performance of their staffs to a greater degree than before. In reality, not all managers had been adequately prepared for this task. The manager in the city where I was working fell into this category. He was not a particularly people-oriented person, favoring a command-and-control style that obviously did not sit well with the people underneath him.

The wine cellar enclave eventually evolved into a series of meetings between the city manager and the department heads in which we worked on understanding:
- The necessity of learning from mistakes. The primary purpose of city governments is to serve the citizens well. The primary role of management is to create a work environment where employees are equipped, empowered, and self-motivated to achieve this goal. Creating this environment requires managers who possess a variety of conceptual, technical, and human relations skills. In reality, no skill is more important than the ability to learn and grow from past mistakes—either your own mistakes or those of others. The majority of mistakes that were taking place in the management

of this particular city were not major issues. They were common mistakes that were easily corrected, once they were appropriately identified and addressed.

- Leadership is not about being the "star." Rather, it is about enabling others to do well. A leader's job is to develop, encourage, and champion the work of their team. In other words, the leader needs to seek and create opportunities to "hand the ball off" to other players. The achievements of an organization need to have the fingerprints of the whole team, not just the manager.

- The profound importance of making whomever you deal with feel important is one of our basic human needs. This factor entails listening to others, being gracious, expressing appreciation, and investing in your staff and those you serve.

By following the aforementioned principles, which apply to any business or organization, the city's employees—from the city manager on down—were able to improve their previously toxic work environment. Even more importantly, they were better able to serve the inhabitants of the city itself.

I am using these same principles now in my work with youth and others—mostly, because I know they work, and partly, because I hope I'm never the subject of a wine cellar enclave!

The Fun Factor

When I coached, I always felt one of my biggest challenges was to create practice sessions that prepared my athletes to compete, while at the same time, didn't bore them to death. The importance of the "fun factor," as I like to think of it, was more fully reinforced on a trip to San Diego's Wild Animal Park with three of my step-grandchildren. We had gotten into a discussion about which sport each of them liked the most. The boys went through their list—football, basketball, wrestling, etc.—and then four-year-old Cara spoke up. "I like baseball best," she said.

"Why is that?" I asked.

"Because they give you candy."

Getting past the sugar part of it, what she was saying is that getting candy is fun. Hence, for her, baseball was fun—because that's where you got candy!

As adults, however, we often overlook the "fun factor" when it comes to our kids participating in sports. A newspaper cartoon by Bill Hinds, called "Cleats," gently poked fun at the intensity adults sometimes bring to what is, after all, just a game. In the cartoon, 10-year-old Jack says to his friend, Abby, and one of her teammates, "Hey, a bunch of us Dawgs want to challenge you Panthers to a soccer match."

Abby replies, "You mean without the coaches?"

"No coaches, no refs, no parents," Jack says.

"You mean play for fun?" Abby asks, incredulous.

Her teammate chimes in, "Are we allowed to do that?"

If kids aren't having fun with a sports or fitness activity, they will quit. It's always amazing to me how many adults don't get that point. In my coaching education workshops, I would always ask coaches if they thought sports should be a fun experience for their players. Of course, everyone said yes. At that point, I would then make them the following offer: "If you can give me an adequate definition of 'fun,' I'll sign off on your certification right now, and you can leave six hours earlier than everyone else." In over eight years, there was not a single winner.

It's vital to encourage kids to be creative and think of ways to make things fun for everyone. I remember hearing somewhere that when Cal Ripken was coaching a Little League team, he saw a mannequin in a ski lodge and got the idea to use old mannequins to help kids learn to hit the cutoff man in the infield grass, while practicing throws from right field. Just imagine how entertaining (and educational) it was when someone hit the mannequin in the wrong spot. When you teach kids to incorporate fun into their activities, you may find that on a particularly hot day, an activity ends with a water balloon fight, or that the "price" of entrance into an activity is to wear your craziest pair of socks. Even something as simple as playing "follow the leader" to warm-up before an activity can be turned into something fun and teamwork-oriented.

As psychologists and educators have learned, children tend to get more vigorous exercise from free play than from adult-designed practice sessions. That's why I strongly believe in putting youth front and center in designing and carrying out unique, inclusive sports and fitness activities. This approach keeps kids of all abilities coming back for more, and serves as the perfect antidote for the declining enrollment and lack of interest experienced by so many of today's youth sports programs. It's like a sugar-rush, without the sugar—fun, invigorating, and healthy!

Triangle

It was a familiar scene. I was sitting at a small table with the senior executive and chief operations officer of a medium-sized company, trying to help them work through their ongoing struggle about how to move their organization forward and stop the downward spiral that was threatening the company's survival.

One thing was obvious—the two executives liked each other (hence, it wasn't a personality conflict) and sincerely wanted to find a way past their conflicts and issues. Hopefully, that would make things easier. Taking a deep breath, I started by drawing the following triangle on a piece of paper in front of us:

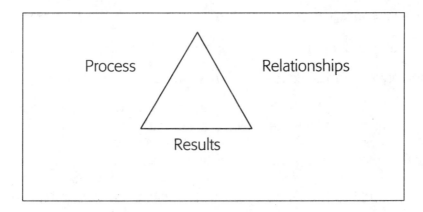

I then asked each of the executives to identify which axis represented their strengths and which one(s) their weaknesses. They thought briefly, before the senior executive said, "Without question, my strength is relationships. I think that is where it all happens. That's where I put my focus and energy."

The COO responded by pointing his finger at "results" and saying, "For me, it's all about results. I work 24/7 to make them happen. I'm practical and concentrate on achieving our purpose—which is to make money. I don't allow myself to get distracted by other matters."

Problem identified, but not solved. More than 35 years of working with businesses, congregations, families, and couples has convinced me that unless there is a balance and equal commitment among relationships, processes, and results, success is unlikely to occur. Unfortunately, that's what happened with this company. Within a year, the COO had left for another job.

In my new endeavor, I am committed to developing and maintaining an organizational balance between one, building relationships with various stakeholders (kids, parents, teachers, administrators, and communities), two, maintaining the processes that develop better leaders and human beings, and three, delivering results that matter to everyone involved. As an organization, we are an equilateral triangle—and we plan to keep it that way.

We Were All Children

Many years ago, I was at the office of Neil Papiano, a college classmate of mine who had distinguished himself as a lawyer on a variety of high-profile cases, including *Finley versus Kuhn* (Oakland A's owner Charlie Finley's restraint-of-trade lawsuit against MLB Commissioner Bowie Kuhn), *Elizabeth Taylor versus The National Enquirer, Joan Collins versus Globe International,* and the *Walter Matthau Estate versus Columbia Pictures*. If that weren't enough, he had also been named one of Los Angeles' "Ten Most Distinguished and Influential People."

We were reminiscing about our days at Stanford, and I was attempting to apologize for how socially inept I'd been back then by commenting. "I was such a child." To which Neil quickly retorted, "George, we were all children."

I understood what he meant. While we were all immature back then, I really did feel like everyone around me had their act much more together than I did. Part of it, I'm sure, was the by-product of growing up in a dysfunctional family. The anti-Semitism of the time probably also played a role. All I know is that I lacked awareness of myself or why I was even at college, except to continue to play basketball and baseball.

For the most part, I camouflaged my lack of awareness and fear of the unknown by focusing on sports and working hard—really hard—to answer the most basic of all questions on the road to adulthood and maturity: Who am I, and what do I want?

I bring this point up, because these questions are ones that kids still struggle with today. In reality, many of them feel very isolated, as they wrestle with these questions. The idea that everyone wants and has a deep need to belong—to affiliate with others and be socially accepted—is one that has been supported by psychologists (Maslow, Adler, etc.) throughout the years. It is why many of our children turn to gangs. It is also one reason why I am doing what I am doing—to provide kids with a positive outlet for finding this sense of belonging and a safe environment in which to grow.

Teachable Moments

I have spent over 35 years offering workshops and trainings to volunteer and professional coaches. One question I almost always ask the participants is, "Do you believe sport teaches life skills?"

The answer is always a unanimous and resounding, "Yes!"

Then I ask, "And how does that happen?"

Some coaches will say, "Well, it just happens." Others don't say anything at all. The more thoughtful ones, however, will reply, "Through teachable moments."

A teachable moment is defined as an unplanned opportunity that arises at the time where one person has an ideal chance to offer their insight to another person. For example, I recently had the opportunity to teach 17 high school students in a leadership class. Before one of our sessions, I watched the kids as they played an informal soccer game on a rough, somewhat grassy field on the campus of the National Hispanic University in San Jose. They were playing with complete abandonment and joy—calling their own fouls, showing respect for each other and the game, and obviously enjoying every minute.

When the time came for our class, I opened by sharing what I had observed as they played—their self-regulation and self-motivation, the fun they were having, and the sense of friendship and community that marked their interactions. This setting lead to a 20-minute discussion of how they could implement these values and experiences in what we were doing and how they could even transfer what they learned to the traditional classroom.

Young people usually have a short-term horizon. The immediacy of "right now" tends to dominate their attention. As adults, we are supposed to see the bigger picture. It is critical that we keep in mind that the teachable moments are precious, and we can't afford to miss them.

Lessons From a Two-Year-Old

Several years ago, I was in San Diego visiting my youngest son, his wife, and my granddaughter, Kennedy. Kennedy was around two-and-a-half at the time. All of the adults were scattered around the floor of the apartment, participating in our favorite activity—Kennedy-watching. At one point, Kennedy was about to do something—I don't remember what—that could have been dangerous. My daughter-in-law, Jenny, immediately said, "Kennedy! NO!" From Kennedy's reaction, you would have thought Jenny said, "Kennedy, your dad and I have decided to move to Southeast Asia, and, oh, yeah—we're not taking you." Kennedy's eyes welled up, and she started sobbing as only a broken-hearted two-year-old can do.

Immediately, Jenny and my son rushed to Kennedy's side, hugging her and reassuring her that they loved her, and everything was okay. Kennedy immediately stopped crying and calmed down, upon which Jenny kindly (but firmly) said, "Now, Kennedy, are you ready for your time-out?"

Jenny knew—much better than I did, when I was a young parent—that the needs of children must come first before addressing their behavior. Why? Because children—like all humans—are emotional beings. Our first response to any event or occurrence in our lives is a physiological response, i.e., anger, fear, anxiety, joy, etc., which is where we stay until we decide to move on. Kennedy's response to her mother's "No," was self-doubt, anxiety, and fear that perhaps she had lost her parents' love and affection. Although those thoughts were not rational or reasonable, they were her body's natural response to a perceived threat. Once assured that everything was okay, and that she had not lost what she most needed, Kennedy was ready to accept her discipline and learn from it.

Another example of how "needs before behavior" should work can help clarify the point. For example, hypothetically, the defensive back on a football team allows the opposing receiver to catch a touchdown pass. His furious coach yanks him from the game, shouting, "Sit down! I'll get somebody in there who can do the job!" The player is naturally anxious and upset and wonders if the coach hates him, and if he's lost his position on the team. In reality, a coach who knows to put needs first and behavior second would meet the player as he comes off the field and say something like, "Bill, you're my guy, and I'll get you back in the game in moment. I just want to go over several things before you go back in." Because the player's needs and concerns have been met, he is more prepared and more likely to listen to the coach and learn what will help him play better when he returns to the field.

The aforementioned examples offer a number of learning points. For example, too often, we tend to address a child's behavior first and their needs second. There are a lot of reasons for this, one of which is that behavior is easier to see. Unlike needs, which often take some digging to get to, behavior is on the surface. After my chat with Alan Gregerman, I gave a lot of thought to what kids need that I might be able to give them. Among some of the things I discovered are the following:

- Kids need to be listened to. Listening—really listening—to a kid is like pouring water on a plant that's been sitting in the sun for a week. They just soak it up! That's why even though there are adult advisors involved in my program, their job is to do more listening than talking.
- Kids need to have opportunities to learn how to make good choices. When a three-year-old insists on wearing snow boots in the middle of summer and *is allowed to do so*, they quickly learn that their feet get hot and sweaty, and those snow boots weren't such a good choice after all.
- Kids need to have fun. This point seems like one of those, "Well, *duh!*" statements, but the fact is that the number one reason kids give for dropping out of youth sports programs is lack of fun. For any type of youth program to succeed, fun has to be a huge component.
- Kids need to learn how to solve problems. Experts who have researched the subject of suicide in youth and adults say that one of the biggest indicators of resiliency is the ability to solve problems. When we give kids opportunities to solve problems ("It's raining and we were supposed to play flag football today! It's a good thing we planned for broom hockey as a back-up!"), we help enhance their level of resiliency.

Kennedy is currently a happy, well-adjusted young girl, because she has parents who not only love her, but who understand what she needs to be able to handle the "no's" of life. When needs are met, behaviors improve and happiness increases … for everyone!

Stop, Thief!

Some years ago, a former college basketball player (his name is best left unmentioned) was about to head off to play in an international league. This player, who had just completed a life skills program I had developed entitled *Building Complete Players*, asked if he could borrow my program and notes "to make sure I get the full benefit of your program." He promised to return everything before going overseas.

He never returned the program or the notes, and one day, I saw his name on Google™ announcing "his" life skills program in several cities across the U.S. and overseas. While I cannot be sure he is using MY program, it should be noted that if it walks like a duck and quacks like a duck, it's usually not a horse. Needless to say, I have felt a lot of anger over the years whenever I've thought about the possibility he stole my work—especially since I would have been more than willing to work out a partnership of some kind if he'd only asked.

This incident, however, has caused me to think a lot about my own moral compass (values). Values comprise the things that are most important to us. They are deep-seated, pervasive standards (separate from our personal preferences and opinions) that influence us and help us evaluate what is right and wrong, as we make judgments, respond to others, and commit to personal and organizational goals.

Our society allows far more compromising of values than it used to. Values have become gray and fuzzy. Expediency rules the day. We value the end product more than the process that helps us reach our goals. We've too often (myself included) traded in our moral compass for a personal GPS that tells us the fastest way to reach our destination.

I am well aware that I've made some choices along the way that, had I been more mature and paid closer attention to my moral compass, I would have done differently.

Values matter! Nothing shapes our lives more than what we value. Not fate, not circumstances, not childhood experience. If we want to grow, mature, and be the best we can be, we must know what we value.

I am fortunate to have a group of people on my team whose values are shared and modeled in everything they do. Alan Gregerman, Harold "Hap" Wagner, Charles "Jiggs" Davis, Gary Riekes, Bob Leet, Linda Best, Alex Gomez, Duncan Beardsley, Dr. Michael Gibbs, David Carver, Jeffrey Davis, Dave Barram, Gary Petersmeyer, and Alan McMillen have made rich, personal and organizational contributions that impact and provide direction to every aspect of our work with youth. Their words and actions give validity to the well-tested axiom: you can only lead others where you yourself are willing to go.

In a world where expediency rules the day, where making it big often precedes values, our goal is to equip children and youth with a moral compass that will help them make wise decisions as they enter the unknown territory of adulthood.

"Gunner" George

Although I had regularly been the high scorer on all my basketball teams, I prided myself on being a team player and team leader. While writing my book *Court Sense: The Invisible Edge in Basketball and Life*, however, I began to worry that perhaps I had also been something I had never wanted to be: a selfish player.

Around that same time, Compton High had a basketball reunion. At the reunion, I saw an old friend—Bill Barnes. Bill was an excellent player, coach, and college administrator, and he knew his basketball as well as anyone.

As Bill and I talked basketball, I eventually worked up the nerve to ask him: "Was I a gunner?" It is important to realize that to basketball people, being called a "gunner" is not a compliment. A gunner is someone who never misses a chance to take a shot at the basket and is usually not a great team player.

Bill responded without hesitation, "Yes, George, you were a gunner!" My heart sank under the weight of his comment. After all, my greatest need was to belong and be liked, and nobody likes a gunner. On the other hand, Bill continued, "But, George, I never saw you take a bad shot!" While I might debate the validity of that last comment, it was reassuring to know that Bill never felt I sacrificed my team's well-being for the sake of my own ego.

In sport and in life, a team attitude is a "we" and "our" attitude, instead of a "me" and "my" attitude. When you become part of a team—whether it is your family, your athletic team, your classroom team or a work team—you're not giving up individual goals. You're not sacrificing your personal success. You are setting your sights on an even greater goal—one that requires being unselfish, which is hard. Ours is a society that struggles with the proper balance of individualism and the common good. For many individuals, the pendulum has swung too far toward individualism at the expense of finding common ground for the sake of the common good.

I hope that if the kids I work with learn nothing else, they learn the value—and fun— of teamwork … because nobody likes a gunner.

A Coach's Story

It was the third in a series of five workshops I was conducting, based on my book, *Coach Sense: Coaching to Make a Difference*. Fourteen coaches from a variety of youth sports organizations were in attendance to learn how to better understand, communicate with, teach, and motivate their athletes.

When I asked if anyone had any stories to share about how they'd applied what they'd learned in our previous workshops, Lori immediately raised her hand. She had been assisting at a club volleyball program in the Fairfax area, when she suddenly received a call from a close friend of hers who was stationed in Norfolk, VA. The friend, who had been coaching a local high school girls' volleyball team, had unexpectedly been deployed for the rest of year, and her team had a tournament that week, which she would not be able to coach. Could Lori come to Norfolk and take over immediately?

Lori arrived the next day, only to find a team full of rude, unresponsive players. They weren't buying anything she was selling—approach to defense, offense, teamwork— nothing. In desperation, Lori remembered what we had discussed previously—that communication was about meeting people where they were. As a result, she stopped giving orders, approached the girls and said, "Okay, what's going on? How can we work together?" Almost immediately, a girl stepped forward and said, "That's all we needed to hear. Let's go to work, ladies!"

What happened? The power of respect and recognition owned the day! Not only had the girls been hit with the sudden and unexpected loss of their coach, but it was their program and their team, and they wanted to have a voice in how it was run. Lori's approach signaled very clearly that she understood what they were going through and accepted that it was indeed their program. This situation was a great example of respecting and recognizing the voice of athletes and working collaboratively with them.

Young people (kind of like old people, or any people) do not like being bossed around. *"Give me 50 (push-ups),"* is a command we hear all too frequently from dictatorial coaches. Young people like to have opportunities to express themselves. They want to participate in decisions that impact their lives.

Effective collaboration is about building trust that allows people to work through adversity (such as a coach suddenly being deployed) and prevent pitfalls that could defeat the team. As Lori learned, it's about more than just using a carrot-and-stick approach. It's about treating kids as the individuals they are and the people we know they can become.

Two Sides to Perfect

A client of mine—a senior-level corporate executive—was having difficulty with his staff. A huge perfectionist, he was famous for trying to control every aspect of what went on around him. The more perfection he demanded from people, the more they rebelled by producing inferior work. In the process, the anxiety, tension, and fear he created became obstacles standing in the way of productivity. Everyone was miserable.

When he asked me if the solution to the problem might be to get rid of people (as in "pink slips," not "cement boots"), I suggested the real issue might be the environment he was creating. I said, "Is anyone enjoying their work? Is anyone having any fun? How do you think they would rate their job experience?" It took several sessions, but slowly, he began to see that he was losing perspective on his own job, as well as pushing and forcing his narrow opinions and views on the rest of the staff. In the end, he made the decision to call a meeting with his staff to discuss a new direction and a new focus— one that would emphasize collaboration and how they might enjoy their work, with a minimum of perfection and control.

The personality trait of perfectionism can bring either good or bad, profits or perils. Perfectionists, by definition, strive for the best, try to ace exams, be top dog at their jobs, and never fail as a mate or parent. Life, however, has taught me (rather harshly at times) that our greatest strengths can be our greatest weaknesses. For example, my perfectionism served me well in athletics—I worked on my shots, passing, dribbling, and defense constantly in basketball, always trying to improve, to reach perfection. In any number of ways on the court, it paid off. Almost every mistake I have made in life, however, is a result of that same perfectionism.

Striving for perfection can be a good thing, an important ally in reaching our goals. On the other hand, it can also mean mental pressure when mistakes are made, and we resist asking others for help for fear of revealing our imperfect self.

A lot of perfectionism exists in sports and fitness. There is the drive to have the perfect shot, the perfect game, or the perfect body. As has previously been noted, that can be both good and bad. When we take stress off kids by emphasizing fun, not perfection, and by teaching kids how to choose realistic, flexible goals, while minimizing "right and wrong" or perfectionist thinking, we open up opportunities for celebrating success that perfectionism cannot see.

Success Is in the Details

When I was the coaching consultant for the Anaheim Unified School District, a promising young coach was referred to me who had received a poor season evaluation by his supervisor. The coach was quite upset. "We took second in the league and were battling for the title until the last week of the season. I know my stuff," he declared. "I'd match my knowledge of the game against anyone's. I work my players hard on the fundamentals, and they are always prepared for their games. Why am I getting a bad evaluation?"

I asked him to tell me more about his season and his approach to sport. As he talked, it became quite clear to me that if teaching and coaching your players were all there was to being a coach, then he was right—he had done a masterful job.

But—and it is a big but—coaching involves more than just winning games. Coaches have many responsibilities, in addition to teaching and coaching, that are essential to managing their programs. They need to be an administrator, a public relations specialist, a sales person, an equipment manager, and so on.

This particular coach was excellent at teaching the Xs and Os of his sport, but had no interest and little patience for making travel arrangements, writing letters, and filling out the myriad forms that are associated with high school athletics. As a coach, he soared. As an administrator, he sucked. Hence, the bad review.

The moral of the story is that if you want to be a successful coach, you overlook the boring details of sports management at your own risk—and sometimes that of your players. Filling out forms, maintaining open channels of communication with parents and administration, inspecting equipment and facilities, and so on, can be tedious and mind-numbing, but it is all part of the coach's responsibility.

It is the same situation with most jobs. There are parts we enjoy doing and parts that we don't enjoy doing. On the other hand, all parts must still be done if we are going to be successful. The aforementioned is why, when I work with kids, they don't just learn the fun stuff—they also learn about everything that needs to be done BEFORE the fun stuff happens. They learn about getting permission slips, checking equipment, and taking safety precautions. They learn about scheduling facilities and practice fields, as well as meetings. They learn about making assignments and evaluating the success of an activity. While these may not always be fun things to do, they are a very necessary part of running a successful program. They are also skills that will serve the youth well, as they progress through their lives.

The key point to always remember is that success is in the details—even if those details are boring.

Whose Game Is It?

As I sat watching the two professional basketball teams go at each other, I found myself becoming more and more frustrated. I couldn't understand it. This sport was the activity that I used to love all aspects of—the sound of the ball *thwacking* the floor, the thrill of catching my man off guard and sinking a shot, even the smell of a gym full of sweaty bodies. The older I got, however, the harder it became to watch professional and, to some degree, college basketball games. As a result, I decided to put on my "psychologist" hat and go for a walk to see if I could figure out what my resistance was all about.

Finally, it occurred to me. What was bothering me was the sight of the coaches parading back and forth in front of their bench, constantly shouting instructions to the players. It was disturbing to me that these coaches, most of whom were excellent teachers, could not trust their athletes to make intelligent choices on the court. Apparently, there was no one on the team the coach could count on to know what needed to be done on a play-by-play basis. Have these players not been adequately trained to know how to work with their teammates to meet the challenges presented by their opponents? I think it's sad when athletes are not given the opportunity to develop the competencies or confidence to execute a game plan, without the coach calling out instructions on nearly every play.

Maybe, I am being overly nostalgic when I recall the days when coaches remained on the bench and trusted the team captain to know how to make adjustments to the moves by the opposition. I know that it may seem quaint to today's athletes that there once was a day when quarterbacks called their own plays, based upon how the defense lined up, without any help from the coaching staff. Increasingly, athletes have been robbed of the opportunity to assert leadership on the playing field.

I have vivid memories of the joys of sandlot sports, where we established our own game plans and enforced our own rules without any interference from experts, unless it was one of our older brothers who gave us unsolicited tips when we screwed up or showed us the way by beating us to the basket. We learned to take responsibility for our own actions, to take control of our lives in sport. As a result, we experienced the joy of mastering and performing sports skills on our own terms. That was enough for us. The sheer enjoyment of being engaged in competition brought us enormous satisfaction and kept us on the courts until darkness set in.

What I am trying to do is to empower youth by creating a culture of creativity, individuality, independence, and interdependence in their games and activities. One of my primary concerns is that today's culture of sport increasingly promotes dependency and immaturity. Maturity requires both courage and compassion, which involves having kids make their own decisions and govern their own actions. Maturity can only be promoted when youth are assigned rights and responsibilities in games and activities that are tailored to their level of experience. Then, and only then, can their games and sports become a source of empowerment that helps kids develop into mature adults and full-fledged citizens in their own activities.

Zen and the Art of Skateboarding

I would like to begin by stating I have never been on a skateboard, and at almost 80 years of age, I don't plan on taking up the sport anytime soon. Yes, however, this is a story about skateboarding.

Many years ago, I met with some parks and recreation folks from Laguna Hills, CA, to discuss a program I was running at the time, called "The Promise of Good Sports." Apparently, Laguna Hills had been experiencing problems (as were a lot of other communities) with youth sports run amok—including excessive parental involvement, ridiculous coaching policies, an overemphasis on winning, and kids dropping out of the activities at alarming rates. It was hoped that by introducing our program to the local youth sports organizations (AYSO, Little League, club soccer, etc.), we could reverse some of the damage that had been done.

We met at the beautiful Laguna Hills Community Center and Sports Park—a 40,000 square-foot facility that included meeting rooms, a banquet area, gymnasium, classrooms, a dance room, and so on. The Community Center was designed around the paleontological history of the area, and the lobby included fossil displays and murals that depicted the area's rich history. The surrounding park included a Prehistoric Playground that housed a 1/3 replica of a bowhead whale, two full-size soccer fields, a baseball field, a roller hockey rink, a group picnic area, a snack bar, and a skate park.

The skate park and the dozen or so kids working on their routines really caught my attention. I learned that many of the skaters had dropped out of other sports (probably because of one of the aforementioned reasons listed) and would spend hours working to master just one maneuver—even though the failure-to-success ratio was approximately 100 to 1. I also learned that skateboarders are often described by teachers and community leaders as unmotivated and lazy students.

Since those two facts seemed rather contradictory, I turned to author and researcher Richard Sagor to find out a bit more about the subject. Sagor interviewed dozens of skateboarders in an attempt to understand their extraordinary perseverance and commitment to boarding, which stood in contrast to their stated lack of motivation in the classroom. He found that on the skateboard track, they were evaluated solely on their own performance, and their progress was measured only in comparison to their accomplishments of the previous day. Every skateboarder was aware of the skill levels of the other skaters. Rather than competing against each other, however, they taught one another, supported each other's efforts, and learned from one another. Compare this culture to the environment that they experienced in the classroom, where the motivational tools consisted of testing, competition, and even punishment. On the track, they measured their progress against themselves; in the classroom, their progress was measured against others or against some arbitrary expectation level.

I think skateboarding is an excellent analogy for what I am now trying to do. First, I am not telling kids, "You will play this sport and do this activity." They choose what THEY are interested in doing. Second, I focus on cooperation versus competition. Yes, times will occur when kids are competing against one another or against another team, but they learn that even within that competition, there must be cooperation. As the old saying goes, "It takes two to tango." Third, I teach kids that the only person they are really competing against is themselves—and I teach them how to evaluate and measure their own personal growth.

Finally, I recognize how critical it is to make learning fun. When you look at kids who are undermotivated and struggling in the classroom, but energized and highly motivated on the playing field, the biggest game-changer is they find one activity enjoyable and the other not so much. The kids I work with, just like those skateboarders I watched in the park, are learning all kinds of crazy skills. Only instead of skateboarding tricks, they're learning how to plan and organize events, promote activities, and solve unexpected problems. Most importantly, *they're having fun while doing it*, which makes all the difference.

Golden

One, day my office phone rang. On the other end of the phone was a bright, young executive who had worked for a company I had consulted with a few years earlier. The company had since fallen on hard times, and the young man was now CEO of his own start-up.

After we spent several minutes catching up, he asked me, "Doc? Why do you think the company went into the toilet?" It was a good question. There were probably several factors at work, but after thinking about it for a moment, I replied, "I think it boils down to a huge disconnect between the stated values of the organization and how people were actually treated."

I cannot remember when I first heard the "Golden Rule" (summarized by the ancient Jewish scholar Hillel as, "Do not unto thy neighbor what is hateful unto thee; that is the whole law"). On the other hand, I see Hillel's words as a universal guide to success for any type of relationship.

I am reminded of the story of the business student who was acing her final exam until she came to the last question: "What is the name of the person who cleans your dorm?" She was incredulous. How could she be expected to know the answer to that? Furthermore, what did it have to do with her business degree? Finally, she asked the professor if the question really counted on their final grade.

"Indeed it does," he replied. "Most of you dream about being the president and CEO of a successful company. Success, however, is a team effort. A good leader takes nothing for granted and recognizes the contributions made by everyone on the team— even those people who appear to do the most insignificant jobs."

The aforementioned point emphasizes the importance of treating people with respect, fairness, and honesty. Treating others the way that we would like to be treated is a personal, professional, and business practice that is obvious in its merits, but is often overlooked in its application. We need to reinforce respectful, fair, honest treatment of others in everything that we do in life and work.

This factor applies to everyone, no matter their age. We all need to experience an atmosphere and environment that is nonjudgmental and demonstrates mutual respect. A successful program makes everyone—kids and adults alike—feel welcomed and supported. That's the kind of thing that makes a program—and the people involved in it—golden.

Don't Know Much About Racquetball

I first met Terry Badger in 1953, when we went on a double date to the spring dance. Terry's date was his future wife, Lynn, while I went with Lynn's friend, Sally. I'm sure Terry and I probably exchanged a few pleasantries. Other than that, however, our paths didn't cross again until we met up at the tailgate party at our 40-year Stanford reunion.

At one point in our conversation, I remember asking Terry what he did for exercise. He said he played racquetball. I had never played racquetball before, but I had fallen off the exercise wagon and was looking for a way to get back in shape. As a result, I asked Terry if he'd be interested in teaching me the sport.

"Sure!" he said.

"When can we start?" I asked.

"I'll call you when I get home," Terry responded.

Subsequently, we set a date to play at the NAS Miramar racquetball courts. I met Terry there, and he explained the rudimentary rules of the game to me. He then proceeded to pretty much clean my clock. I was obviously neither a natural racquetball player, nor was I in any semblance of shape. I had to stop to catch my breath at least three times in the first game. The second game was even worse. Mercifully, Terry said, "I think that's enough for your first time. You'll get the hang of it quickly, I'm sure." In reality, he didn't sound sure at all. Terry later told me that he was afraid I was going to go into cardiac arrest right there on the racquetball floor.

As I slowly followed Terry back to the men's locker room, we walked past the basketball court, where a couple of young men in their 20s or 30s were playing one-on-one. As I heard the familiar *thwup thwup* of the ball slapping the floor, it was like a shot of adrenaline straight to my heart. In the locker room, I was quiet for a minute, and then I said to Terry, "Let's go play them."

"Play whom?" he asked.

"Those two guys on the basketball court."

I'm sure Terry thought I was nuts. "George," he whined. "I haven't played basketball in 30 years. I can't do it now!"

"Yes, you can," I said, as I grabbed Terry by the arm and pulled him back out to the basketball court, my racquetball fatigue completely disappearing.

"Hey, do you guys want to play two-on-two?"

The two guys looked at Terry and me—both of us old, short, senior citizens—and smiled. "Cool," they said, with some degree of relish. Imagine their surprise when the senior citizens beat them handily!

I'm still not much of a racquetball player, but those racquetball sessions with Terry spurred me to get back to playing senior basketball and refereeing high school games. They reminded me of how good it felt to be physically active and in shape.

In the past 25 years, the number of kids age 2 to 19 classified as obese is up nearly 20 percent; in the 6 to 11 group, it has tripled. Obesity is a major health problem in our country. According to the National Center for Health Statistics, as of 1991, about one in every three Americans ages 35 through 45 was obese—36 percent more than it was in 1962. In a new study (reported in *USA Today*), it was predicted that 42 percent of American adults will be obese by the year 2030, which represents a tremendous threat to the health and economic welfare of our country.

I think that while children have a natural tendency to want to be active, the older they get, the fewer outlets they have for fun, meaningful activity. Not everyone is going to like or be good at the same sports. On the other hand, if you give kids enough options—whether it's basketball or broom hockey—they are more likely to discover something that engages them enough that they want to continue. That factor is how a lifelong habit of physical fitness is created. That is how healthy, active adults are developed. That is how I was provided with the shot of adrenaline that has kept me going, despite numerous health issues that could have killed me years ago.

While I may not know much about racquetball, I do know it probably saved my life. Hopefully, it won't take our kids as long to learn that lesson as I did.

The Stanford Breakfast Club

You know the old joke, "A rabbi, a priest, and a minister walk into a bar ... ?" Well, in the case of the Stanford Breakfast Club, it would be more like, "An aerospace engineer, a cardiovascular surgeon, and a CIA operative walk into a bar ..." Of course, you would have to add a few more people to the story, like the advertising exec and the millionaire, and the famous comedian's son. Oh, and me. You get the idea, however. To call this group "diverse" would be an understatement.

For the past nine years, since I moved to Northern California, I have traveled almost monthly to San Diego to enjoy and be nourished by a group of friends from my days on the Farm (as Stanford is affectionately known by alumni the world over). How did such a diverse mix of individuals get together in the first place?

The Stanford Breakfast Club started when Den Kennedy and Wes Marx, both Stanford alums, bumped into each other at the 2001 Carlsbad Oktoberfest. At the urging of Wes's wife, Den and Wes—along with John "Skip" Schumacher, another graduate from the Class of '56—started meeting for lunch. Not long after, when I was looking for input into a book I was writing at the time, they brought me, Brad Leonard, and Terry Badger into the mix. The lunches turned into breakfasts, and then more people got added to the group. Currently, we have an average monthly attendance of about 6 to 8 men, with sometimes as many as 13 individuals showing up.

For a bunch of guys who are supposed to be way over the hill, I am always struck by the energy that is present in this group. Though old, we are still growing. Allan Goodman—cardiovascular surgeon—still working. Tom Waterhouse—CIA—still working. Jerry Govan—author, developer, spiritual counselor—still working. We continue to seek, to chase our potential. Unendingly, we strive to remain vital. We travel, take on new challenges, and try to expand our knowledge and opinions about life and ourselves. While many people at this point in life may elect to simply go through the motions, the individuals in this group refuse to run out of steam.

Marie de Hennezel, a renowned therapist and author of the book, *The Art of Growing Old*, notes that individuals should look forward to embracing everything aging has to offer in terms of human and spiritual enrichment. On the other hand, aging, at least in American society, is often viewed more as a necessary evil, rather than something positive. I can honestly say, though, that the numbers of this group have the insight to appreciate the process.

What does my experience with the Stanford Breakfast Club have to do with what I'm doing now? First, it illustrates the importance of making connections through shared experiences, and how those connections can influence us for decades. Second, it illustrates how much we have to learn from one another. These wonderful individuals whom I am privileged to meet with on a regular basis have not only just given me suggestions and ideas for various projects I've been working on, they've also served as examples of how to courageously deal with life's challenges—including death, divorce, and other struggles.

Finally, I believe the Stanford Breakfast Club illustrates the value of continuous learning in our lives. The key point is that you're never too old to learn. Or too young, for that matter.

Cracking the Code

I was well into my coaching education workshop, "Coaching to Make a Difference," at Modesto Christian High School, when one of the coaches raised his hand. "Dr. Selleck, can you help me with a problem?" "I don't know. What's the problem?"

"I have this athlete with Division I talent. He's really good, but he's lazy! I don't know what to do with him!" I thought for a minute and then asked the other coaches, "Do any of the rest of you have this problem? Gifted athletes who are lazy?" Every hand in the room went up.

I had a feeling what I was about to say wouldn't make me any friends with this group. "You know, there is no such thing as a lazy kid."

You could have heard the proverbial pin hit the floor as everyone looked at me with shock and puzzlement. I went on: "There is no such thing as a lazy kid. Laziness is simply how a person is handling their problem. The problem may be that they are in conflict with their coach or a teammate; they may be injured and afraid to reveal their injury for fear of losing their position in the starting lineup; they may have a personal problem; they may be having trouble in the classroom, or they may just be burned out on the sport. Laziness, however, is not the problem—it is the symptom."

After that, we had a great discussion on how to get to the root of why an athlete might be underperforming and what to do about it. At the end of the workshop, I drove the 95 miles to my home in Pinole. It was late when I arrived, but I could hardly wait to tell my wife how smart I was! She listened patiently to my story, and then matter-of-factly said, "Oh, yes—we teach all our potential teachers (she is a professor of Early Childhood Education at Contra Costa Community College) that kids communicate through their behavior. Then, we teach them how to 'crack the code.'"

Cracking the code? What was that? Fortunately, I'm married to someone who could explain it to me. As my wife noted, behavior is a code—much like a code used to send secret messages. A young person's behavior is their way of communicating what they need or want, e.g., encouragement, support, skill assistance, conflict or stress reduction, options, correction, etc. Behavior also provides clues about specific challenges and difficulties that the young person is experiencing. A person who wants to decipher the coded message must understand the code to know what the signals means. In other words, they need to "crack the code."

At the present time, of course, in my workshop, I talk with coaches about "cracking the code," and they love it. In reality, it goes over a whole lot better than telling them they are wrong, and there is no such thing as a lazy kid!

We teach the same thing to the adult advisors in our current program. Understand the behavior, and you'll understand the kid, because there are no lazy—or bad, or good, or sneaky, or rebellious—kids. There are just kids—kids who sometimes exhibit lazy or good or bad behaviors. That's a critically important difference to recognize.

When Things Go Wrong

We could hear the shouting through the CEO's closed door. A conflict had been brewing between the CEO and her chief operating officer over his ideas for moving the company forward and the way she wanted to continue doing things. The storm finally erupted as they screamed horrible things at each other. As a consultant to the company, I was concerned. Emotions were running high, and it was impacting the thoughts, opinions, and productivity of the employees. The prospects of things working out did not look good.

The next day, I met with the CEO and her COO. Tempers had cooled, and they were both feeling a little foolish about the way they had behaved. Apologies were extended. That's when I went to work. Putting on my problem-solving hat, I said, "Let's identify your concerns and see if we can agree on what needs to be done."

Conflict. We all have to deal with it. It occurs when two or more people with differing perceptions, beliefs, or values attempt to occupy the same space at the same time. This space can be physical, psychological, or emotional.

Contrary to the widespread belief that conflict is bad and should be eliminated, conflict is actually natural and can be a good thing. My goal in the meeting with the CEO and COO was to minimize or eliminate the dysfunctional disagreements and seek a constructive resolution to the identified issues.

Dealing with confrontation creatively can strengthen, rather than destroy, relationships. The goal "when push comes to shove" is to help individuals or groups see the healthy aspects of conflict. Legitimizing conflict is essential for individuals, groups, and organizations to move forward.

Making conflict work constructively can involve a number of steps, including the following:

- *Step #1: Establish ground rules.* The ground rules should encourage everyone involved to be open, honest, and respectful in their communications.
- *Step #2: Identify and establish ownership of the problem.* What is the conflict? Who is involved? To whom does the problem belong? What is the history of the conflict? What are the consequences?
- *Step #3: Identify the barriers to communication.*
- *Step #4: Identify possible solutions.*
- *Step #5: Develop a plan for moving forward.*

The great thing about working with kids is they are often a lot more open to resolving conflicts than adults are. It's fun to be able to teach them how to resolve conflicts successfully. As a result, when they're 40-something business owners and operators, they won't be screaming at each other behind closed doors. Instead, they'll be acknowledging their differences and calmly working them out.

Musings Over a Diet Coke®

I had more than one opportunity to interact with Bill Walsh, former head coach of the San Francisco 49ers and the Stanford Cardinal football team. The first occurred when I did a two-day workshop for Stanford's athletic department. There was also the time when Walsh returned to Stanford after his successful professional coaching career and asked me to work with his football staff for a couple of days. My favorite, however, was probably when we got together in a meeting room on the Stanford campus and just chatted over a couple of Diet Cokes.

At one point, Bill commented that he couldn't remember ever having taken as many notes as he had in my workshops. He followed up by asking for more details and examples on some of the points I had made.

That experience had a profound impact on me. After all, Bill Walsh was an icon. An icon was taking notes about things I said. I have to say, I found myself feeling pretty good about me!

It also made me aware of one of the keys to Bill Walsh's success. A lot of coaches have power, but not all of them are successful. Bill had plenty of power, but he also had the ability to make you feel good about yourself. That, to me, is the first rule of salesmanship. People don't buy things or ideas because they like YOU, but because they like themselves when they are around you. Bill's ability to positively influence his players, coaching staff, and others was a crucial part of his ability to lead effectively. In a similar vein, my leadership development program for kids is built on the belief that real power does not come from titles, degrees, or how loud you can yell, but from your ability to quietly influence those around you.

Over the years, influence has been described in ways that almost make it seem mystic. One definition describes it as a kind of spiritual or moral force. Other definitions describe it as authority, prestige, or credibility. Personally, I believe that influence is the ability to secure a desired outcome without the apparent use of force or direct command. Influence arises from the confidence that kids have in the ability of our adult facilitators and staff to either take them where they want to go or demonstrate a better alternative.

It is also important to note that yes, on occasion, Diet Coke is involved.

It Started With a Phone Call (India—Part I)

It started with a phone call, subsequently, a face-to-face meeting, and then a few more phone calls. The next thing I knew, I was on my way to India to work with Saumil Majmudar, Jayashankar, and Jitendra Joshi—the founders of SportzVillage. These young, very bright and talented men, all with MBAs and corporate experience, were looking to do something more meaningful with their lives, and they wanted to do it in sports. Furthermore, they thought that I might be able to help them figure out what they should do.

Our initial project involved leasing land, on which I helped them develop the sites for games, as well as sports activities and programs, for kids in the neighborhood and surrounding communities. The program marginally supported their families until the price of land shot up. Anxious, they asked what I thought they should do next.

After very little thought, I said, "You guys have learned a lot through this project. Why don't you take what you've learned to the schools of India?" Thus, EduSports was born. At the present time, it is India's leading private initiative providing integrated sports management services to schools. EduSports works with schools all over the country, helping them fulfill the dreams of millions of youth for high quality, holistic education. In the process, we've reached more than 300 schools, 175,000 children, 5,000 teachers, and 50,000 parents. The parent program I designed is used in schools across 70 cities, and I have written more than 100 articles for *Education World*, India's leading education magazine.

A critical question that needs to be answered is what exactly had Saumil, Jayashankar, and Jitendra learned that enabled them to make SportzVillage into the highly successful company it is now? They had learned how sports and fitness go hand-in-hand with the educational goals schools have for their students. Sport wasn't just a footnote to the school day. Rather, it was a tool that educators could use to teach and reinforce skills that would empower kids for a lifetime.

I helped draw the distinction between education in the *narrow* sense and education in the *broad* sense. In the narrow sense, education refers to all the knowledge, skills, and values that we learn in an academic setting. In contrast, education in the broad sense includes all that we learn within and outside of the school walls.

I wanted to shift the focus from what kids are being taught to what it is they are learning. The personal and inter-personal learning kids acquire through homework, sports, and play or when applying for work or college, constitutes a vital part of their educational experience.

I framed all of this as an EXTENSION OF THE CLASSROOM. For example, games, sports, and physical activities that mix skill development, integrity, fair play, respect, and striving to do your best are key ingredients for success in whatever kids elect to do in life. SportzVillage has been able to employ this philosophy to drive their marketing and sales activities.

The SportzVillage vision is to build a sporting culture in India and make sports an integral part of a child's education and upbringing. The company wants to transform the way children and parents look at sports, and use sport to help build a healthy society and better citizens.

That's very much like what I am trying to do in this country, using students themselves to drive the process, which sounds like a very good thing for the youth of America, as well as the youth of India.

Let the Magic Begin! (India—Part II)

In 2003, I had the remarkable experience of being able to travel to India to advise a young company called SportzVillage in their efforts to create a physical education and sport program for kids. In 2009, I returned to India on behalf of EduSports, a SportzVillage subsidary company that was designed to provide sports management services to schools.

My 16 days in India were spent traveling to seven cities in the southern part of the country. During this period, my goal was to help this young company of dedicated individuals introduce and implement physical activity (physical education) and sports to a nation whose schools not only lacked these programs but also lacked time in their school days and the space and facilities to conduct such efforts.

I saw few, if any, playgrounds or grass fields in India. What I did see was a great need for knowledge in the classrooms about physical fitness and its contribution to health, as well as the other wonderful benefits of physical activity and sport (i.e., integration of mind and body, development of life skills and lessons, the incentive of almost daily progress, etc.).

I was at a school in the fifth city on my journey, when something magical happened. I was told that a group of 8th graders were expecting me to talk to them. The director of the school announced it as a "pep talk." Like all real teaching should be, however, it ended up with the teacher (me) learning every bit as much and maybe even more than the students.

As I waited in a large room, 150 students in their school uniforms marched in and sat on the floor in rows. Being quite uncomfortable with the idea of standing above those young people, I sat down on the floor with them and invited the rows to move closer and fill in the spaces. I then said that because real teaching and learning occur when the teacher and student learn together, I would get us started, but I fully wanted to learn from them.

As these young people from this faraway country gathered around me, barriers came down, and we exchanged thoughts, ideas, and questions. The truly wonderful thing, however, was their body language. They listened like no other group I have ever addressed or with whom I have ever interacted. The expressions on their faces and in their eyes clearly were signs of deep involvement and connection. My few minutes with these kids turned into about 45. While my old body had a tough time sitting on the ground that long, the feeling that we were fellow searchers for the truth will live with me forever.

Throughout my career, I have sought to point out the wonderful learning environment that physical activity and sport provides. It is a true laboratory for learning because it is:

- Visceral (it happens inside of kids, not simply in their heads)
- Hands-on (kids learn by doing and discovery)
- Fun (when done correctly)
- A place where kids (for the most part) want to be

Sports and fitness activities, just like art, music, drama, and other co-curricular activities, are an extension of the educational process that enable students to expand their knowledge, as well as enjoy an experience outside the classroom in a way that is consistent with the overall philosophy and goals of today's education. Furthermore, I believe that as we work to develop the whole child, we need to focus on the contributions that physical activity and sport make to learning life lessons that can be applied to the classroom, relationships, and careers. This is part of the magic of sports.

To which I say, let the magic begin!

The Scared CEO

For a number of years, I had been providing training seminars, personal and professional development assistance, and management coaching to a mid-size company. The work was interesting, fun, and challenging. As the world and business climate started changing with accelerating speed, however, the company began to show signs that it was slipping behind its competitors.

The head of the company was a well-meaning and caring person. As bad news repeatedly came rushing in, however (e.g., the loss of a long-term contract, the departure of important employees, the failure to win a contract, stronger competition from bigger companies, as well as the usual operational problems), it became clear to me that this executive was making hasty and impulsive decisions, as the perfect storm of outer and inner turmoil continued its destructive path toward the company.

Frustratingly, the more I wanted to help, the less I was consulted. A big part of the problem was that with each new threat to the company, the executive would immediately react to the threat, instead of pausing to reflect and consider different options. In this person's desperate attempt to relieve their own anxiety and fear, time was not set aside to properly consider what the best course of action might be.

I think it was easy for me to recognize this pattern, because it was something that I had done throughout most of MY life, as witnessed by the fact that when a class syllabus was handed out on the first day of college, I would be in the library that night working on the term paper that wouldn't be due for months. I've watched myself do the same thing with relationships, career decisions, etc. Instead of taking a breath to learn and reflect on situations, I only wanted to do whatever would make the anxiety and discomfort go away as quickly as possible.

All the really important battles of our lives are internal. As I've slowly learned, I need to take charge of my own life. This realization was not an easy victory to achieve, particularly when my need to be accepted and belong led me to please others first. Fortunately, I have finally realized that commitment to self precedes commitment to others, because it allows me to grow and develop and ultimately bring more to the party—to my wife, my kids, and those I seek to serve.

We need to teach our kids to become students of their own selves. A student, by definition, is a person who is involved in self-discovery. It is what I like to think of as the adult task of seeing yourself and your place in the world more clearly and with more ideas. As a consequence, you know the difference between fantasy and reality. You make better decisions. You're more aware of your strengths and weaknesses. You take responsibility for your goals, priorities, choices, and actions. While putting your internal house in order is hard work, it is good work, because it is the most important work of your life. It helps keep anxiety at bay. It helps keep you from running scared.

The Class From Hell

I was having lunch with Mark Stanios, a new friend at Professional and Scientific Associates, a company for which I had been consulting for over five years. After talking about PSA's newly developed sports division, Mark brought up the subject of the program I was starting. "So, what's this thing all about?" he asked. "It sounds interesting."

After giving him a quick introduction, then I mentioned I was on pins and needles to see how the leadership training program I had designed (based on experiential, or project-based, learning) would go over with 7th and 8th graders. Subsequently, Mark pricked up his ears when he heard "experiential learning" and excitedly said, "Have I got a story for you!"

When I was a senior in high school, I was required to take a U.S government class to graduate. By the time I signed up, the only class remaining that had space was an advanced placement class that would count for college credit. I was less than thrilled, figuring the class would be very time-consuming and boring.

The first day began with the teacher glaring at us, like we'd just been caught stealing candy from a store. He barked at us all to get a desk and that would be our assigned desk for the remainder of the school year. He then rattled off the class rules: "No one late for class! No late work accepted, and no partial credit given for late work. No food or drink allowed in class. No bathroom breaks. No talking unless you're assigned to do so, or if you are working within a group. You will be assigned to a group, and no changing groups. You will work as a party in the legislative branch of the government. You will write bills and debate, and either pass or reject them. Your grade will be 80 percent based on your participation within the process of the activity. Bring only your textbook and binder to class. No backpacks. The highest grade most of you will obtain in this class will be a 'C.' No extra credit work accepted!"

My stomach tightened at the thought of suffering through a half year of this guy, just to get a 'C' in this class.

He then took the remainder of the class time to explain the process of government and the creation of bills and laws, their value, and their importance in our day-to-day lives. It was absolute hell.

The next few class periods were as dry and boring as anticipated. By the second week, however, things began to pick up. We were divided into groups and given instruction. We were told that any bill voted on and passed by our legislative body would be law, and he would have to honor it. It was only then we realized we could change everything in the class and get rid of all his stupid rules if we were able to do it as a bill and have the class pass the bill into law.

With this golden revelation, the entire class worked feverishly that first month not only to abolish the class rules, but also to pass a bill giving the entire class an 'A' for the semester.

As we progressed through the semester, learning and exercising our rights as legislators, I was amazed to find that this class was becoming my favorite of the year. Even the work—and there was a lot of it—was fun and welcomed. The teacher not only baited us the first day, but also reeled us in. As such, we were all captured by his approach to discover the value of government and the processes involved in making change.

I love this story, because it highlights what I've always believed: meaningful learning occurs when students understand its relation to their life and their future. True learning requires two crucial and related ingredients: engagement and activity. Clearly, they were present in Mark's government class.

I believe kids WANT to learn. Our job is to facilitate such learning. We do this by: one, creating a positive (fun, engaging, non-threatening) climate for learning; two, clarifying the purpose of the learning; three) making all necessary learning resources available; four, balancing the intellectual and emotional aspects of learning; and five, sharing our thoughts and feelings with the students, without dominating the learning process.

Hopefully, one day, the kids I work with will be talking to someone when the subject of learning comes up, and they will be the one to say, "Have I got a story for you!"

Awesome Ain't Easy

The life expectancy for individuals who have ALS (Lou Gehrig's disease) averages two to five years from diagnosis, according to the ALS Association. My brother-in-law, Dennis Burke, began his battle with the disease somewhere around 2003, and passed away in 2009.

Dennis spent 10 years ministering to the inmates of San Quentin, teaching everyone from drug addicts to lifers. He captured the essence of this experience in his highly-respected book, *Doing Time*. It was a moving and provocative exploration of the minds and lives of men, struggling daily to find meaning behind the walls of our massive, oppressive, and unforgiving prisons.

For me, one of the most wonderful things about Dennis—in a long list of wonderful things—was the attitude he displayed throughout his battle with ALS. Even when he lost the ability to walk or talk, it didn't stop him from sharing the faith, kindness, and caring that was a big part of his life and career. His attitude delivered the message that we should keep doing what is important, no matter the circumstances. Contrast that with the attitude conveyed by a bumper sticker I saw a while back that said, "I love my bad ass attitude." What that bumper sticker says to me is, "I have no skills or ability to control my life, except to develop an attitude that makes it difficult for people to work with me."

Our attitudes are choices. In any given situation, these attitudes may be productive. A list of several examples of non-productive attitudes includes the following:
- "It's my way or the highway."
- "Sorry. That's just the way I am. Deal with it."
- "I'm never going to get it right, so why bother trying?"

- "That kid will never amount to anything."
- "A leopard can't change his spots."

Although a lot of non-productive attitudes are chosen as a protective strategy or coping mechanism, they are extremely limiting on a person's level of development and success. It is also important to note that if we can help today's youth choose productive attitudes, there will be fewer adults with non-productive attitudes in the future. Is it necessarily going to be easy? No. On the other hand, as Dennis would be the first to say, "Awesome ain't easy." Maybe we should put THAT on a bumper sticker.

Lunch With the Beebe's

I had accumulated thousands of frequent flyer miles commuting from Oakland to Dulles International Airport over the course of six years. Now, however, because JetBlue® had discontinued servicing that route, I was in danger of losing precious award tickets if I didn't quickly book a JetBlue flight somewhere.

Ah! Since I fly to San Diego once a month to see two of my grandchildren, I could fly Jet Blue to Long Beach and save my mileage. The key issue for me, however, was how would I get from Long Beach International Airport to San Diego?

It was then that I decided to contact an old friend from my days playing at the Long Beach YMCA in 4th and 5th grade—Selden Beebe. Selden had also been a Stanford classmate of mine. Subsequently, we decided to have lunch and talk about old times. Selden and his wife would then drive me to a rental car agency, where I would pick up a car to drive the rest of the way to San Diego.

At lunch, Selden happened to share the following memory: "We were about nine or ten years old, shooting around one day on the small basketball court at the 'Y,' and I remember asking you why you shot so well. You told me you never took a shot without trying to make it." Truth be known, I had no idea I was so profound at that age.

What I meant was that becoming good at anything—in this case putting a ball through a hoop—had much more to do with deliberate practice than any natural or physical attributes that I or any other player might have had. "Deliberate practice" has been defined by Geoff Colvin in his 2008 book, *Talent is Overrated*, as an activity designed specifically to improve performance. Though I obviously had no knowledge of this back in the 1940s, I had already started a process of thinking, self-correction, and adjustments to improve my shooting versus mindlessly repeating what I was doing, without regard for whether it was achieving my goal of putting the ball in the hoop. I was consciously breaking down my shots into parts, and working intently with my own observations and feedback to improve each part that needed to improve. In short, I was purposeful and focused.

Regardless of whatever goals or objectives we might have, it is not our innate ability or talent that we need to concern ourselves with—it is our focus and ability to self-correct. It is not about a person's athletic ability or natural gifts. It is about being aware that success is determined more by your desire, commitment and focus.

There are no shortcuts to success. If we want to be the best we can be—in sports, academics, relationships, etc.—we must commit ourselves to the process of deliberate practice and not take those shots without trying to make them.

Natal, Brazil

In the summer of 2011, I accepted an invitation to join Team USA to play in the Senior World Games in Natal, Brazil. I was just shy of my 77th birthday.

I knew it would be a challenge. We would be playing five-on-five on a full court. In addition, since there were only five teams in the 75-and-over division, we would have to play two games against the young punks in the 65-and-over bracket.

Warming up before our first game against a strong team from Argentina, whose players were all at least 10 years younger, I did something that was not very smart. With the Argentine coaches and players intently watching us going through our warm-ups, I shot lights-outs from all angles and distances on the court, particularly from behind the three-point arc. Stupid! I should have missed every shot and perhaps limped a bit on my sore knee. The Argentines, eager to defeat the Americans, took note and didn't miss a thing.

For the entire 40 minutes of play, I was guarded by the fastest and strongest players from the Argentine team, as they rotated fresh legs and harassed me throughout the contest. We lost by one basket.

My second mistake came sometime during the third quarter. The ball got loose and went rolling between several Argentine players. Forgetting my age and the issues with my knees, I dove to the floor between the opposing players and secured the ball for my team. The Argentine players and the crowd in the stands looked at me as if I were crazy. This behavior wasn't how old people were supposed to act! Needless to say, my knee came out of the pile a loser, which hindered my play and enjoyment for the next six days.

Accordingly, it might be asked—was it worth it? I think so. I took a risk, both in agreeing to play in the first place and then in diving for that loose ball. They were calculated risks, however. The potential reward was worth the potential loss. I believe that to succeed in life, we have to take those calculated risks. We must seek to go beyond established limits. We need to be a little uneasy with the status quo, as well as need to live on the edge of our competency, which is what I'm doing now. At my age, no one would begrudge me if I were to sit back in my armchair, with a good book and an occasional walk around the block for stimulation. Instead, I'm out in life, learning how to promote and run a program (using skills that are very much outside my comfort zone), because I believe the potential reward for our kids is totally worth any potential loss I might face.

To have the opportunity to change a kid's life? I'd dive on the floor for that any day.

Thank You, John!

One day, I was combing through the Internet in search of some information, when I noticed a reference to Bay Area basketball. It was a blog called "The Golden Age," which covered the University of California basketball team. My curiosity piqued, I went to the blog and found several posts, including one interchange between—surprise!—my oldest son, John, and another gentleman. I felt like I'd unexpectedly walked in on one of my kids talking to his friends about me:

> [John] .... My dad played in the same back court as Tomsic at Stanford, and roomed with Bill Russell in New York for the East-West All-Star game.

> I can only say "Wow." Your dad must have had some great memories, and some great stories to tell. How did your dad react when you told him you had decided to go to Cal? Did you play any hoops at Cal?

> Oh yeah, my dad has lots of stories—his freshman team beat Russell's USF freshman team at the last minute, when he improvised a fumbleruski play. The two years that he and Tomsic played together, my dad was the point guard and mostly set up Tomsic. Subsequently, he was then the big scorer his senior year. He played in Stanford alumni games well into his 70s—very amusing to his grandkids. One year, he was the runner-up to Casey Jacobsen in the three-point shooting contest. He was just inducted into the Pac-12 Hall of Honor this spring.

> My dad had taken me to see both campuses and was ultimately pretty accepting of my choosing Cal over Stanford ... Saved him a lot of money, and my younger sister ended up going to Stanford, so it all worked out.

> No, I did not inherit or develop any basketball talent and only played intramurals at Cal. My younger brother was a really good point guard (AAU and led our high school to the L.A. City finals) and ... ended up playing PG for UCSD.

> What a story. Thanks for telling it. I've always respected your posts. I know we've had a couple of disagreements, but now I'll have to defer to you on everything. You probably learned more about basketball at the dinner table than I did in years of playing and following it.

You can imagine how tickled I was to read this interchange. My work with kids and parents over the years has convinced me that every kid has issues with their parents—no matter how old the kid or the parents are. As a consequence, it really was a wonderful surprise to run across these words of apparent pride from my son.

It also brought home to me how much it means to be on the receiving end of positive feedback. If an old guy like me lights up like a Christmas tree after reading something like this, imagine what it could do for a young person. Unfortunately, a lot of the feedback our kids get tends to be more negative than positive. "If you had spent more time on your paper, you could have gotten a higher grade." "You call *this* music?" "What in heaven's name made you think sticking a bean up your nose was a good idea?"

It's important for kids to learn how to give each other lots of positive feedback. "Wow, what a catch!" "Awesome poster!" "Great idea!" "Lookin' good out there!" In reality, it doesn't matter if you're 8, 18, or 80—you're never too young or too old to hear something good about yourself.

Where Are the Kids?

Recently, I was driving slowly through a nearby neighborhood when I turned a corner and saw something I had not seen in years—maybe even decades. It was a group of kids, somewhere between 8 and 12 years old, playing baseball in the street. *In the street!*

While that might not sound strange to those of you who live in a small town (or a time-warp), here in the East Bay of San Francisco, a scenario involving kids playing in the street has gone the way of transistor radios and analog televisions.

This group of kids obviously had to recruit whatever friends were available to get enough players to make a couple of teams. I imagine that it didn't matter how old you were or how good you were, if you wanted to play you were in.

I still smile every time I think of it. Because you know what I usually see when I drive through neighborhoods these days? Empty driveways. Empty parks. Empty yards. Empty sidewalks. The kids have vanished.

Granted, there are probably a fair number of kids who are inside their houses playing video games or texting friends or chatting on Facebook™. This hypothetical possibility doesn't completely explain the emptiness, however.

More kids are playing sports than ever, but now they're doing it at specialized football camps or baseball academies or seven-on-seven tournaments or super leagues. Either that or they're in a weight room, preparing for next season. Sandlot ball is dead, which leaves out millions of kids who don't have the skill level to appeal to the elite sports community, or who do not have the money to attend camps, or who just want to play for fun.

Those are the kids to which we need to reach out. They're the kids who drop out of sports by the age of 13; they're the kids whose schools have drastically reduced their physical education class requirements; they're the kids who lack the confidence or the skills to participate at a higher level, but who still want to participate.

While we may not be able to bring back the sandlots, we can bring back the kids.

Dominos

My wife and I are domino nuts. Whenever we can find the time, we will work in a game. Despite my competitive streak, when it comes to our domino matches, Barbara is the undisputed champ. I console myself by thinking, "Well, of *course* someone who has worked with kids all her life would be good at dominos!" When I can, I also try to distract her by talking about random things.

Barbara has a 42-year history with the Montessori method of teaching children, beginning in 1970, when she first taught pre-school, and moving up through her recently retired (June 2014) position as professor of early childhood education and director of the Early Learning Center at Contra Costa Community College.

One day, while playing our customary game of dominos, with Barbara way ahead and me trying to think of something disarming to talk about, Barbara mentioned that adults look at things differently than children do. She said adults tend to have product-based outcomes or goals for their children (i.e., graduate and get into a good school), while children are more into the process of the thing—making friends, having fun, etc. That comment started bouncing around in my head and Barbara went on to win the game, all of which proves that she is not only very smart, she is also very *sneaky*.

For those of you unfamiliar with the Montessori method, it is both a philosophy of child development and a rationale for guiding that development. It is based on two important needs children have: the need for freedom within limits, as well as a carefully prepared (learning) environment that provides experiences that will result in kids developing intellectually and physically. It is an environment that is built on their desire to learn and their unique abilities to develop their own capabilities. Essentially, kids need adults to expose them to the possibilities in their lives, while the kids retain/determine their response(s) to all the possibilities.

What Barbara said about how kids learn solidified what I had long felt and espoused in my own work with kids, as well as what I am now trying to do. What I do is about learning, as opposed to the lifeless, sterile, futile, quickly forgotten stuff that is often crammed into the minds of kids. Rather, we are about learning that it is the insatiable curiosity that drives young people to absorb everything that moves them forward, that it allows them to do, that it improves the efficiency and speed of their goals. We are about the student who says, "I am discovering, I am drawing in from the larger world and making it part of what I'm doing and am about." What we are striving for is conversations like this: "No, no, that's not what I'm talking about, wanting, looking for … Yes, THAT'S closer to what I had in mind, what I'm interested in, what I need."

I like to think that we are building the future dominos champs of the world. Unless they play my wife, of course.

Happy Birthday!

The day before my 78th birthday, my wife, Barbara, and I arrived in San Diego to visit my son, Peter, and his family. Because it had been a long, hot drive, I didn't even bother to change into a swimming suit—I just pulled my wallet out of my pocket and jumped into the pool to play with the grandkids.

Later, as we were toweling off, I asked Peter if he was playing basketball that night. (He had been an outstanding player in high school and college and still played several nights a week in various leagues in the area.) He said "yes," and then, to my everlasting joy, he asked, "Would you like to play?"

It is important to note that I hadn't played basketball since my trip to Brazil the year before to participate in the World Senior Games. Furthermore, I definitely hadn't been hitting the gym as much as I should have been. There was also the whole "turning-78-the-next-day" thing to contend with. I then thought it over for a whole .5 second, before saying, "Sure!" It was all I could do to keep from jumping up and down and adding, "Can we go right now? Can we? Can we?"

Peter explained that they were short a couple of players because one guy had injured himself in the previous game, while another had to stay home with the kids, because his wife was out of town. "So you'll help us out?"

Well, we ended up winning the game by one point in the closing seconds. I took two shots from the outside and hit one—a three-pointer—and made a couple passes that made me think, "Not bad for an old guy." The highlight of the game, however, was when Peter came off the bench to replace me and held his hand out for the customary teammate-to-teammate high-five. I will cherish that sign of camaraderie, approval, and love from my son until the very last seconds of my life. It was the best birthday present ever.

As I reflected later on this experience, I thought back to a meeting I'd had earlier that same day with Jay Giles, the producer of KSNN (Kids Sports News Network). We were discussing my current work, when Jay rather pointedly asked me, "Why are you doing this?"

In reality, Jay, there are a lot of reasons why I'm doing this. Most of them can be encapsulated into that one moment of pure joy that I felt, as my son and I passed each other on the court. There are many things about sport that are wonderful. Sport and exercise can have a tremendous positive impact on us, both physically and mentally. The greatest impact, however, comes through the relationships we form and the experiences we share with others. It saddens me when I think of the number of kids who are missing out on these relationships and experiences, and I want to do something about it.

After all, why should I have all the fun?

Beth

Some of my classmates from college have suggested that my basketball days at Stanford were the high point of my life, but I would have to disagree. I think my greatest life accomplishment is the beautiful, blended family I now have, which includes not just my own children, but also my current wife, Barbara, and her two children (one of which I just walked down the aisle, along with her own father), and my dear son-in-law, Keith, with whom I lived when I was commuting to work in Virginia. In addition, probably to an outsider's surprise, it also includes my first wife, Beth, who currently lives with my son, Peter, in San Diego.

Beth and I married when she was 20, and I was 25 going on 14. After we divorced, Beth went back to school to obtain her Ph.D. as a psychologist and then spent her career working at Metropolitan State Hospital in Los Angeles County. It was a challenging work—not just because of the typical work associated with a state-run psychiatric facility—but also because she worked with a lot of doctors who didn't like women (especially women psychologists who were far more intelligent than they were). Beth has always been smarter and more well-rounded than me, and fortunately our kids take after her.

I spend a lot of time with Beth. Of course, I see her every time I visit Peter, but she also joins us on the family vacations that we take with the kids. People occasionally ask what it's like when my ex-wife and my current wife get together. Frankly, I have to state that it's actually quite wonderful. They are both mature women; individuals who share many values and interests. In fact, the last time Barbara and I were in San Diego, while my son and his wife took their kids to the baseball game, Beth, Barbara, and I went out to dinner together.

I think that when we are young, we tend to see things as very black-and-white. Children can be best friends one day and bitter enemies the next, all because of a chance remark or unintended slight. As we get older, however, I think we see not so much the shades of gray, but the colors of possibility. I hope this factor is something that kids I work with can also see and absorb—the beautiful colors of the personalities and people around them. If they don't, they will miss out on a lot. Take it from me—and Beth, and Barbara.

No Yelling Allowed

As often as I can, I fly back to Virginia to visit my grandson, Spencer. I'll never forget picking him up at the bus stop one day after school and asking him, "What are we going to do today, Spence?" With a child's directness, he replied, "I hope to play baseball without the coach yelling at us."

Spencer's comment reminded me of something that I learned back in the early 1980s when I was at Michigan State University to conduct a sports recruiting workshop for their coaches. The day before the workshop, I had been given a tour of the University's Institute for the Study of Youth Sports, which is a leader in sports research throughout the world.

During the tour, I asked the director of the Institute, Dan Gould, if there was any recent research on youth sports that he could share with me. Excited, he handed me a pamphlet. Apparently, MSU researchers had just spent several years asking sports-involved adolescents, "Why do you participate in sports?" The three top choices were consistent: one to have fun; two, to be with friends and/or to make new friends; and three, to improve sport skills and learn new skills. The study also found that about 33 percent of youth dropped out of sport participation each year. The three top reasons for doing so were: one, no fun; two, too much pressure; and three, too much emphasis on winning. At the time, this information was fairly radical. Until then, it had been accepted that one of the main reasons kids played sports was to win. Winning, however, was clear down in 12th place on the reasons why kids participated in sports.

This situation caused me to reflect on what "fun" is for kids. Subsequently, I decided … fun is participating in meaningful activity. It is being with people who encourage you. Fun is using a ball, a bat, a glove, a stick, or a racquet as often as possible. It is hitting a softball, shooting hoops, playing games, pitching balls, kicking goals, splashing water, being with friends, eating pizza, and experiencing success.

Fun is NOT being yelled at. It is NOT enduring long and boring practices, coaches who talk too much, or sitting on the bench. Fun is play, venturing out, trying new things.

Fun is being understood. Fun isn't just a good thing—it's a necessity!

When we know what fun means to kids, then we have a better chance of creating it in our activities and programs. We are better able to meet the needs of our youth.

I am seeking to meet to the needs of kids by making sports and play fun for them, so that hopefully, someday, somewhere, another grandfather picking his grandson or granddaughter up from school will ask, "So, what are we going to do today?" In turn, the response will be, "Oh, Gramps—we're going to have *fun!*"

"I've Got Next"

When I exercise these days, I try to do the treadmill at the local fitness center for at least 30 minutes, reading the paper or a book while I plug along. Then, maybe, I'll go do a few sit-ups or some arm work. It's pretty boring, to tell you the truth.

Sometimes, however, I'll wander down the stairs to the basketball courts. The adrenaline starts to kick in, and I think, "I'd really like to get into a game!" Seldom do I ever get up the nerve to do anything about it. After all, I'm 79 years old and getting shorter by the day (not that 5'8" was ever tall). On rare occasions, however, I'll stand on the sidelines among a crowd of players, and with increasing anxiety, call out, "I got next."

It's scary. I feel like an outsider. I'm once again that little Jewish boy of my childhood. Once in awhile, someone is unexpectedly nice, or another person remembers me from a previous game. They support my request—may even offer to play on my team. As people are kind or friendly, or make the effort to reach out to me, all my present and ancient anxieties vanish like a puff of smoke.

All kids experience anxiety to some degree. An important part of growing up is learning how to face and overcome these anxieties. We don't want our kids to forever be afraid of the dark. In reality, however, there is a lot of anxiety that can be avoided or lessened through the simple actions of others. The kid who feels like an outsider because they have autism, or ADHD, or are overweight, or don't speak English well, or don't wear name-brand clothing—all it takes is for someone else to reach out to them, and suddenly those things matter a lot less. That's what it's all about—kids reaching out to kids so that everyone's "got next."

Win-Win

Barbara's son, Dominic, had recently been accepted at Cal Berkeley and had moved into an apartment near the campus. I was excited for a number of reasons, including the fact that his room in our condo could now become my office.

Then, however, I thought of Barbara's daughter, Kathy. After graduating from college, Kathy had gotten a job with a non-profit organization that, like many non-profits, didn't pay enough for her to live on her own. With Dom living with us, Kathy moved in with her biological dad. Personality-wise, it was like mixing oil and water.

Mentally saying, "maybe later" to the home office in my mind, I approached Barbara, with the possibility of having Kathy moving in with us. She liked the idea, too, although she knew it could be a potentially disastrous way to begin a new marriage.

In reality, what could have been a disaster turned into a win-win for everyone. Kathy was able to go back to school, earn her master's degree, and marry a wonderful young man. Living away from her dad gave them the time and space to mend their relationship. Living with us gave me the time to get to know Kathy in a way I wouldn't have otherwise. Watching this beautiful young woman grow into an empathetic, forgiving, hopeful adult has been an unbelievable joy. To think that I almost gave it up for a home office.

How does this situation relate to my current work? I think it's about keeping our minds open to possibilities. Kids can be quick to hold a grudge and slow to let go when they think they've been wronged. On the other hand, get them working and playing together and getting to know the person they're mad at, and nine times out of 10 they'll say, "Oh. That person really isn't so bad, after all." We give kids the opportunity to know each other on that level. We open them to the possibility of being friends with someone they might not normally be friends with—so that someday, when they're faced with the choice of office space or someone else's well-being, they won't even have to think twice.

The office will lose every time.

The White Dress

It is very difficult to write about death, much more so when it is about your daughter. Everything about me wants to deny the loss, to believe it has not happened or to figure out some way to bring her back. Alison is gone, however! Alison is gone, and the hole in my heart seems to get bigger with every passing day. On July 15, 2007, she died in her home, at the age of 43, after a long, courageous battle with brain cancer.

I have, as any parent would, many memories of my little girl. I see her hiding in my pastoral robe as I greet parishioners after Sunday services. I see her laughing as we try to beat our consecutive string of volleys across the tennis net. I watch with pride as she becomes one of the first girls to play on the boys' Little League team and as she continues to play co-ed softball, even as she fights for her life.

There is one story that I remember in particular. Alison loved to have her dad take her shopping for clothes. It was great fun. From her earliest years, she would try on outfits and parade in front of me, waiting for my reaction. Alison had great taste and always knew what she liked. On the other hand, she would "go along" with dad by modeling this and that to get my opinion, and dad would "go along," knowing that she knew what she wanted, no matter what I might like or think.

One year, when Alison was around 10 or 11, we were shopping in Mexico City. Alison knew exactly what she wanted to get—a white dress with colorful embroidery around the shoulders. Before we started on our shopping excursion, I explained to her how shopping went in Mexico—you bartered, and you bartered, always trying to gain the lowest possible price. I explained the process to her several times.

After visiting maybe a half a dozen shops, Alison found her dress. The salesman began doing his thing. "That will be 30 dollars, señor!"

I replied, "Twenty-seven?"

Back came his reply, "No, no."

I shook my head, implying that 27 dollars was already outside my budget.

"Twenty-five dollars?" the man suggested.

Ah. We were then getting somewhere. This time it was my turn to reply, "No, no." I noticed Alison getting a bit nervous, but I persevered. I could tell I was getting closer to the real price of the dress.

"Twenty-three dollars?" the salesman asked.

"Mmm … no, no," I said, convinced that the dress was probably only worth 10 dollars at most. However, Alison, scared that her dad was going to cheapskate her out of the most perfect dress in the world, began to cry. Caving, I told the salesman, "That will be fine." To this day, I wonder how much lower we could have gone.

When Alison died, my world, unfortunately, did not stop. My busy schedule forced me to think about other things. It also interfered with my work of mourning, so that even today, I continue to mourn. I am usually distracted throughout the day, but when night arrives, I grapple with trying to bring her back in whatever way I can.

I have learned that grief does not come with an expiration date. It was Robert Benchley who said, "Death ends a life, not a relationship." I am learning more and more about my daughter and myself, as I rethink and rethink our relationship almost daily.

My kids have always been keenly important to me, but I have always wondered if they know the depth of my feelings for them. With Alison, I no longer get to work on that.

I think the situation with Alison is just one of the many reasons I throw myself into my work with kids. It's not just about sports or fitness. It's about letting kids know that they ARE important—that someone cares about what they think and what they do. Someone wants them to be successful and happy in their lives. I hope they know that. And I hope that Alison knows that, too.

No Emotion

Sometime, after my daughter was diagnosed with a brain tumor in 2003, Barbara and I invited Alison and her husband, Keith, to join us on a Mediterranean cruise. It was a bittersweet time. Alison was on chemotherapy pills that made her nauseous and uncomfortable, plus, as a doctor, she probably had a better sense of what the rest of us were still in denial about—which is that her tumor would most likely kill her. Nevertheless, being the trooper that she was, she made it to all the port excursions, as well as to dinner every night. How happy I am that my wife and I were able to share this precious time with Alison and Keith.

I first met my daughter's future husband when they were students at Stanford. Keith, like me, played basketball for Stanford, becoming a two-time, honorable mention All-American, two-time conference scoring champion, and two-time all-conference selection. Like me, he was drafted by the pros (in his case, the Los Angeles Lakers), and also like me, he followed a different career path and is now a successful executive with Kaiser Permanente.

My knowledge, respect, appreciation, and love for him really grew after Alison's passing. When an event management company in Reston, VA (only a couple of miles from Keith and Alison's home in Fairfax) hired me as a management consultant, I spent every other week in D.C. for more than four years, doing my consulting work, conducting monthly workshops for the State Department's *Sports United* Program, and working with the Fairfax County Public School system. While there, I stayed with Keith and my grandson, Spencer, in the house where my daughter had once lived. I watched as Keith took upon himself the mantle of widower and single father.

Keith, Spencer, and I were each grieving the loss of Alison in our own way, and it was not an easy time. There were days when I thought that it would be impossible to survive such grief. Out of this adversity, however, came a deep and important connection between Keith and Spencer and our entire family. Keith and Spencer have joined us for our annual summer get-togethers, they came out to California for my step-daughter Kathy's wedding, and they were part of the family cruise we took at Thanksgiving.

Keith and I have the kind of relationship in which we may go days without talking to each other, and then have a four-hour, non-stop conversation about anything and everything. How many fathers-in-law are fortunate enough to be able to say that about the men their daughters marry? I count him not just as a son-in-law, but as a mentor, coach, and guide, who has kindly and patiently supported my journey with helpful insight on how to get from where I am at to where I wish to go.

Keith is going to be inducted into the Stanford Basketball Hall of Fame and has asked me to present him, but requested I do so with "no emotion." Frankly, that will be impossible. On the other hand, he and I have accomplished the impossible before.

Overtime

This is the "overtime" period of my life. I am almost 80 years old. I have battled prostate cancer, skin cancer, and heart issues, as well as an extremely painful and ongoing bout of shingles. I'm sure no one would hold it against me if I spent my remaining years playing dominos with my wife and sitting on the deck watching the sun set.

I can't do that, however. For better or worse, I still feel driven to make a difference, which has brought me to Leading2Play. This is the program that was begun in Alan Gregerman's office. Actually, it was probably begun the first day I ever set foot on a basketball court.

Leading2Play believes that kids, by working together, can tap into their unlimited potential and create opportunities for all of their peers to experience the magic of sport, the joy of lifelong physical activity, and the challenges and rewards of leadership.

Until now, all the stories in this book have focused on my personal experiences with family, friends, school, sports, and work. I've used these stories as tie-ins to various principles and lessons related to Leading2Play. In this final section, however, I'm going to be talking about the Leading2Play program. There will be some odds and ends ("shingles" comes to mind), but for the most part, I want you to learn more about the project that will probably be my last hurrah on this earth. I believe it is more than just another program. I truly believe that what I am doing now has the possibility of becoming a movement that can transform sports and education as we know it. More importantly, it holds the possibility of changing children's lives for the better.

I can think of no better legacy to leave.

Rookie Mistake

The first Leading2Play pilot program—initially called the "A-Games"—took place in Richmond, California, with a group of nine students from various schools in the San Francisco East Bay area. We spent eight months meeting in the basement of Salesian High School, while the kids worked on designing, developing, and implementing a community Sports & Play Day that was eventually held at a local park.

The kids were wonderful—attentive, interested, friendly. Our progress was slow, however. Painfully slow. It worried me. Were future Leading2Play activities going to be like this? Was I missing something? If so, what?

After much thought, it occurred to me that I had made a big mistake. For someone who talks so much about meeting kids "where they are," I really hadn't done that. I simply did not understand the context in which these young people were operating. "Sports and play" meant something entirely different to them and their peers than they did to me.

In contrast to my youth, kids were not outside riding bikes or playing basketball in the driveway. I had failed to notice this factor as I moved in and throughout Richmond.

No one was playing pickup games of football or baseball in yards, parks, or empty lots. Driveways were empty. Parks were empty. Yards were mostly non-existent. If kids were playing basketball, they were doing it indoors on their Wii™.

In my enthusiasm and eagerness to introduce fun and play to these kids, I overlooked the fact that they had little or no history of playing games or sports, which is why it took eight months to put together one community activity. It was simply another example of a teacher/leader not practicing what he preached. On the other hand, I learned several valuable lessons from the experience, including the following:

- All learning begins with prior knowledge. I needed to start with the kids, not with my preconceived ideas. What was their understanding of playing sports or games for fun? This factor should have been my starting point. I needed to get into and stay within their range of their learning environment. Less is more when youth or adults are unfamiliar with the subject. A few simple questions from me might have made a huge difference.
- Real learning only takes place when it provides the young person with the opportunity to make a connection between what is being taught and how it affects them. My role was supposed to be more of a guide or coach, rather than a source of knowledge and information. Unfortunately, that situation got switched around much too often to the detriment of the program.
- Taking in new information and ideas and really understanding them takes time—sometimes, at least eight months' worth.
- Context should have been used more abundantly. Instead of talking about the games and sports activities, we should have played those games. We should have taught in the context of what we eventually wanted to provide to others.
- Finally, I learned that while my goal was to work myself out of a job, I didn't do this undertaking as well as I should have. It was a rookie mistake. On the other hand, since I also teach that mistakes are valuable learning tools, this is one area where I DID practice what I preached.

Full Circle

In the 1980s, I got my first taste of non-profit work. I had just written my book, *How to Play the Game of Your Life*, and decided that it would be fun to put together a program that would help kids get the most out of their sports experience. As a result, Sports for Life was born.

Subsequently, I probably conducted more than 50 Sports for Life programs at various high schools throughout California and other parts of the country. In reality, however, I had clearly bitten off more than I could handle alone.

My former Stanford teammate, Dave Epperson, was on my initial board. While he was a good friend and supporter of my efforts, I think that he knew all along that I lacked the knowledge and experience to succeed.

As Sports for Life struggled for air (and people and money), Dave suggested that we narrow our efforts to focus on helping parents of athletes be better sports parents. Together, we wrote *From the Bleachers with Love: Advice to Parents with Kids in Sports, and Beyond the Bleachers: The Art of Parenting Today's Athletes.* We then created the Parents for Good Sports organization and "took our show on the road," so to speak. We had a great website, many programs, and a lot of people who seemed interested in what we had to offer. Eventually, however, I was the main guy in the field, and it simply wasn't enough to support my family.

With two failed non-profits under my belt, you'd think that I'd be hesitant about starting another one. I learned a lot from my previous efforts, however. As a result, I have a greater understanding of how to build a successful organization, including the amount of money it takes and the number and quality of people you need to have on your team.

I also learned that if you're going to throw your heart and soul into something, it needs to be something in which you believe. Not that I didn't believe in the work Dave and I were doing with sports parents, but my passion really lies in working with and making a difference for kids.

At this point, I have come full circle. I am back in the non-profit game once more. This time, however, I have improved my shot, and my bench is much deeper. The final horn has yet to go off, but when it does, I am hopeful that Leading2Play will be in the winning column.

A Good Day

My first meeting with Amika Guillaume, the dynamic principal of Cesar Chavez & Green Oaks Academy K-8th in East Palo Alto, had taken place early in November of 2012. Six weeks later, after meetings with the school's vice principal, physical education instructor, and a potential Leading2Play adult advisor, it was time to rendezvous with Amika and prepare for our next steps with the students and faculty.

As the appointment time approached, Sam Carver—the bright and energetic young man who was interning with us before starting college—and I sat excitedly outside of Amika's office, going over some final details. It was then time to meet with Amika.

I have to say that while there are a lot of meetings I don't enjoy, this wasn't one of them. With Amika taking the lead, we worked together to outline a program for her students.

We decided it would begin with a Student Leadership Training Program that would be held at the Four Seasons® Hotel. Since most of our training locales don't get more exciting than the school library, being able to bring the kids to such an upscale location would not only add to the fun of the training, but would also impress upon them the significance of the undertaking in which they were involved. We were fortunate that the hotel provides the school with a once-a-year opportunity to hold activities there, including a brunch for all of the participants.

We also decided the planning would center on recess opportunities, a summer program, and other potential opportunities, such as physical education and after-school programs. More specifically, it was suggested that the 7th and 8th grade student leadership team should select and promote games for their peers and younger school students, and follow a weekly practice of selecting and implementing games and activities—first for their classmates (fellow 7th and 8th graders) to develop confidence, and then to deliver and oversee the younger kids (3rd to 6th graders) participating in those games and activities. Finally, we agreed that the leadership team would meet Monday mornings at seven to plan the week's activities. I would be present, along with Sam and the school's adult advisor.

I left the meeting positively giddy at the thought of not only launching another Leading2Play site, but doing it with such incredible support. I was reminded once again that relationships, rather than programs, change lives. A program, however, can provide the opportunity and the environment for relationships to grow and develop.

Taxi Driver

While commuting to my consulting job in the Washington, D.C. area, I would often take a taxi from the airport to either my office in Reston, VA or my son-in-law's home in Fairfax. On one of those trips, as I sat in the back of the taxi, trying to check my phone for messages (it was a new phone, and I was still trying to figure out how to work the thing), the taxi driver asked, "And how was your flight?" Instead of replying, "Fine, thanks," and going back to my phone-wrestling, I decided to talk to the driver. What a brilliant decision on my part!

Instead of dealing with technology stress, my new friend and I had a delightful chat about world affairs, national issues, and other matters of interest. At the end of our conversation, the driver lamented the fact that most people are too busy with their cell phones to talk to him anymore. The thought that taxi drivers get bored with driving the same routes every day and actually like it when people to talk to them had never occurred to me. I just figured they were at work (at work *driving*, no less) and might not want to be distracted. In reality, it would appear that taxi drivers—like the rest of us—need to have that human connection.

I have thought a lot about that experience, as I encounter kids, teachers, school administrators, and potential contributors to the development of Leading2Play. While everyone seems to have something to say, few connect.

What do I mean by "connect"? In this context, it refers to the give-and-take that occurs on both a conscious and unconscious level. It includes the ability to identify with another person and relate to them in a way that improves or increases your influence with or impact on them. I've always loved the understanding of this factor, based on the Latin word *communis*, or "common." Connection is about creating a common ground, a situation in which people stand side by side. It involves more than words. It requires that we value the other person and bring our total presence to the encounter.

Connecting with another person goes beyond mere communication. When I think of this kind of connection, I get a mental picture of two railroad cars coming together. When the couplers engage, the identity of neither car is altered. On the other hand, they then have the power of two, instead of one.

Almost anyone can communicate, but connecting is a choice. It is a choice to which we are firmly committed at Leading2Play. We know it may mean putting down our cell phones for a few minutes, but the pay-off—being able to know what others know, feel, or want—is worth it. It was definitely worth the cost of a taxi ride.

Abrupt Ending

For over three years, I had been consulting on a bi-monthly basis for Professional and Scientific Associates (PSA), an events management and communications company based in Virginia. Not only did I like the work—executive and management coaching and training and leadership/career development—I enjoyed the relationships that I had with the employees. I also felt that I was making good progress in supporting the organization's efforts to transition into a more professional, competitive, and cutting-edge business. In addition, working for PSA gave me the opportunity to be with my son-in-law and grandson during and after the loss of my daughter, Alison.

As the threat of sequestration neared, however, the company lost a couple of major contracts. As a result, things quickly went from bad to worse. The annual retreat, which I was preparing to lead, was abruptly cancelled, and so was my consulting contract. Just like that, my work and life in the D.C. area ended.

Part of me was relieved to be able to spend more time at home with my wife and family and to put all of my energy into growing and developing Leading2Play. Part of me, however, was angry and hurt that I had not been consulted on this decision. I was also embarrassed at having been terminated, even if it was purely about money and not my performance.

I had been teaching people for years that we need to define success for ourselves and not fall into the trap of measuring our success by what other people think of us or want us to do. Getting fired made it hard to do that. On the other hand, I remembered what my old YMCA coach, Shorty Kellogg, taught about what it meant to be a champion. As a result, I picked myself up off the floor and continued moving forward.

I was disappointed, though, that I wouldn't be able to give the presentation I'd prepared for the retreat—a presentation that was an effort to summarize all I had learned in more than 60 years of working with people as a pastor, as a clinician, and as a corporate consultant. I realized, however, that the essence of that presentation is included in every aspect of what we do in Leading2Play. The key points include:

- Do we listen to learn or listen to defend? Whenever anyone opens their mouth, our response is either to learn or to defend. Listening and learning is still the number one sales/managerial tool, as well as the top priority for building relationships.
- The problem is never the problem. Because the problem is usually a symptom of a deeper issue or breakdown, we must dig deeper to resolve the conflict vs. simply treating the symptom(s).
- We can't afford to believe our own interpretations in the people business. If we do, we will not be open to the many other possibilities that are out there and will, in all likelihood, act upon our beliefs and fail to meet the other person where they are.
- You can't have two crazy people in the room at the same time. If the other person is being irrational, you have to give up your irrationality, or nothing but disaster will follow.
- Bath time is important. Not literal bath time, but time for quiet reflection. A solid 30 minutes a day (more if you can) recharges your mental juices and helps improve your creativity.

These are things we try to teach the students who lead Leading2Play, and they, in turn, share these lessons with their peers. Hopefully, these lessons will help them deal with—or avoid—abrupt endings in their future.

Far More Than a Gym

I've been blessed with some wonderful role models over the years, but I was not always aware of their importance at the time. It is different now. Accordingly, when a good friend of mine said, "You need to meet Gary Riekes—you two have a lot in common," I immediately set up an appointment.

Gary is the founder and executive director of the Riekes Center for Human Enhancement, a non-profit mentoring organization that is designed to help students define and accomplish their goals and interests through athletic fitness, creative arts, and nature awareness. Collectively, the organization strives to improve the character, self-confidence, and peer relationships of the more than 4000 kids who participate annually in its programs.

Gary and I have a lot in common. We both went to Stanford, we both have sports backgrounds, and we are both invested in helping kids. Our first meeting took place at the Riekes Center, where I was given a tour of the facilities. The tour began with introductions. The introductions, however, only consisted of first names. It was a subtle difference, but a very significant one for the simple reason that it created an immediate sense of familiarity.

A Leading2Play intern, who had previously been involved with the Riekes Center, shared a story with us that when he was a 12-year-old tour guide, one of his first tours was a father-son duo. I had been instructed by Gary to insist that everyone use their first names. As a result, when the father introduced himself as "Mr. Jones" (not his real name), I had to say, "Sorry, sir, but I need your first name."

"Mr. Jones is quite alright," the man said.

"No, sir, it isn't. I need your first name so we can begin the tour."

"Mike," He growled reluctantly.

I cite this example, because it sets the tone for the powerful culture of the Riekes Center. The tour, as with everything about the Riekes Center, is about making people feel at home. I was fascinated by the music rooms, the nature study rooms, the weight room, and more. For me personally, however, one of the highlights of the tour was the kitchen. Apparently, there is almost always someone in the kitchen, either making or eating a sandwich. It was subsequently explained to me that everyone has access to the kitchen and its food, with the only stipulation being that you leave it cleaner than when you arrived.

Since that initial meeting, Gary and I have been able to partner on several Leading2Play efforts. Gary likes to say that he comes away with something profound every time we meet, but I think it is the other way around. Gary has built a real community at the Riekes Center—a community people want to be part of. He has a masterful touch when it comes to working with kids, helping them pursue their dreams, and achieve their potential. Just as he has created a facility that is far more than a gym, he has been an example to me of how to create something that is far more than a program.

4 a.m. Wake-up Call

In January of 2013, I would climb in my car every day before 4 a.m. to make the 74-mile trip from my home to the campus of the National Hispanic University in San Jose. I would arrive at the local McDonald's® a few minutes after it opened, purchase my Egg McMuffin®, coffee, and *USA Today* and settle in for three hours of work, before heading over to conduct a Leading2Play Leadership class with 17 students from the Summit Prep High School. (In May, I did the whole thing all over again, in partnership with the Riekes Center for Human Enhancement.)

I don't know if it's going to make me healthy, wealthy, or wise, but I've definitely got a lock on the "early to rise" part of Ben Franklin's adage! What a wonderful experience it was, working with these young people as they put their newly learned leadership skills to use in designing, developing and implementing a Leading2Play activity.

At the conclusion of the month-long class, the leadership team proudly presented the *BALLIN' FESTIVAL!* This effort involved more than 300 who students participated in six different games, including a 3-on-3 basketball tournament, kick ball, capture the flag, dodge ball, tug-o-war, and a whipped cream gummy bear hunt (yes, that last one was as fun as it sounds). At the end, there were smiles and congratulations all around. As a result, those 4 a.m. mornings didn't seem half as bad as they did at the beginning.

What I learned from these kids is that life is short, and school is part of life. Furthermore, if we want kids to buy into the education process, then at least some portion of their school day needs to be meaningful for them. On the other hand, how do we structure the school day to meet the need for meaningful activities and experiences? We do this by engaging kids in the process.

In contrast to education that is imposed on kids by adults, we need to involve kids far more in both the process and the eventual experience of their education. In essence, we need to ask kids to help us learn how best to teach them, which is one reason why Leading2Play seeks to take direction from the youth who are involved, instead of the other way around. I think if I had been part of an educational system that encouraged me to do more critical thinking, as opposed to rote memorization and regurgitation of facts and dates, I would have been much better off in the long run. Furthermore, if they'd thrown in a gummy bear or two, well—so much the better!

Visionary

A while ago, a friend suggested that I read a book by Dennis A. Jacobson called *Doing Justice*. In it, the author quotes one of my favorite verses from Proverbs, which states, "Where there is no vision, the people perish." Jacobson, however, went on to add a crucial caveat: "… without organization, the vision perishes. Vision without organization is fanciful. Organization without vision is moribund. To become realized, a vision must be organized. To remain dynamic, an organization must be visionary."

The world is awash in visions that have never gone anywhere. Truth be known, half of them have probably been mine! As such, I am determined that the Leading2Play vision—"To create a youth-driven program that puts kids front and center in designing and carrying out fun, inclusive, and unique school and/or community-based health and fitness programs"—will be different.

Leading2Play is more than a vision. We are an organization acting to create a movement—a movement to give all kids, but particularly those who are left out of today's sports world for one reason or another, the opportunity to play and have fun now.

At Leading2Play, we believe in the unlimited potential of today's youth. They may dress differently than adults, watch different TV programs, see different movies, listen to different music, communicate in different ways, hang out in different places, and pay attention to different ideas and people, but they are committed to making the world a better place. They are also remarkable in the breadth of their diversity and appreciation for and comfortableness with each other.

Leading2Play is about hearing the voice of these kids and bringing them together through fun and friendly sports and fitness activities. These activities are not only designed to help kids have fun, but also to help them develop critical leadership, as well as organizational and social skills that will position them for the future.

Now that we are well into the new millennium, society has begun to recognize the seriousness of the issues that kids are dealing with today—issues like bullying, violence, obesity, and poverty. Finding solutions to these issues isn't an easy task. It requires vision and organization. With the help of some incredible advisors and partners, Leading2Play has been positioning itself as an organization that can offer viable, easily implemented solutions to many of these issues.

Recently, I was introduced to the music of the Indigo Girls. One of their songs goes, "My life is more than a vision. The sweetest part is acting after making a decision." I can say without hesitation that is true for me. Seeing Leading2Play blossom, from a vision to a reality that has already influenced the lives of hundreds of children, has been sweet, indeed.

All the Fun, None of the Worry

"Isn't this terrific?" I said to my daughter-in-law one day while watching my granddaughter's soccer game. It's amazing how much more fun and relaxing it is to watch your grandkids participate in sports versus the gut-wrenching anxiety that often came when my own children were out there. Furthermore, because there's less anxiety, I find I'm able to be more supportive of my grandchildren (and by extension, their parents).

The nice thing about being a grandparent is we can sit back and admiringly watch our grandkids play, without being concerned about whether they are winning or losing. We find it easier to say, "Did you have fun?" rather than "Did you win?" Just watching our grandkids be who they are, regardless of how they perform, is enough to evoke joy in the hearts of most grandparents. The grandparents I know who have grandchildren in sports seem to have more awareness that our primary function is to be "under-standing." That is, to stand under them, so that if they falter, we can be there to soften the fall.

Keeping in mind the potential of grandparents to positively influence the world of youth sports, I've come up with what I call "Golden Rules for Golden Oldies." These are things any grandparent (or senior citizen acting in a grandparent-type role) can do to improve sports for their grandkids and generations of children to come.

Golden Rules for Golden Oldies

1. Become a Senior Ambassador for Good Sports

The youth sports community needs all the wisdom and perspective it can muster. Many seniors have learned, through a lifetime of experience, the best way to support their grandkids, whether is in the living room, in a family setting, or after a sports outing, is to *be there* for their grandkids. Most seniors have matured to the point where they have developed *perspective*. They have learned when to take their grandchildren out of harm's way, and when to allow them to chart their own course so that they are able to get satisfaction from solving their own problems. I would like to suggest these seniors become ambassadors for *good sports*. They have the wisdom, patience, experience, and time to make a difference in the world of sports for kids.

2. Help Envision a Better Sport Future

Through our realization that we are not going to be on this earth forever, many grandparents, including me, start to evaluate what is really important in life. Why not use this wisdom to make the world of sports for kids a better place? We know that sports can inspire, educate, and unify. We also appreciate that, in most cases, sport is being underutilized as a tool for improving the life of our grandkids and their families. Sport can empower the main actors in the youth sports drama: kids, parents, coaches, and spectators. On the other hand, to realize this empowerment goal, it will be necessary for sports parents, with our counsel and support, to evaluate current and future sports policies and practices. They will need to determine how all of us, working together, can eliminate the toxic influences that threaten the spirits of our kids and their families.

3. Resist Offering Unsolicited Advice

It is essential for seniors who wish to contribute to the enhancement of youth sports to resist offering unsolicited advice. It is frequently difficult for any of us to use restraint when we think we know what is best for others. As senior ambassadors for good sports, however, we can be most effective when we direct the discussion with sports parents and their kids so that *they* consider the costs and benefits of the various solutions to the problems they are facing. Effective ambassadors for good sports are those individuals who have learned to draw solutions from all parties involved. We do that by being good listeners. Listening is one of the most underdeveloped skills in society. It is a problem for all generations. For seniors who understand that their extensive experience has given them an advantage in coming to grips with what is going on in the world, it can be especially difficult to resist the temptation to preach to younger people. To be effective, we must learn to listen to what is being said, to paraphrase what we hear, and then to raise questions that will provoke thoughtful answers.

As a "Golden Oldie" myself, I could restrict myself to sitting in the bleachers and cheering for my grandkids. There is nothing wrong with that. On the other hand, I like to think that I have the potential to do even more good by equipping myself with the sensitivity and the skills that allow me to work effectively with youth in Leading2Play to promote and achieve a vision of sports, play, and fitness that will benefit all.

Shingles

About halfway through this book and in the middle of working almost 24/7 to bring Leading2Play to reality, I started feeling some pain in my right arm and shoulder. At first, I thought it was just a sore muscle. The symptoms then got worse—like "heart attack" worse. Since I have a history of heart disease, I was sent to the hospital and subsequently released. No heart problem!

That was the good news. The bad news is that I continued to get worse. The pain spread to other locations, and eventually a red rash appeared on my face, neck, and chest. The diagnosis: shingles.

Let me just say that everything you may have heard about shingles is true. They hurt. They really, really hurt. At this writing, it's been nine months, and the pain shows no sign of abating. The pain pills they've given me just make me nauseous and sleepy. Apparently, the only real cure is complete rest—which is simply not going to happen.

In reality, this book would lack a lot of integrity if I didn't admit that I've spent too many years and made too many decisions in my life without paying attention to the unconscious self that is now telling my conscious self that I need to slow down or—horrors—go on the "disabled list."

If we are to know ourselves well, we must be aware of our unconscious, as well as our conscious self. Although I have done a great deal of counseling, initially as a pastor and then later as a psychotherapist, I must admit that my own therapy had more to do with getting me through some particular crisis in my life, rather than exploring my unconscious and discovering some things about myself with which I may not have been ready to deal. It is only as the months have turned into years that I have begun to open a corridor between the conscious and the unconscious, and the two selves have begun to become collaborators.

Why is this factor important? Well, we all know that knowledge is power. This point applies to internal knowledge, as well as the ability to add one plus one and come up with two. What we are aware of empowers us, and what we are unaware of controls us. Awareness should be a priority, then, because it drives what we can control, versus those issues or realities about which we are unaware, which tend to exert control over us. The critical issue is how does this principle apply to Leading2Play?

Leading2Play doesn't just work on activities to keep kids physically fit. It also strives to keep them mentally fit by helping them discover the importance of self-discovery and self-awareness. As a result, by the time THEY hit their late-70s, they're relaxing on a beach somewhere, instead of complaining about how much their shingles hurt. (Did I mention they hurt A LOT?)

Getting Real!

As part of our Leading2Play effort in San Jose, I held a two-month leadership class with 17 absolutely wonderful high school students who attend two charter schools (Tahoma and Rainer) that are located on the campus of the National Hispanic University. I was part of a team of three teachers, with the other two being very bright, capable individuals. As usual, I wondered what I could possibly bring to the party.

My first thought was to share tips, tricks, and techniques that would help these kids stay awake in their classrooms. After all, staying awake seems to be half the battle in school these days. Then I decided to do something different. I decided to share with the group what was happening with me as I was working with them. I guess you could say I got "real."

Yes, we talked about the list of things that I had already come up with that I thought would apply to them as members of what I call the "iY" generation (with the "I" standing for all the technology they're exposed to, as well as the fact that as a generation, they're a little bit spoiled). As we talked about artificial maturity versus real maturity, however, the dangers of relying too much on technology to communicate, the trend toward permanent adolescence, and other subjects I hoped would give them some insight into successfully navigating the path from youth to adulthood, we also talked about:

- The constant and sometimes almost unbearable pain I was experiencing with shingles.
- How I spent 12 years attending world-class universities and never learned a thing, because I had not learned how to be responsible for my own education.
- My own issues in the long and still-continuing journey to becoming a complete person.
- My hopes and dreams for Leading2Play—how it began as one person's project and how it will hopefully grow into a movement that involves many, many people.

Finally, I told the students that the most important conversations they will ever have in life are with themselves. While I did not have any new ideas concerning how to do that, other than the familiar ones (silence and reflection, taking long walks, reading, keeping a journal, finding a friend who would listen), I hoped these ideas would move them in the right direction. I ended by saying, "This will not fix you, but it will help you to be a friend to yourself at a deeper level, as well as to cultivate a sense of identity and integrity that will allow you to feel at home with yourself, even as it has for me in this late stage of my life."

I have had to learn the hard way the benefits of personal insight. I'm sure these young people will have to learn many things the hard way, too. That's part of life. Hopefully, however, their participation in Leading2Play means that they'll be a little bit smarter about the journey than I was. After all, if technology can evolve and improve over the generations, why can't people?

The Difficulty of Doing Good

As I walked back to my car, it occurred to me that I probably hadn't been the best date Bob Leet had ever had. I had met Bob about six months earlier at a lunch arranged by my former Stanford classmate Charles "Jiggs" Davis, and we'd had several meetings since then. Bob had many years of experience in the financial industry, specializing in consulting with owners and manager of small to mid-sized businesses—a skill set I definitely lacked and much needed.

It's not like I didn't have anything positive to report to Bob. Good things were happening with our Virginia pilot sites. We'd established a partnership with the Riekes

Center for Human Enhancement, and had a field trial lined up at Helms Middle School near my home. On the other hand, I still needed to complete the curriculum packages before school started. In addition, the paperwork needed to be done to establish our non-profit status. Furthermore, we were still recruiting a board of directors and a team of advisors, and so on. Oh, and I kept dipping deeper and deeper into my savings to compensate staff without whom I couldn't move forward.

As I drove home I thought, "All I want is to do something good in the world. Why does it have to be so hard?" I worried that maybe I had come across as a bit of a Debbie Downer to Bob, so the next day I sent him an e-mail:

> *Bob—thanks for yesterday! It is always enjoyable and helpful to spend time with you. I must apologize for being a bit down, tired, and discouraged. I certainly hope it didn't undermine your energy for this most amazing potential effort.*
>
> *Until next time,*
>
> *George*

Bob replied later that day:

> *George—it did feel as though you were a bit short of energy and your usual enthusiasm yesterday, but I am not surprised. I always appreciate the opportunity to visit, given that I gain a better understanding of Leading2Play on every occasion.*

Bob went on to suggest several answers to my question of why doing good isn't always easy:

- It can be a lonely journey. For me, Leading2Play is something I live and breathe. It's the culmination of a life-long commitment to helping kids, adults, and families grow and develop as human beings. On the other hand, just because Leading2Play is the most important priority in MY day doesn't mean that it holds the same importance for others.

- Not everyone wants to collaborate with kids. The good news about Leading2Play for school and community organizational leadership is that it adds no significant additional effort to their already busy schedules. The bad news is that collaborating with kids—which is at the heart of Leading2Play—means that adults must be supporters and cheerleaders who respect and appreciate the efforts of youth. Sadly, many adults continue to hold negative stereotypes about the capabilities of teenagers.

- Not everyone wants to try something new. Just as some people would rather put their money into a bank account with a low, but guaranteed, interest rate versus investing in a risky stock with the potential for higher returns, there are people who would prefer not to rock the boat and think the way things have been done for the past 20, 30, or 40 years worked just fine for them and their kids, so why should we change anything?

- Not everyone "gets" how tremendous the potential contribution of Leading2Play to kids and society is. As Bob said, it may be quite clear to me, but may be less so to others. The challenge is to convey our vision and mission in such a way that people do "get it" and want to be part of it. Unfortunately, with so many other programs fighting for people's attention, that is not an easy task.
- People are burned out. The access to cosmic amounts of information (no, I am not condemning the Internet to eternal damnation) means that we have become so besieged by the world's sufferings that the act of giving one more iota of our resources can seem to be a herculean task.
- Finally, it's hard to be patient. When things don't happen fast enough—when a person you're trying to help keeps sliding back into bad habits, or when a potential funding source turns you down—it can be easy to get frustrated and give up. John Wooden used to tell his players, "Be quick, but don't hurry." You have to be quick in basketball, but if you don't have the patience to set up plays and wait for openings (in other words, if you hurry), you make mistakes, and you lose games.

All of the aforementioned are very valid reasons why it can be difficult to push forward as we try to make a positive difference in the world. It is important to remember, however, that they are only reasons—not excuses to stop trying.

Get Uncomfortable

Almost every day, I'll find myself walking through Pinole Park or shooting hoops at my local 24-Hour Fitness Center or working with a Leading2Play program at a school. At some pint, I often come across a kid or group of kids struggling to correctly shoot a basketball.

That's when my innate shyness does battle with my desire to see kids succeed. The latter usually wins out as I approach the youngster(s) in question and ask, "Would you like me to help you with your shot?" I am seldom greeted with eagerness. Usually, I am greeted with a look that clearly says, "Why is this old guy bothering me?"

If they humor me, I will ask the shooter to stand about three feet from the basket, place the ball in one hand, and with the elbows in and the ball touching their fingers and free from their palms, push the ball toward the basket. If they follow my directions, within minutes, they will start making baskets. After they've succeeded at this suggestion, I show them how to use their unused arm and hand to position the ball in preparation for their shot.

My success rate is almost 100 percent with the kids who are willing. Too often, however, I am met with resistance. "It feels uncomfortable," is the standard response. Of course, it feels uncomfortable! It's supposed to! In any endeavor in life, if we want to reach our potential, we need to be willing to step outside our comfort zone.

Dealing with discomfort enables what psychology professor Mihaly Csikszentmihalyi calls a "flow experience." He describes flow as that state when our confidence in our abilities equals the challenge we face. If the challenge appears too much, we experience anxiety, maybe even panic. When the challenge is beneath us, we get bored. On the other hand, when we are close to a balance, we experience a good, fun challenge.

On a larger scale, Leading2Play aims to create what Malcom Gladwell in his 2002 book *The Tipping Point* calls a "social epidemic"—in our case, a youth-driven sports, health and fitness program. It involves working hard for a long time, often with little discernible impact, and then, suddenly, tipping. The tipping point is that magic moment when an idea, trend, or social behavior crosses a threshold, tips, and spreads like wildfire.

Tipping is inherently uncomfortable, whether it's falling off a ladder or feeling overwhelmed by daily challenges. Unwillingness to endure that discomfort can prevent us from reaching our goals. For Leading2Play to reach its tipping point, dealing with discomfort is part of the journey. That's why, just as I sometimes have to push myself to help kids I don't know make a decent basket, I also have to push myself to walk up to someone I've never met—such as former San Francisco mayor Willie Brown—and introduce myself and Leading2Play. All factors considered, you never know when that little push is going to cause something to tip.

Seven Empty Courts

It was a beautiful gym with, among other things, EIGHT basketball courts. Its spaciousness, bright lighting, and colorful décor were proudly pointed out by the manager of the facility who was leading the tour. As we walked through the facility, something caught my eye. On one court, there were eight players (pretty good players, by the looks of them) who were having a great time trading baskets, kidding around, doing some friendly trash-talking, and clearly having fun with each other.

The other seven courts, however, only had—at most—a few players on them. There were no games, no talking, no interaction—just individuals with decidedly fewer playing skills, as well as, in my opinion lacking the confidence and the experience to get a game going. That picture has never left me as I have continued my efforts to develop Leading2Play.

A well-regarded teacher once said that he didn't spend too much time focusing on the smart kids, because smart kids are going to do what they're going to do—which is pay attention, do their assignments, participate, and get good grades. He also didn't spend excess time on the trouble-makers, because they, too, were going to do what they were going to do. Furthermore, if he taught well, they would, hopefully, decide to drop the attitude and learn. What he DID focus on were the quiet kids—the ones who didn't get noticed much. Those were the kids that he felt he could really influence.

One of the most powerful and persuasive things we have to offer one another as human beings is to listen and pay attention. When we choose to listen to kids, we give them one of our most cherished resources—our time. This factor alone is a powerful symbol of our intentions toward them. By listening, we affirm their worth and communicate in a clear manner that they matter. In the process, we fulfill their basic need to be understood and to feel important.

At Leading2Play, our goal is to give our full attention to those other seven courts—to the kids who might be hanging back, because they don't have great sports skills or they're a little shy. Regardless of how great your facility is, seven empty courts is seven too many.

Not My Problem

It was an encouraging beginning. I had just met with the principal of a large suburban high school in Northern California. The principal, a former physical education teacher, was excited about Leading2Play. He loved the idea of his students being front and center in designing and carrying out the activities. He and his enthusiastic athletic director quickly agreed that we should work together to recruit a leadership team and initiate a lunchtime program.

With momentum on my side, I said, "Let's talk about after-school possibilities." Immediately, the principal responded, "That's a problem. We don't have after-school transportation. These kids all have their own cars, ride with friends, or are picked up by their parents."

I quickly replied, "That's not our problem!" Noting the puzzled expression on the faces of the principal and athletic director, I continued: "The problem belongs to the kids."

Adults have set the bar far too low when it comes to the ability of youth to learn and use leadership skills. Leading2Play believes kids come alive when they are given responsibilities and when they can help each other. We believe that within every kid, there is an innate drive and yearning to grow and mature, to become capable and responsible, and to fulfill his or her highest potential.

I once came upon this statement in a brochure, announcing a national conference on teaching and learning:

IT'S A FACT

Many students have no direction and lack motivation. These students have little knowledge of the social skills necessary for teamwork and negotiation. They're bored and passive in situations calling for action, and belligerent and destructive in contexts requiring reflection.

I don't think that the statements in the brochure are true at all. I believe that kids are a tremendous untapped and underestimated resource. In any number of ways, they are an asset that can help our schools and communities meet the ongoing challenges that exist in society today. Young people are not brain-dead, as some would argue. They simply have been marginalized in our society.

The unique power and success of Leading2Play stems from the fact that youth are not marginalized—they are the ones in charge. They drive the design of Leading2Play activities. They create sustained fun and engagement. They make a commitment to inclusiveness, affordability, and adaptability. Leading2Play programs succeed because students, not adults, develop, implement, and actively manage their own experience. Furthermore, on occasion their role includes figuring out how to get people to and from an after-school activity.

It's All About the Dollars

I had just attended a four-hour planning session for an upcoming intercession program at two public charter public schools in East San Jose. It was an impressive meeting. About 30 people were in attendance. Administrators and teachers were well-prepared, organized, and professional. Their presentations were informative and helpful. The energy in the room was obvious. Excellent questions were raised, and equally impressive answers were given. The school's administration had done a bang-up job of detailing what they expected of the students, teachers, and community providers.

Something was troubling me, however, on my long drive home that afternoon. In the entire four hours, there had not been a single mention or minute of time spent on what the students might want. What I wanted to know was, "How come?" Clearly, everyone at the meeting cared deeply about young people and was committed to them.

I was eager to talk with Barbara about it, figuring that with her background in early childhood education, she might be able to help me understand. The next evening, after sitting down to our customary game of dominos, I presented my concern. Boy, did I get an earful in response!

"George," she said, "it's a systemic problem. Though administrators and teachers would love to listen to the voices of their students in planning and carrying out their responsibilities to educate them, they don't make the decisions on what takes place in their schools. The legislators determine that, and they are mostly men who do not have a developmental perspective. They dole out the money, and they say what it will be used for. At no time, do they consider the voice of kids. It is all about the dollars. Teachers know the importance of the early years and the superiority of a student-centered curriculum. We know that we could probably be much more successful if we listened to the kids and allowed them to tell us what works for them. Unfortunately, the legislators are telling us what to teach!"

After listening to Barbara, the challenge teachers and kids face became much clearer to me. We live in a culture that increasingly insists success is about numbers—test scores, graduation rates, salaries. On the other hand, we know that success is multi-faceted and includes a wide range of skills and character traits, such as integrity, creativity, and cooperation—things that aren't easily measured. We also know that students need to be *engaged* in the education process. In reality, however, neither measurable nor hard-to-measure goals can be achieved if kids are bored, apathetic, hostile, tuned-out, or otherwise disengaged.

The aforementioned is why listening to the kids, working *with* them, and letting them drive their own learning process is probably the most important part of Leading2Play. Yes, we want kids to get moving, be active and healthy, and learn leadership skills. None of that will happen, however, at least not on a long-term basis, if the kids aren't the ones behind the process. In Leading2Play, it's not all about the dollars. It's all about the kids.

The Ultimate Open-Book Exam

One day, I was having coffee with an old friend. After catching up on work, family, and relationships, my friend turned to me with a serious look and asked, "So, George, how would you sum up your life experience?" It was a pretty heavy question, but fortunately one for which this book had prepared me. My response was that life was something I pretty much had to learn as I went along.

There is a book by Tina Seeling, executive director of the Stanford Technology Ventures Program, in which she identifies life as "the ultimate open-book exam." That description struck me as pretty apt.

Of course, this description is a huge contrast to my actual educational experience. In reality, we rarely, if ever, had open-book exams. Instead, we were required to read, study, and memorize the material beforehand so that we could regurgitate it at an appropriate time, when the tests were passed out. That was the kind of education I excelled at, since I usually had some idea of what was expected of me.

In contrast, life has been totally different. I have had to become my own teacher (which took me a long time to figure out), charged with determining what I needed to know, where to find the information, and how to absorb it. I have also had to learn to tap into the myriad of resources waiting to be recognized and utilized, as I have faced endless challenges and problems related to my work, family, friends, and the world at large.

My school tests were typically multiple-choice, with one right answer for every question. In life, however, there is usually more than one answer to every question, as well as more than one of which can be correct. In reality, facing so many choices can be overwhelming. While other individuals can offer their advice and support, it is essentially our responsibility to pick our own direction. What I have learned is that we don't have to be right the first time. In school, failing was not acceptable. In life, however, failure is what helps us learn. Failure, or making a choice that doesn't work out, isn't the end of the world. A number of opportunities to experiment and recombine our skills and passions exist. My failures, as well as my successes, are what have helped create Leading2Play.

Personally, I hope the "open-book" theory is something Leading2Play participants take away from the program. That way, when they're sitting in a coffee shop years from now, they'll be prepared when a friend asks them, "So, how would you sum up your life experience?"

Dear Coach Lapchick—Get Me Out of Here!

In March 1947, tiny Holy Cross College, with an enrollment of 1,400 men, won the NCAA Division I men's basketball championship. Playing a key reserve role on the team was a freshman who went on to become one of the greatest players in basketball history. Due to a combination of homesickness and his feeling that he should have played more minutes during the just completed season, the freshman wrote a letter to legendary St. John's University coach, Joe Lapchick. In his letter, the freshman relayed his unhappiness at Holy Cross, and asked Coach Lapchick if he could transfer to St. John's, located only a few miles from his home.

A decade later, this former freshman, who at the time was the most valuable player in the NBA, shared Coach Lapchick's response in his book, *Basketball Is My Life*:

Dear Bob,

You're not in college primarily to play basketball, but to get an education, and you're getting a very good one at Holy Cross. If you should transfer to St. John's, you wouldn't be gaining anything in that respect. Your coach at Holy Cross, Doggie Julian, is one of the finest basketball coaches in America, and someday you'll be proud you've played for him. He doesn't want to hurt you and isn't doing so deliberately. I know he is depending heavily on you in future years, and would be very much upset if he knew how you felt. Aside from everything else, transferring from one college to another is, at best, a risky move. You don't know if you're going out of the frying pan into the fire. And college rules dictate that you must wait a year before being eligible for varsity competition. This would hardly make it worthwhile for you. Be patient. You're only a freshman. Your turn will come. Stay at Holy Cross. You'll never regret it.

Sincerely,

Joe Lapchick

The restless freshman was Bob Cousy, who went on to become a star with the Boston Celtics, playing on six NBA championship teams and leading the league in assists eight years in a row. On many occasions, Bob expressed his appreciation for Coach Lapchick's advice and his great admiration for Lapchick's act of principle. (From *The Encyclopedia of Sports Parenting*, by Dan Doyle with Deborah Burch)

Several times a week, I pull my weary, arthritic body together and head for the gym to exercise. I start out on the treadmill and then eventually wander downstairs to find a pick-up game—preferably half-court. I like half-court. Not only is it easier on the knees, there is less opportunity for guys to go coast-to-coast and fire a three-pointer—because let me tell you, after a while that gets boring. On occasion, it seems that it's all the younger players want to do. From youth sports to pro sports, it is hard to find players who understand that *Sports Center* is about entertainment, and that sport itself is about participating, testing your skills, enjoying the experience, and learning from it. These are called "life lessons." Frankly, I don't believe kids are learning them as much as they should or could be.

One of the things that I'm developing with the leadership team of kids, who are primarily responsible for running Leading2Play in their school or community organization, is a series of "leadership papers" that are designed to help them reflect upon the skills it takes to become a good leader. The following is an example of one of these papers:

The Leadership Papers

Skill: Self-discipline

> *"We are what we repeatedly do;*
> *excellence then is not an act, but a habit."*
> —Aristotle

Definition:
self·dis·ci·pline: Correction or regulation of oneself for the sake of improvement

Questions to Think About:
1. Who:
   • Who are some people I can think of who have a lot of self-discipline?

2. What:
   • What is something that is hard for me to be self-disciplined about?

3. Where:
   • Where do I need to show self-discipline in order to be a good leader?

4. When:
   • When are some times when being self-disciplined has paid off for me?

5. Why:
   • Why do self-discipline and hard work go hand-in-hand?

6. How:
   • How can I encourage others on my team to be self-disciplined?

My goal, as it is with just about everything I do, is to help kids experience various life lessons. For example, they need to realize that physical activities, such as sports, fitness, athletics, and running around until you're a ball of dripping sweat, are fun. Each of these lessons can be so much more than what they appear to be on the surface. Like Bob Cousy, for example, kids can learn the value of hard work and patience—a lesson that will stay with them long after they've lost the ability to run a full-court press.

I Dreamed a Dream

Even though I graduated from college more than 50 years ago, I still have this recurring nightmare, where I'm back at school during finals week, and I can't remember what final I'm supposed to be taking or where the classroom is. It's a very aggravating, frustrating, and anxiety-laden dream.

Although I trained as a psychotherapist, I did not go through psychoanalysis or gain expertise in dream interpretation in my career. I do, however, understand that recurring dreams are quite common and are often triggered by specific life situations, such as a transition, a personal weakness, fear, conflict, or an inability to cope with something in our lives.

At the same time, I believe that dream interpretation is a very inexact science. We need to be careful in our attempts to make sense of and learn from our dreams. That being said, I accept the fact that events and emotions in our waking lives trigger our dreams. As such, a recurring dream is our subconscious trying to send us a message and reveal some valuable insights.

School is a popular dream locale, because the dynamics of the school setting continue throughout our lives. School is where we first learned the importance of being on time and meeting deadlines. It is where we learned how to prepare and "do our homework." It is where we learned how to deal with scrutiny, how to move up the ladder, and how to fit in. It's where we learned many of our basic work and social skills. School dreams are most often connected to our work life and, on a lesser basis, our social and family life.

The question arises concerning what do I make of my rushing around the halls looking for a class that I can't find, because I do not know its name, and consequently, where it meets?

I am pretty much convinced that my school-centered dream about being lost, unprepared, uncertain, and vulnerable has its basis in guilt. Depending on when the dream occurs, I am probably feeling undeserving of my achievement or else feeling that I'm not doing enough and letting others down. Guilt. It gets us all.

Healthy guilt is connected to objective transgressions, such as breaking the law or breaking an internalized code of conduct. If you walk into a department store and walk out with an unpaid-for object under your jacket, you will probably feel a healthy sense of guilt. If you don't, then you have a bigger problem than shoplifting. On the other hand, if you feel sick to your stomach for getting a B+ instead of an A on a test you studied very hard for, then you have unhealthy guilt. Unhealthy guilt, as analyst Selma Fraiberg wrote, behaves "like a Gestapo headquarters, with the personality mercilessly tracking down dangerous ideas and every remote relative of these ideas, accusing, threatening, tormenting in an interminable inquisition to establish guilt for trivial offenses or crimes committed in dreams. Such guilt feelings have the effect of putting the whole personality under arrest."

I have no doubt that I will continue to experience feelings of unpreparedness, uncertainty, and vulnerability in whatever activities I undertake—whether it's preparing Leading2Play for a new school or preparing to go on vacation. I've come to learn that's just the way I'm built. I also know that when I have these dreams, I need to sit up and pay attention. My dreaming mind puts me back in school, because it wants me to succeed in life, as well as wants me to shed the unhealthy guilt that threatens to keep me from moving forward and pursuing my real-life dreams.

In Leading2Play, we don't get into dream interpretation (although that might make for a very interesting session). We do. However, talk about how important it is to know yourself—to be able to look within and confront what you find, no matter how difficult it is. It is only then that we learn the really wonderful things about ourselves, in addition to the things we need to work on to succeed in life. We learn that it's vital to have dreams—dreams of being able to sink a free throw, or of making the winning shot, or of owning your own team someday. Our dreams—both conscious and unconscious— are what drive us and make life worthwhile. Understanding them is very important. Understanding our dreams enables us to understand ourselves.

I Only Know One Way to Play the Game

My bout with shingles has put me in an extremely emotional state—probably the most emotional I've been since losing my daughter almost six years ago. It's very frustrating— just as Leading2Play appears to be taking off. Placing a heavy demand on my time and energy, my shingles show no sign of abating. According to my physicians, I am currently experiencing postherpetic neuralgia, which manifests itself in pain, headaches, and nerve problems that last anywhere from 30 days to several years. The pain associated with postherpetic neuralgia makes it difficult to eat, sleep, and perform daily activities. It can also increase my risk for depression, which explains why I was not comforted when my wife commented, "Well, George, maybe you won't be able to work and go all out like you've done all your life."

My visceral reaction to Barbara's remarks was, "But, I only know one way to play the game!" I feel like there is so much unfinished business I still need to … well, finish.

I worry that I might not have resolved all my issues with my boys. They know they are deeply loved and respected, but have we put to rest past disappointments and failures? Furthermore, what about Alison? Did I leave anything on the table before her passing? What about friendships and other relationships—like the one between Barbara and me—that I feel are just getting started?

I don't want to stop and smell the roses. I want to plant the bulbs, grow the flowers, and maybe even invent a new species or two. No wonder, I'm not always the easiest person to live with. I am driven. I fully admit it. I think that I'd like to learn how to be less driven—I just don't want to do it right now. Without question, I certainly don't want to be forced into it.

Most of all, I worry about Leading2Play. If I slow down—or stop completely—what will happen to it? On the other hand, as Cesar Chavez once remarked, "If your mission can be accomplished in your lifetime, it probably wasn't big enough." The goal of Leading2Play is to touch the life of every child in this country, and maybe beyond. That's a pretty big mission. Realistically, I know it won't be accomplished in my lifetime. Since I only know one way to play the game, it's not going to stop me from trying.

The Journey

If you're reading this page right now, one of the main reasons is because a colleague of mine suggested that I ought to write a book introducing Leading2Play. To which, I rather defensively answered, "No way! I started Leading2Play, because I didn't want to write another book. Not only do relatively few people read my books, the darn things never end up paying for themselves!" A week later, I began writing. So much for famous last words.

At this point in this book, I'm almost done. I will be happy to stop getting up in the middle of the night to write down a thought, or arriving at my desk by 4 a.m. to get some writing in before my REAL workday starts, or pushing the "stop" button on the treadmill because there are only so many hours in a day. Yes, finishing this book will feel wonderful. It is important to remember, however, as several friends who have climbed Mr. Everest have shared, it's not standing on the summit of the mountain that they really learn from. It's the journey to the top.

I have definitely learned more from writing this book than I will gain by finishing it. In reviewing my scrapbooks, talking with friends, taking long walks, discussing thoughts with my wife, and reflecting more deeply and realistically than any time previously in my life, my perspective has been transformed. I have seen my childhood and adolescence with fresh eyes and a more open and forgiving heart. I have begun to embrace my achievements, rather than focusing on my limitations. I am learning how the experiences of my life are gifts that have helped me grow and develop and have prepared me for making the most of my time in this game of life, where the clock is always running, and there are no time-outs.

Journeys are always about much more than just movement from one place to another. Journeys are about learning and growth. They have the potential, as I have discovered, to teach people about themselves and the society in which they live.

I hope that the kids who participate in Leading2Play understand the aforementioned point about journeys. While the end result may be a community sports and play day or a school-wide ballin' festival or something exciting like that, the real value of being part of Leading2Play—whether they're part of the leadership team or just participants in the activities—is what they learn along the way. It's the growth they experience. It's the friends they make. It's the journey.

Seeing Fish

One time I was invited to take a fishing trip in Canada. It was a totally new experience for me. At our first stop, my host said, "Tell me what you see." I told him I saw a beautiful lake with the sun reflecting off the surface of the water. He then asked, "Do you see any fish?"

I looked a little harder, wondering if I was missing something. Nope. No fish. At that point, my friend then handed me a pair of polarized sunglasses and said, "These will help." Immediately, everything looked dramatically different. With the sun's glare removed, I looked at the lake and discovered I could see through the water. I could also see fish—a lot of fish. Suddenly, I could see enormous possibilities that I hadn't seen before. Although those fish had been there all along, until I put on the glasses, they were hidden from my view.

The aforementioned situation is, perhaps, the best way that I can illustrate my experiences in developing Leading2Play. Today, I see possibilities that I never knew existed two years ago. In addition to being a way to outsource physical education and athletics in our cost-strapped schools, I've learned that Leading2Play also holds the possibility to become:

- A program to meet kids' need to be heard. I am currently working directly with two K-8 leadership teams, one 7th/8th grade leadership team and two 9th-11th grade leadership teams. My experience has reinforced my perspective that teenagers need to feel they are being heard in order to move forward. Too often, I see and hear students who are used to being told what to do. It doesn't matter how well-intentioned the speaker may be, the young people I encounter daily are dying for an adult in their life who listens to them.
- An alternative for the kids who do not *fit* (i.e., have a place) in our current sports system. Leading2Play provides the opportunity for sports, fitness, and play for all kids, regardless of their athletic ability. This environment helps to offset the 75 to 85 percent of kids who drop out of sports by age 13, as well as the kids who don't get enough physical activity because of diminished physical education requirements in the schools, and those kids who, for whatever reason, never gave sports a try.

- A way for kids to become owners, rather than renters, in their educational experiences. There are a lot of kids who do not care about school and drop out, because they are not engaged in the process. They either find school meaningless or see each stage of schooling as a mere preparation for the next stage. School has to *mean* something to kids for them to succeed at it. Leading2Play is about helping kids to discover the possibilities inside and outside the walls of their schools, communities, and homes and to guide them in piecing together not just who they are, but who they can become.
- A chance for kids to develop their leadership skills. In three separate conversations with school administrators (one superintendent and two principals), the one thing they've all said they like about Leading2Play is that it gives an opportunity to kids who want to lead, but who may not be the usual "leadership types" who get selected for everything. On one hand, maybe, they're a little on the quiet side. On the other hand, maybe, their grades haven't always been the greatest. In Leading2Play, it doesn't matter. If you want to become a leader, you can. Furthermore, maybe that one opportunity is all it takes to help them become leaders in their schools, their communities—even their country. You just never know. The possibilities are as beautiful as a clear, blue lake full of fish.

Saying Goodbye

As this book draws to a close, my thoughts naturally turn to my daughter, Alison. Alison died of brain cancer on July 15, 2007 at her home in Fairfax, VA, at the age of 43. I still miss her every day. While I have not been in a coma of sorrow, I have experienced more than simple grief. I think the grief will never disappear. It is a chronic disease that exists within my body.

Every morning, I wake up to pictures on the dresser only inches from my side of the bed: Alison in her wedding dress. Alison with her two brothers. Alison with Spencer, her only child. While on the Stanford campus not long ago for a meeting with a visiting professor, I passed a grove of beautiful giant redwoods and a particular bench where Alison and I had once sat and visited.

The memories came flooding back. Like most fathers of daughters, Alison was the apple of my eye, the joy of my life. I remember her hiding in my robes at the conclusion of worship service, as members of the congregation and I greeted each other. I remember her days as one of the first girls to play Little League baseball with guys and her high school days, where she was voted the athlete of the year over everyone else in the school. Alison had a lifelong love of sports. She played on the boys' junior varsity baseball team in high school and excelled in tennis. She played on the women's softball team at Stanford, as well as on a variety of intramural and community teams. She coached Spencer's Little League team. So many memories.

I believe memories choose us for a reason. They tap us on the shoulder and say, "Pay attention to me—I want to give you something deep and important." Alison was and continues to be a model to me. Her courage, wisdom, understanding of life and the world, sensitivity to others, honest communication, and sense of personal responsibility instruct me daily. They also call me to be a better person than I would be otherwise.

My kids have always been keenly important to me. I never wanted to miss a ballgame or any other event they participated in, but of course, I did. I have always wondered if they know the depth of my feelings for them. With Alison, I no longer get to work on that.

My daughter was beautiful, strong, and independent. She believed in me, even when I didn't believe in myself. She, who was always so caring and concerned about others, would love Leading2Play. And I, who loved her so very, very much, wish I could share the experience with her.

The Final Chapter

A lot of pressure exists when you write a book to make the last chapter the best one. Mozart used to say that you've got to end with a bang so that people will know you're through. Fortunately, I think I can do that. My final story is about my wife, Barbara.

We first met at a restaurant in Oakland, near Jack London Square. I was early, as usual, sitting at the bar having a drink and wearing my favorite Hawaiian shirt, which I later learned gave Barbara the impression that I was a "player." (Note to men: do not wear Hawaiian shirts on a first date.)

Barbara arrived with one of her colleagues from Contra Costa College, who happened to be married to Warren Lee, one of my lifelong friends. Sue and Warren, taking pity on my less than stellar love life, had arranged for the four of us to have dinner together. I was living in Fallbrook (near San Diego) at the time, but was in the Bay Area as a visiting professor at the San Francisco Theological Seminary.

It didn't take long for Barbara to discover that I was not a player, and for me to discover that you're never too old to fall in love. I can now say without hesitation that my life can be divided into two distinct periods: B.B. (Before Barbara) and A.B. (After Barbara). For the first time in my life, I do not feel lonely. Barbara is always there for me, especially now, as my struggle with shingles and its accompanying pain leaves me weakened and a little fearful about what the future holds.

I once ran across a poem called "Now I Become Myself" by May Sarton, which says:

> Now I become myself.
> It's taken time, many years and places.
> I have been dissolved and shaken.
> Worn other people's faces …

These few lines say a lot about how long it has taken for me to become the self I am today, how much turbulence I have encountered along the way, and how often I have hid from my true self. In that regard, Barbara has provided a safe place for me to grow and become more of who I am.

How critical it is for us to have that "safe place," especially today, and especially for kids. The world can be cruel. People can be cruel. The scars of childhood can take a lifetime to erase. Children need programs that allow them to test themselves, to grow, to make mistakes without shame. Just as I need Barbara, children—*our* children—need Leading2Play.

Thank you for taking this journey with me. Thank you for letting me share my hopes, dreams, and passions with you. I hope you got something out of it.

I know I did.

Epilogue

"Most of us have an urge, maybe more as we age, to circle back to the past and touch the places and things of childhood."

—David Brooks

In an OpEd piece written for *The New York Times*, journalist David Brooks muses on the richness of historical consciousness. He states:

> *Historical consciousness has a fullness of paradox that future imagination cannot match. When we think of the past, we think about the things that seemed bad at the time but turned out to be good in the long run. We think about the little things that seemed inconsequential in the moment but made all the difference.*

When I began this book, I honestly wasn't sure why I was writing it. On the other hand, I think I understand now. I can see how the experiences I had shaped the person I became. Even more, as I have turned 80 and continue to battle the painful after-effects of shingles, I see the value that sport and physical activity can have on a person's life—when experienced the right way.

Unfortunately, a strong possibility exists that the ugly side of youth sports (i.e., pressuring kids to do too much too soon, a misplaced emphasis on winning at all costs, etc.) will rob kids of the things that sports has historically offered—things like the ability to spend time every day actively playing with your friends, or the freedom to choose and run your games yourself, or, most important of all, the opportunity to collectively appreciate human performance and give participants a glimpse of human possibility.

The aforementioned is why I fight on through the shingles, through the pain, through the discouragement a naturally shy person feels when they "put themselves out there" for a cause that not everyone gets, which is why Leading2Play is so important to me. As I noted in a recent grant application:

> *The mission of Leading2Play is to inspire young people to develop their full potential by putting them in charge of creating meaningful sports and fitness activities and experiences that are open to all participants, regardless of athletic ability.*
>
> *Today, only half of America's youth are vigorously active on a regular basis. Studies indicate that less than 20 percent of students receive adequate physical education each week and over 80 percent stop participating in organized sports activities of any kind by age 13. Alarming increases in childhood obesity, diabetes, and other chronic illnesses reflect these trends. The vision of Leading2Play is that all children, regardless of fitness level and/or natural ability, will have the opportunity to participate in meaningful, youth-driven sports and fitness activities, while gaining valuable life skills, such as*

teamwork, discipline, sensitivity to others, self-regulation, and more. The organization does this by creating a safe, engaging context for kids to design and operate their own sports and exercise programs. Leading2Play puts youth front and center in designing and carrying out unique, inclusive sports and fitness activities. Whether they're planning a Frisbee® golf tournament, a Hula Hoop® contest, or a lunch-time flag football game, young people are in charge and everyone's invited.

Leading2Play's adult advisors (teachers, volunteers, etc.) help facilitate and mentor each program's Youth Leadership Team (YLT). YLTs are a critical component of Leading2Play. Each YLT completes "market research" and determines the kinds of activities that are most attractive to the population they serve. The YLT then plans, organizes, and implements these activities. In return, members of the YLT receive hands-on leadership training, with the opportunity to experience group decision-making, strategic planning, program implementation, scheduling, program evaluation, and follow-up. All Leading2Play programs and activities emphasize the connection between leadership, responsibility, health, and greater success in school and in life. Leading2Play's robust curriculum provides clear program options, based on research and proven outcomes, and ensures that adult advisors provide effective guidance, encouragement, and conflict resolution to YLT members.

Leading2Play offers exciting, accessible, innovative, and fun activities that encourage active living. Participating in Leading2Play helps kids improve their physical fitness and develop life-long, positive health habits in a fun way. The program asks kids what THEY want. Leading2Play works to overcome the challenges brought about by a sedentary lifestyle by inspiring student leaders to invite, encourage, and involve their peers in fun and meaningful physical fitness activities. This peer-to-peer model helps to meet the needs of those who want to participate in sports but are out-of-shape or overweight. It fills a gap in service for those who may not have the innate skills to be a great athlete and have dropped out of organized sports, after spending most of the season on the bench. It meets the needs of the kids who DO have innate athletic ability but would like to be physically active in a less-structured environment, with friends who are not on their organized team.

Leading2Play, which was founded in Fairfax, Virginia, in 2010, was originally known as the A-Games. In Virgina, Leading2Play provided programming to create a structured recreation program for three middle schools. In 2012, Leading2Play was introduced to the West Contra Costa Unified School District (WCCUSD) at Helms

Middle School, where we successfully trained a leadership cohort to implement youth-led recreation activities. In 2013, we began a meaningful partnership with WCCUSD's Linked Learning Academies. Working within the Health Academy at Pinole Valley High School, we provided two classes (80 students) with curriculum and training. As their culminating project, the students created a "Recess Day" at Collins Elemenary School, serving 59 5th graders and 61 6th graders. This model was so successful that Leading2Play was asked to present at the California Partnership Academy Conference in Sacramento as a best practice Linked Learning.

WCCUSD has taken note of Leading2Play's service learning model as a best practice for engaging youth and developing leadership. In 2014, Leading2Play began meeting with the executive director for the Pinole Family of Schools, who asked that we expand our work with the Health Academies, using the Leading2Play curriculum to reinvent the physical education classes for Pinole and DeAnza High Schools, making P.E. fun for students by reengaging the disengaged and having students see themselves as central change agents in their community.

Exciting things are happening with Leading2Play—things that started when I began looking backward in order to move forward. I hope that exciting things will continue to happen and that the program will continue to grow. If not, however, perhaps sometime in the future, someone will pick up this book, read it, and think, "Hey, that's not such a bad idea." At that point, something that might have seemed inconsequential at that moment will turn out to make all the difference.

If you are interested in helping Leading2Play make a difference in the lives of young people and their communities, you can contribute by sending your tax-deductible donation to the Philanthropic Ventures Foundation, 1222 Preservation Park Way, Oakland, CA 94612-1201. (In the subject line of your check, put "George's Fund for Leading2Play.")

Leading2Play is a 501(c)(3) organization.

If you would like to bring Leading2Play to your school or community, contact Dr. George Selleck at dr.georgeselleck@gmail.com.

About the Author

George A. Selleck, Ph.D., M.Div., MA, is a member of the Pac-12 Men's Basketball Hall of Honor and a counseling psychologist with more than 35 years of professional expertise.

Dr. Selleck has successfully integrated his knowledge of human behavior and experience as an accomplished athlete and coach (California Interscholastic Federation Player of the Year, Stanford All-American, Stanford Athletic Hall of Fame, Pac-12 Men's Basketball Hall of Honor, two-time *Los Angeles Times* High School Coach of the Year) to become a national sports workshop specialist and recognized author in the field of sports education. In addition to presenting business, athletic, and personal growth seminars to hundreds of organizations (including the NBA Rookie Transition Program, the American Basketball Coaches Association, the American Football Coaches Association, Anaheim Unified School District, Hewlett-Packard, and Dow Chemical), Dr. Selleck is the founder/co-founder of three non-profit organizations—Sports for Life, Inc., Parents for Good Sports, and, most recently, Leading2Play—designed to improve the youth sports experience for young people throughout the U.S. and beyond.

Dr. Selleck is the author of hundreds of articles on youth sports. *Changing the Game* is his eighth book.

Dr. Selleck currently lives in Northern California with his wife, Barbara.

Wendy Fayles is an award-winning writer who has spent over 25 years making sure her clients know the proper use of punctuation. She has a BA in English from Brigham Young University, and lives in Salt Lake City with her husband, three children, and a semi-reasonable amount of cats. When not writing, Wendy works for the National Alliance on Mental Illness (NAMI Utah), offering support and advocacy for the many families and individuals who battle mental illness every day.